Doing Business with the U.S. Government

How to Sell Your Goods and Services
Into the 200 Billion Dollar Federal Market

Herman Holtz

Prima Publishing
P.O. Box 1260BK
Rocklin, CA 95677
(916) 786-0426

Production by Melanie Field, Bookman Productions
Copyediting by Sylvia Stein Wright
Interior design by Suzanne Montazer
Jacket design by Kirschner-Caroff Design
Typography by Dharma Enterprises

Library of Congress Cataloging-in-Publication Data	
Holtz, Herman.	
Doing business with the U.S. government / Herman Holtz.	
p. cm.	
ISBN 1-55958-320-7 : $24.95	
1. Government purchasing—United States. 2. Public contracts—	
United States. I. Title.	
JK1671.H6374 1993	93-13832
353.0071'2—dc20	CIP

93 94 95 96 97 RRD 10 9 8 7 6 5 4 3 2 1

Printed in the United States of America

How to Order:

Single copies may be ordered from Prima Publishing, P.O. Box 1260BK, Rocklin, CA 95677; telephone (916) 786-0426. Quantity discounts are also available. On your letterhead, include information concerning the intended use of the books and the number of books you wish to purchase.

CONTENTS

CHAPTER 7   The Proposal Game   145

CHAPTER 8   The Roles of the Computer
in Proposal Writing   179

CHAPTER 9   Marketing Intelligence and Computers   198

CHAPTER 10   Writing with a Personal Computer   212

CHAPTER 11   Writing with a dbm   231

PREFACE

Years ago I was an executive with a small firm that supported—that is, subcontracted to—the large government contractors who build missiles, aircraft, tanks, radar, and the like. We wrote their technical manuals, drafted their drawings, supplied their technical temporaries and consultants, and did myriad other such chores. Having come from the ranks of some of those major contractors, I immediately started out in pursuit of our own prime government contracts. Other executives in the company jeered at me. They *knew* we were too small, at $8 million a year in volume, to compete for government contracts and wondered where I had gotten such a bizarre idea.

Many months and many millions of dollars in successful bids and proposals for government contracts later, those executives were still shaking their heads disbelievingly: I must be engaging in some kind of sleight of hand to get those contracts. Weren't we too small to do business with the government?

Prejudice dies hard with some people, especially those who believe myths. Yet even I was not totally immune to the disease. Much later, when I left the company to strike out on my own as a free-lance writer, a contracting officer who knew me from "the old days" asked me why I wasn't bidding to him for some of his smaller contracts. He laughed at my protest of being just a one-man enterprise and assured me I was entitled to and would get full and equal consideration for any bid or proposal I submitted that was appropriate for a one-man effort.

Thus I became a small, independent government contractor, often burdened with more work than I could handle. And thus, I began to learn many details of government contracting that I could never have learned as an executive in even an $8 million firm, much less in my earlier experience as a consultant to or an employee of the huge corporations (IBM, GE, RCA, Philco, Sperry-Rand, U.S. Industries, and others).

I learned that while the huge contracts go to the huge firms (which are the only ones that can handle them, of course), the vast majority of government contracts go to medium-sized and small firms. I also learned that, in many cases, small firms have a great advantage over large firms. But the most surprising thing I learned was that my own experience with that $8 million a year firm was not at all unusual: Ignorance of government marketing and the opportunities to be had in the government markets is the rule, not the exception. On one occasion, I listened impatiently to a lecturer, a supposed government-marketing expert, smugly assure a group of near-neophytes that proposals play an almost insignificant role in contract competitions. And he was preparing to teach them how to write good proposals for winning contracts! Nor was that the only time I heard such mythology expressed. In another case, I reviewed a manuscript that made a similar claim—that proposals play a relatively small role in the contract-award decisions; yet the writer also promised to explain how to write winning proposals.

Somehow, the paradox always seems to escape these cynics, who know so many things that aren't so.

Less than 2 percent of the 13 million businesses in the United States do business with the U.S. government regularly, despite the size of the market and the fact that, on many occasions, federal contracting officials are hard put to attract enough bidders to constitute a fair degree of competition. No doubt such myths as the one referred to here are at least partially responsible. But there are at least two other reasons.

First, the government market is not a market; it's a large and complex set of markets—impressive in its sheer diversity. Those markets are scattered throughout many agencies and many geographic locations and represent countless needs, many of them unique (the U.S. government is the *only* customer for numerous items and services), and so many kinds of purchasing arrangements. (The public hears only of huge contracts to build military equipment, but the government is a customer for almost every known good and service.)

Second, the government is extremely limited, by the nature of bureaucracy, in its ability to educate and inform U.S. businesses about its needs and business opportunities. It is confined principally to its own publications to make announcements that reach only those already aware of and usually actively engaged in marketing to the government! This book has, then, two main purposes: (1) to make more business people aware of the business opportunities available from the many government agencies and (2) to try to place these diverse government markets into some sort of framework and perhaps bring order to what appears to the newcomer to be pure chaos.

This is not a philosophical work; it makes no political commentary and engages in no economic theorizing. It is offered strictly as a how-to book. It is based primarily on my own experiences, although it also presents information from official publications. However, I have tried to avoid including those mechanical details that may be found in other, usually official, publications, and I have made it a goal to maximize the kind of information that can be gained only through experience.

Will this book make you an expert on government markets? Of course not. Only your own continuing experience can do that. But it will put you on the right road. It will reveal to you information and inside facts for which I paid dearly. It should save you a great deal of time. It should spare you a great deal of shin-bruising stumbling in the dark. And I hope it will teach you techniques, strategies, and methods that you might never have learned otherwise.

I am indebted to many people for my education in government marketing and for their help and encouragement of my work. I wish also to note that, despite occasional abuses and improprieties in government procurement, the sincerity and dedication of most government officials continue to make our government purchasing systems the best in the world.

CHAPTER 1

The U.S. Government Paid Me $6,000 to Answer Its Mail

(Some of it was two years old!)

The Broad Government Market

The wind-energy branch of what is now the Department of Energy (then the Energy Research and Development Administration) paid me $6,000 to answer its mail. Staff members couldn't keep up with it themselves because the chief of the branch insisted that every letter merited a personal response rather than a form letter. I was hired to help them catch up with a two-year backlog of about 200 letters. The letters I answered came from all kinds of correspondents: college professors, scientists, engineers, ordinary citizens, inventors, and would-be inventors. (Many citizens sent in their ideas in the form of rough sketches on yellow paper, which the chief referred to caustically as "one-page inventions.") In any case, I was forced to exercise my imagination and think up plausible reasons for having taken two years to respond to some of the mail.

I was paid $1,800 by the General Services Administration to critique a training program (which I attended for one week); the Civil Service Commission (now the Office of Personnel Management) paid me $100 each for a series of 80-minute lectures on procurement for federal employees; and I received $600 for an expense-paid two days in Vermont as an EPA consultant. (These are figures of more than a dozen years ago; the fees would be much higher today.)

None of these examples is particularly unusual—I've won both larger and smaller jobs. I've worked as a small, independent government contractor from a suite of offices in downtown Washington, D.C., but I've also won and handled contracts using my own home as an office. And so have many other people.

Government contracts have been let to round up wild horses, rent mules and handlers, referee sports events, supply go-go dancers, bag groceries, produce theatricals, print bumper stickers, make rubber stamps, repair typewriters, fell trees, manage warehouses, run office copiers, rent cabins in national parks, guard buildings, manage subscriptions to government periodicals, scatter sterilized screw worm flies from the air, answer government telephones, operate travel bureaus, organize seminars and conferences, operate government computers, run a bus service, make sandwiches, and perform thousands of other jobs, most of them more mundane than these.

A Few of the Myths

Perhaps the most common myth about contracting with the government is that you have to be a big corporation. As a single individual, I have personally won many thousands of dollars' worth of contracts, many of which were for more than $25,000. Another fable is that you need influence or "pull" to win government contracts. I have no special influence and my "contacts" in government are the ones I made by working with the agencies. I started cold and built my list of acquaintances. Even now, I have no high-level contacts.

Like all myths, these have a tiny speck of truth that has been thoroughly distorted. Certainly, individuals or small firms aren't going to win the multimillion-dollar contracts awarded for some jobs, and influence has been used occasionally to help bring in the really big contracts. But even in those special cases, the effect of "influence" is not nearly as great as the myths would have it, and all the influence in the world is not going to win contracts for those who do not compete well. The use of influence has severe limitations in our system.

Do It Better, Then Sell It to the Government

If you can do something the government is doing or is supposed to do, and you can do it better than the great bureaucracy does, you can sell it back to the government! One enterprising gentleman who became aware of the shortcomings of the official telephone directories each agency publishes compiled his own *Federal Telephone Directory.* He listed 18,000 executives in all the Washington-area federal offices and kept up to date by annual revision. He sold subscriptions, which cost more than $100 per year, to private organizations doing business with federal agencies. But to his delight and surprise, the agencies themselves became his best customers!

More than one small company today publishes periodicals listing federal job openings in Washington and elsewhere, for job seekers. Lo and behold, many federal personnel offices subscribe to these.

When the Consumer Product Safety Commission began, its offices were frequented by a young man who was launching the *Product Safety Letter,* a weekly newsletter intended for industry. But Safety Commission offices have many subscriptions, since commission executives learned they could keep abreast of commission affairs better through that newsletter than through any official means. (Almost all agencies subscribe to a number of privately published newsletters about their own activities.)

Big Government = Big Business

No one knows just how much our government spends each year for goods and services. Estimates, even official ones, vary widely, but the latest *Federal Procurement Report,* an annual issued by the Office of Management and Budget through its Office of Federal

Procurement Policy, lists 20,152,308 procurements by all listed agencies, totaling $210,689,057,000. That doesn't account for the spending of certain government corporations, such as the U.S. Postal Service, and a few other "off-budget" agencies and expenditures. The Postal Service alone spends at least $30 billion annually to buy a wide variety of goods and services.

Government warehouses and supply depots bulge with an inventory of more than six million items. Each year the Federal Supply Service alone buys about $6 billion worth of "common use" items (ordinary commodities).

Many major contracts have been let in excess of $1 billion each, and multimillion-dollar contracts have become commonplace. In fact, anything under $25,000 is a "small purchase" in government circles under current law and doesn't even require a formal contract, but may be authorized by a simple purchase order.

Startling Statistics

To many, the U.S. government is a maze of bulky, monolithic buildings frowning over busy streets just east of downtown Washington, D.C. In fact, the U.S. government is more than that. It includes the following:

- Approximately 2,800,000 civilian employees, with more of them in California than in Washington, D.C.
- More than 34,000 facilities or activities
- 405,000 buildings owned by the government
- 54,000 rented buildings, plus rented space in other high-rise buildings
- About 760 million acres—one-third of the U.S. land area

Even that is only the beginning:

- The U.S. Army has the largest fleet of wheeled vehicles in the world, but the U.S. Postal Service is second in size, with well over 100,000 vehicles and more than 300 repair shops (vehicle maintenance facilities).

- To pay for all this, the U.S. Treasury must issue some 800 million checks every year.
- Because all this buying requires a great deal of work, there are about 15,000 purchasing offices employing about 125,000 procurement specialists.

In addition to a great deal of buying every day of the year, our Uncle Sam must maintain several centralized procurement and supply organizations:

The Federal Supply Service (General Services Administration)

The Postal Service supply organization

The Veterans Administration supply organization

The Defense Supply Agency

The Structure of the Bureaucracy

There are 14 departments in the government—Treasury, Labor, Commerce, Transportation, Interior, Energy, State, Army, Navy, Air Force, Housing and Urban Development, Health and Human Services, Education, and Veterans Affairs. (There's a bit of an anomaly here because the Department of Defense is listed as a department, but so are the three major military arms that are the major parts of DOD; yet only the Secretary of Defense is a cabinet officer.)

There are more than 60 "independent agencies"—NASA, EPA, GSA, and others, as well as a number of quasi-official agencies, such as the American Red Cross. Department status is not related to size. Some of the independent agencies are larger than some of the departments.

Within agencies, which I'll use as a generic term for all federal organizations, are many large subdivisions, some of them better known than the agency itself. For example, the well-known and large Forest Service is part of the Department of Agriculture, although everyone admits its missions are better suited to the Interior Department.

This adds up to hundreds of agencies—the best estimate is 1,800—but even that doesn't tell the whole story. Most of these have a number of offices throughout the United States, many of which do at least some of their buying independently. Thus, there is a complex set of markets, rather than a single market, that includes thousands of customers who pay with U.S. Treasury checks.

The government divides the United States into ten federal regions, and most major agencies have a regional office in each one. However, some have many other offices. Commerce and the Small Business Administration have about 80 each, for example (see Appendix 1 for a listing), and there are even more for some agencies. In addition, all of the many military bases in the United States and overseas do some independent buying.

Programs and Missions

Some of the agencies, particularly the older and better-established ones, have straightforward missions, indicated by their names. The Government Printing Office, for example, does printing, typesetting, and a few related tasks. The Treasury handles fiscal matters and disbursements. The Postal Service delivers the mail (most of the time).

But it's a different story with the newer agencies. As the government and the society it governs become more complex, so do the organization and missions of the many bureaucracies within the great bureaucracy.

The Department of Labor, concerned with working people, has been assigned missions relating to training unemployables, through Job Corps, for example, to administering labor laws and standards, and to occupational safety and health.

The Economic Development Administration of the Department of Commerce is also concerned with jobs—with creating them. It is usually assigned the chore of administering such things as public works grants.

The Bureau of Indian Affairs is in the Department of Interior, to which it was transferred in 1849 from the War Department (which no longer exists).

The Inevitability of Change

If death and taxes are inevitable, so is change, especially in government. Each new administration will work some changes, creating new departments, shifting agencies and missions around. Among the more recent creations have been the Department of Energy and the Pension Benefit Guaranty Corporation, but other agencies (for example, the Department of Transportation and the U.S. Postal Service) are creations of recent years. And the Office of Economic Opportunity (OEO) dwindled from a large operation to an invisibly small office, handing off its major programs to other agencies.

Some agencies are highly visible and well known because they touch on matters of great concern or at least interest to almost everyone; others are relatively obscure because their work is so highly specialized. For example, who hasn't heard of the Social Security Administration? But how many citizens know that there is something called the Community Services Administration? That very fact has an effect on contracting: Because the National Cancer Institute is highly visible, it had to retain a contractor to answer its telephones and mail and send out information to the concerned citizens who call and write.

Redundancy in the Agencies

Many people, including presidential candidates, decry the redundancy and duplication of effort among federal agencies and call for reform to eliminate such duplication. However, there is often a clear distinction among the missions of agencies that appear to duplicate each others' functions.

For example, a small business may apply to the Small Business Administration (SBA) for a loan guarantee. Or it may apply to the

Economic Development Administration (EDA), within the Department of Commerce. But each would require a different type of justification. For SBA assistance, the business must qualify as a small business according to the standards established by SBA. For EDA, the business must demonstrate that the loan will either create new jobs or save jobs that are threatened. And it would also have to demonstrate that the jobs would be created in a "labor surplus" area (as designated by the Labor Department). In short, it is important to understand such distinctions if you are to do business with the agencies.

Perhaps an even finer distinction is that between the Occupational Safety and Health Administration (OSHA), in the Labor Department, and the Environmental Protection Agency (EPA), an "independent" agency. OSHA is concerned with the health and safety of workers in their workplaces; EPA is concerned with the health of the general public, that is, with health hazards arising out of pollution. Suppose you have some device to reduce the pollution arising from some industrial process. Do you offer it to OSHA or EPA? You do either or both, but in one case, you must address the protection of the worker and, in the other, the protection of the atmosphere and the general public.

If you have a device to make some consumer product less hazardous, you might want to talk to the Consumer Product Safety Commission, although it might have application to other agencies' missions as well. For example, if it has to do with automotive safety, it might interest the Highway Traffic Safety Administration in the Department of Transportation; if it would affect boating safety, take it to the U.S. Coast Guard, also in Transportation.

Overnight Experts

You've probably heard that "Man proposes and God disposes." In Washington, Congress legislates and the bureaucrat procrastinates.

But not without some justification. Frequently, what Congress legislates is a hot potato for the administration and its bureaucracy.

Let's take the case of the Pension Benefit Guaranty Corporation (PBGC), formed under new legislation in 1974 to protect workers denied their pensions because of circumstances such as a union pension fund going into bankruptcy. Suddenly, an organization exists, largely on paper, and the administration must begin a frantic search for people who can implement the new program.

When an agency is an entirely new entity, it borrows from various other agencies people who appear to have at least some of the right qualifications and assigns them to form a temporary cadre for the new organization. In the case of PBGC (a new government agency quickly becomes identified by its initials), it took the temporary staff two years before they had begun to assemble a staff of actuaries and other specialists. And then, woefully short on all but professional bureaucrats and new hires, they began to seek contractors to write programs to train the new staff in all the special fields they needed to know.

When the Energy Research and Development Administration (ERDA) was formed, initial staff was drawn from technical agencies such as the National Science Foundation and the National Bureau of Standards. But even when the staff is reasonably well qualified, there are never enough people available right away, when enthusiasm and funding are high and when Congress wants to see immediate action. The answer is, of course, to call on industry and issue contracts.

Prior to ERDA, there were few "energy experts," and no one had, in fact, used that term before. But once ERDA announced it wanted help, and in a hurry, there were numerous applicants who assured ERDA they were indeed experts. Those who got in on the ground floor and won some of the first contracts established their reputations quickly, although they may never have worked in that field before. It was not long before we had many energy experts—whole companies of them!

One of the most dynamic situations revolving around new agencies and new programs sprang up almost overnight when Lyndon

Johnson took office and announced the advent of his Great Society and his War on Poverty. The effort centered immediately on the new Office of Economic Opportunity (OEO) at 19th and M Streets, NW, in Washington, D.C.

Shortly after OEO opened its doors and staffed its building on 19th Street with a few government bureaucrats and many recruits from the nation's universities, the building began to swarm with people from companies large and small. Most had been affected by the recent slowdown in defense spending and were attracted to what they thought was going to become a multibillion-dollar market in training, education, and social welfare programs. The erudite contracting officer of OEO, Milton Fogelman, summed it up laconically this way: "Look at them. They're like dogs around the butcher shop: They smell the meat, but they don't know how to get at it." Nevertheless, OEO (and the Office of Education [OE], which soon followed) transformed the neighborhood: It soon buzzed with psychologists, sociologists, and educators of many kinds.

One could literally wander through the offices of OEO and emerge with a contract, not quite sure how it had all happened. On one occasion, while strolling past an office in the building, I was summoned by a harried OEO program manager and challenged. "Look at that requirement," he said, handing me a typed statement of need, "and tell me if you could do that job in 30 days and for how much." (We settled, ultimately, on 45 days and just under $50,000 for the project.)

Dozens of small companies sprang up, fueled initially by contracts from OEO, and some of the larger companies—General Electric, Westinghouse, IBM, and Xerox, for example—organized or bought education and training companies and went after OEO contracts.

Those days and that frenzied atmosphere are long gone, as is the Embers, the ground-floor watering place for OEO and its habitués. Some of the consultants and small companies in demand by the program are gone, too. But many have survived and are today carrying out projects to aid other agencies in their many "social intervention" programs, working to provide child care, help for the elderly, education, and aid for the handicapped, minority enterprises, jobs programs, alcohol and drug abuse programs, mental health programs, and so on.

Trends and Projections

For years, the trend has been to more and more programs to help those in need and distress, and that trend shows no signs of abating, despite inflation and a ground swell of taxpayer protest. But not all new programs and trends are "social" in the sense of succoring the unfortunate and the underprivileged. Safety and environment are prominent programs, as is energy. And despite the lower profile of NASA since the Apollo program was completed, NASA's budget is still quite large.

There will continue to be work for psychologists, sociologists, educators, scientists, engineers, and specialists of many kinds. The government, despite nearly three million employees, has not nearly enough hands and feet to carry out all its programs. In fact, many agencies are hard-pressed to find people to manage the contracts let to private industry. Without the contracted help of private industry, almost all the programs would falter and fail from sheer lack of nourishment.

Some of the markets are vertical ones. Engineers and scientists in the physical sciences will find their projects among technical agencies: NASA, the military departments, EPA, the Department of Energy, and, to some extent, the Department of Transportation. Educators, sociologists, psychologists, therapists, and others in related fields will find their chief markets among such agencies as HHS (with its many bureaus), the Department of Labor, and, to some extent, the military.

There are horizontal markets, too—those totally unrelated to the mission of the agencies. All agencies use computers and data processing, for example, and computer specialists may find projects almost anywhere in government. The same considerations apply to writers and certain other kinds of specialists.

The architect-engineer may find good prospects at HUD, as may real estate specialists. But a daily scan of the *Commerce Business Daily* (CBD) will reveal that few agencies turn their new-construction needs over to the General Services Administration's Public Buildings Service, so almost any agency may request bids on architectural and engineering requirements.

Printers will find the Government Printing Office the source for virtually all government printing contracts, of which there are many every day, although there are a few exceptions to this general rule.

What the Government Typically Buys

By now, you should be starting to appreciate that the U.S. government is necessarily a customer for virtually everything, both goods and services. The military forces must be fed, clothed, housed, armed, and equipped. The thousands of buildings and other facilities must be repaired, maintained, cleaned, and serviced. New construction must be carried out. The programs require studies, surveys, analyses, reports, execution, and evaluation. The computers need to be fed their thousands of programs, and the large, mainframe computer systems must be operated by humans, who are frequently specialists under contract.

Agencies' needs for outside help are of several types. Some represent simply the need for more hands and feet than the in-house staff can provide. Some are for skills and abilities that do not exist in-house. Some are for physical facilities the government does not have.

Specific arrangements vary, depending on the circumstances and the agency's regulations. Contractors may work "on site" (at the government's facilities) or "off site" (at the contractor's facility). Some jobs may be performed anywhere the contractor chooses; others must be performed within some prescribed proximity to the government's issuing facility. The government will let one-time contracts to meet specific, discrete needs, but it will also issue annual contracts year after year to satisfy permanent, ongoing needs. Among

this great diversity of needs, many contracts are for standard commodities, in both goods and services, but many are for custom-
designed goods and services. And government requirements are often
somewhat unusual. In fact, for many things, the U.S. government is
not only the biggest and best customer; it is the only customer. (Who
else would pay you to run a travel bureau or sell prophylactics on the
streets?)

Small wonder, then, that many suppliers to the government have
tailored their operations to satisfying unique needs. For example,
"management consultants" are usually individuals and companies
who will respond to a wide variety of government solicitations with
proposals to design unique products and services. To give you an
appreciation of the diversity of goods and services bought frequently
and routinely, here are just a few of those agencies purchase almost
daily.

Services

Typewriter repair
Writing, editing, and proofing
Automotive repair and service
Laundry and dry cleaning
Advertising road building
Shoe and clothing repair
Air-conditioning repair
Striping parking lots
Moving and hauling
Construction
Janitorial work
Trash removal
Electronics maintenance
Architecture, engineering
Making sandwiches for
    immigrants
Architectural design

Typesetting
Food services, catering
Typing
Printing and duplicating
Answering mail and telephones
Making rubber stamps
Computer programming
Mailing
Hiring consultants
Lecturing and training
Maintaining subscription lists
Renting cars, trucks, and buses
Managing conventions
Mapping
Providing temporary office
    help
Drafting and illustrating

Photo finishing
Photography (still and aerial)
Providing subscriptions, books
Movie making
Bagging groceries
Studies and surveys
Managing government facilities
Parking cars
Repairing machinery

Rug cleaning
Research and development
Administering correspondence
Auditing and accounting
Civil engineering
Title searches
Painting, plumbing, and electrical
Medical and dental services
Laboratory services

Goods

Foods, raw and processed
Lumber and mill work
Valves, machinery
Computers and computer supplies
Office supplies and equipment
Construction materials
Paints, solvents, and brushes
Furniture (home and office)
Rope, cable, and marine supplies
Photo lab equipment
Clothing and insignias
Aircraft and aircraft parts
Tires and inner tubes
Missiles, weapons, and ammunition
Vehicles (all types)
Textiles and findings
Paper goods (all kinds)

Air conditioners
Wrapping supplies
Dinnerware and flatware
Cameras and photography equipment
Lubricants
Waxes
Books, subscriptions, and maps
Ships and boats
Automotive parts and accessories
Bearings
Cranes and hoists
Ores and minerals
Training aids and devices
Shoes, leather goods, and findings
Metal bars, sheets, and forms
Hand tools
Abrasives

Laboratory and scientific equipment

Measuring tools

Hardware

Fire-fighting and safety equipment

Pumps and compressors

Pipe, tubing, and hoses

Medical and dental supplies

Lighting fixtures and lamps

Hospital supplies and equipment

Communications equipment

Chemicals and chemical products

Tractors and agricultural machines

Electronic parts and supplies

Electrical supplies

Crude materials (metallic and nonmetallic)

Nursery supplies

First-aid equipment, supplies

Earth-moving vehicles

Household furnishings

Cleaning materials and supplies

Alarm and signal systems

Even that is far from all of it. See Appendix 4, which lists Federal Supply Schedules, for an indication of the range of goods and services bought by the government. The government buys goods and services in over 100 general categories; each category has many subcategories, and each subcategory has many individual kinds of items. There are "miscellaneous" categories, too!

The government buys almost everything. And if the budgets and purchases of the CIA and other federal intelligence services (for example, the National Security Agency and the many military intelligence services) were not secret, I could probably eliminate the word "almost" from the first sentence of this paragraph. (Newspaper stories have revealed, for example, that the CIA has paid members of the oldest profession to help carry out its missions.)

Among the thousands of contracts announced regularly by the government are many large ones to large companies, but there are also many small ones to small companies and individuals. Contracts under $25,000, however, are not usually announced because the law does not require it. But here are a few small contracts let to individuals and small companies, just to illustrate that it is not only manufacturers and wholesalers who can and do sell to the U.S. government:

CANDY MILES, Alexandria, Virginia: $11,600 to revise the FCC *Broadcast Procedures Manual*

JAMES E. BONE, Columbus, Georgia: $41,187 for "repairs to garages"

MARVIN MARKOWITZ, Miami, Florida: $139,680 worth of kitchen cabinets sold to the air force

LEM'S COUNTRY KITCHEN, Nashville, Tennessee: $285,900 worth of cakes and pies

MIKE BASS, Potomac, Maryland: $5,000 to write test questions for an OSHA home-study course

EDDIE'S CONSTRUCTION COMPANY, Honolulu, Hawaii: $92,285 to reroof seven buildings

BYWATER SALES AND SERVICE, Louisiana: $31,900 worth of paints, sold to GSA

PACKTICS, Baltimore, Maryland: $40,000 for bumper stickers

SUGARMAN BROTHERS, Massachusetts: $104,915 for paper bags, sold to GSA

VINCELLI'S TIRE SERVICE, Redding, California: $25,000 for tires, sold to GSA

JAMES KENDRICK, Washington, D.C.: $5,200 to revise a draft manual for OSHA

TATE SPARGUS, Washington, D.C.: $63,000 for photo services

CHUCK GOODMAN, Reston, Virginia: $1,400 for writing services for the Department of Labor

Note that these companies and individuals are scattered around the United States. None is a large company; in fact, many who sell merchandise are retail dealers. Although my own office is near Washington, D.C., I have done work for agencies in Missoula, Montana; Topeka, Kansas; Norman, Oklahoma; Orlando, Florida; and other places. I have had jobs as small as $75 and jobs that have run into thousands of dollars. (And government agencies have bought my books and reports on how the federal procurement system works!)

Anyone can do business with the government.

CHAPTER 2

Understanding

the System

It's actually several systems.

Competition as the Basis

The government is a complex structure of 1,800 departments, bureaus, administrations, offices, and other agencies, located throughout approximately 34,000 installations, with about 15,000 procurement offices and 125,000 procurement officials. The procurement offices are guided by a now unified set of Federal Acquisition Regulations (FAR) (compiled from four original sets, plus a myriad of memoranda and bulletins). In those voluminous regulatory excursions, contracting officials can find the basis for doing almost anything they want to do. However, in the vast welter of policies, procedures, and practices, a few unifying features can be found.

The basis for all government procurement is competition. That word, as you will learn, has more than one meaning in federal procurement, and there are some exceptions to the basic rule of competition. The underlying intent of all federal procurement practice and law is to utilize competition and procure what is "in the best interests of the government."

At the most fundamental level, there are only two kinds of procurement or purchasing: price competition, which the contracting community refers to as "formally advertised" or "sealed-bid" procurement, and technical-quality competition, formerly referred to officially as "negotiated" procurement but now called "competitive proposals." These lead to two basic types of contract: fixed-price and cost-reimbursement. The complexities arise from the exceptions and from the variants or hybrids of these basic types.

It's a simple matter when the U.S. Army wants to buy a quantity of 105mm howitzers. The army issues a specification, to tell bidders exactly what they must manufacture and deliver, and accepts bids, to be delivered sealed and then opened publicly at a set time, place, and date. Given no unusual technicalities, the lowest qualified bidder will win the contract.

It's quite another matter when the army wants a special howitzer, to be mounted on a vehicle, equipped to fire special ammunition, or with other departures from the usual specifications and standards. In such a case, the army cannot furnish detailed specifications because the item has yet to be designed. It's an R&D (research and development) job.

No one knows with any certainty how long it will take to get the new weapon out of the laboratory and ready to be manufactured, much less what it will cost or just what the final hardware specifications will be. The army can furnish some performance specifications—what it would like the new weapon to be capable of doing—and perhaps some hardware specifications, such as "not to exceed three tons weight"; but that's about it.

Such a contract usually calls for a cost-reimbursement arrangement, perhaps the famous "cost-plus" contract. The government will reimburse the contractor's costs plus a fixed fee or profit, within some estimated amount. But how does the army select a contractor for such a job and keep the basic procurement competitive?

In a procurement of this type, price is only one consideration—and not necessarily the most important. The government is also concerned that the contractor be fully qualified to do the job and that he furnish assurances that he will, in fact, be able to do the job and deliver as promised. Low price is not going to mean anything if the contractor cannot deliver. In short, the army (in this example) wants a contractor who

1. fully understands what the army wants
2. has the necessary know-how, people, and other resources to do the job
3. has a track record of experience and demonstrated competence in such work

This, then, becomes a "negotiated" procurement, which means that the army is not bound to award the contract to the low bidder, but may use its judgment as to which bid is "in the best interests of the government, price and other factors considered." (This is standard language to explain the conditions under which the successful bidder will be chosen.)

To establish competition, proposals are requested. Each bidder writes a proposal that demonstrates an understanding of the requirement, describes the plans for carrying out the program, and presents his qualifications. The government takes all this into account, along with the cost estimates, and decides to whom the contract will be awarded. But that decision is not entirely arbitrary or subjective. An "objective rating scheme" is used to help ensure that each bidder gets fair consideration in what is primarily a technical competition and only partially a price competition.

Types of Solicitations

Because there are only two basic types of contracts, there are only two basic types of solicitations. For formally advertised procurement, in which the bids are sealed and opened publicly, the government issues an information for bid (IFB). The fact that it is an IFB trumpets the announcement that it is a sealed-bid procurement. When the government wants proposals and a negotiated procurement, it issues a request for proposal (RFP).

In most cases, the same form, Standard Form 33, is used. The first and fourth pages of this four-page form are shown in Figure 2–1. As you can see, item 4 on that form ("type of solicitations") has two boxes, where the contracting official who issues it may check off IFB or RFP to advise the bidder immediately what type of solicitation and procurement is contemplated. The form also states when the bid or proposal is due, where it is to be delivered, and where the public opening will be held. It also provides a space for the bidder to sign.

There is a third type of solicitation, which is really not a solicitation at all, technically, but is often used as one: the RFQ, or request for quotation (Standard Form 18). (See Figure 2–2.) This form is supposed to be used simply to give the government an idea of how much an item or service will cost; the quotation furnished is not binding on either party, as the small print stipulates. However, many agencies use this form to solicit proposals, particularly for small jobs, and it is also often used to decide who is lowest in price and then issue a purchase order. The RFQ, however, is not itself a contractual document, as Form 33 is, and cannot be used as such. Therefore, if the contracting official wishes to issue a contract on the basis of quotations furnished via the RFQ, he must issue a formal negotiated contract, although he may use a purchase order if the award is less than $25,000.

If you look closely at Form 33 (Figure 2–1), you'll see that when the bidder signs, he or she has actually signed a contract. Should the contracting official sign in the place provided for his signature, the contract exists immediately. In practice, this is rarely done. Usually, if the contract is sizable, and sometimes even if it is small, there is a negotiating session in which the contracting official tries to whittle the price down a bit. Even for a small job in which the official is quite satisfied with the price, the contracting official usually calls and has the bidder verify willingness to contract before the document is signed and copies are sent to the bidder.

The purchase order (see Figure 2–3) is even simpler. The contractor's signature is not required at all. The purchase order simply authorizes the contractor to proceed with the work at the price stipulated.

Rules of Small Purchases

Under the current Small Purchases Act, competitive bids are required for purchases up to $7,500. For purchases above $7,500 but not above $15,000, government officials are supposed to get three bids, but they may be oral bids. For purchases above $15,000 but not above $25,000, the bids should be written but may be quite informal. In practice, in most agencies, a purchase order for work not exceeding $25,000 may be awarded rapidly and without formality to anyone the agency wishes to award it to.

Note the phrase "in most agencies." There is always the matter of agency policy. Although the law permits certain practices, it does not always mandate them. An agency chief may restrict small purchases to some figure less than $25,000, be firm about getting written bids on everything, no matter the size, or restrict the use of whatever the law permits in any way he or she sees fit. Therefore, what you can do in one agency you may not be able to do in another. You may find in one agency that price is highly important, even in a negotiated procurement, although it is of little importance in negotiated procurements in another agency. You must therefore know what the procurement regulations permit, but you must also know what policies exist in the agencies you want to do business with and how they choose to interpret certain of the procurement regulations.

Where the Regulations Came From

Strange as it may seem, the United States government had no organized set of procurement regulations until World War II. In fact, except for earlier wars, it hadn't been much of a customer and didn't perceive a need for formal procurement regulations, even in World War I, when the government did buy weapons in quantity.

World War II changed that. The government was forced to buy on a scale never seen before. This came on the heels of a number of years during which the great bureaucracy had grown to a far larger size than ever before, as the president and the solons on Capitol Hill combated depression and unemployment with federal bureaus.

OMB Approved No. 9000-0008

SOLICITATION, OFFER AND AWARD

| 1. THIS CONTRACT IS A RATED ORDER UNDER DPAS (15 CFR 350) | RATING | PAGE OF PAGES |

2. CONTRACT NO.

3. SOLICITATION NO.

4. TYPE OF SOLICITATION
- [ ] SEALED BID (IFB)
- [ ] NEGOTIATED (RFP)

5. DATE ISSUED

6. REQUISITION/PURCHASE NO.

7. ISSUED BY   CODE

8. ADDRESS OFFER TO (If other than Item 7)

SOLICITATION

NOTE: In sealed bid solicitations "offer" and "offeror" mean "bid" and "bidder".

9. Sealed offers in original and _____ copies for furnishing the supplies or services in the Schedule will be received at the place specified in Item 8, or if handcarried, in the depository located in _____ until _____ local time _____
(Hour) (Date)

CAUTION — LATE Submissions, Modifications, and Withdrawals: See Section L, Provision No. 52.214-7 or 52.215-10. All offers are subject to all terms and conditions contained in this solicitation.

| 10. FOR INFORMATION CALL: | A. NAME | B. TELEPHONE NO. (Include area code) (NO COLLECT CALLS) |

11. TABLE OF CONTENTS

(✓)	SEC.	DESCRIPTION	PAGE(S)	(✓)	SEC.	DESCRIPTION	PAGE(S)
		PART I — THE SCHEDULE				PART II — CONTRACT CLAUSES	
	A	SOLICITATION/CONTRACT FORM			I	CONTRACT CLAUSES	
	B	SUPPLIES OR SERVICES AND PRICES/COSTS				PART III — LIST OF DOCUMENTS, EXHIBITS AND OTHER ATTACH.	
	C	DESCRIPTION/SPECS./WORK STATEMENT			J	LIST OF ATTACHMENTS	
	D	PACKAGING AND MARKING				PART IV — REPRESENTATIONS AND INSTRUCTIONS	
	E	INSPECTION AND ACCEPTANCE			K	REPRESENTATIONS, CERTIFICATIONS AND OTHER STATEMENTS OF OFFERORS	
	F	DELIVERIES OR PERFORMANCE			L	INSTRS., CONDS., AND NOTICES TO OFFERORS	
	G	CONTRACT ADMINISTRATION DATA			M	EVALUATION FACTORS FOR AWARD	
	H	SPECIAL CONTRACT REQUIREMENTS					

FIGURE 2–1. Standard Form 33

OFFER *(Must be fully completed by offeror)*

NOTE: Item 12 does not apply if the solicitation includes the provisions at 52.214-16, Minimum Bid Acceptance Period.

12. In compliance with the above, the undersigned agrees, if this offer is accepted within _____ calendar days *(60 calendar days unless a different period is inserted by the offeror)* from the date for receipt of offers specified above, to furnish any or all items upon which prices are offered at the price set opposite each item, delivered at the designated point(s), within the time specified in the schedule.

13. DISCOUNT FOR PROMPT PAYMENT *(See Section I, Clause No. 52-232-8)*	10 CALENDAR DAYS %	20 CALENDAR DAYS %	30 CALENDAR DAYS %	CALENDAR DAYS %

14. ACKNOWLEDGMENT OF AMENDMENTS *(The offeror acknowledges receipt of amendments to the SOLICITATION for offerors and related documents numbered and dated:)*

AMENDMENT NO.	DATE	AMENDMENT NO.	DATE

15A. NAME AND ADDRESS OF OFFEROR	CODE	FACILITY	16. NAME AND TITLE OF PERSON AUTHORIZED TO SIGN OFFER *(Type or print)*

15B. TELEPHONE NO. *(Include area code)*	15C. CHECK IF REMITTANCE ADDRESS IS DIFFERENT FROM ABOVE - ENTER SUCH ADDRESS IN SCHEDULE.	17. SIGNATURE	18. OFFER DATE

AWARD *(To be completed by Government)*

19. ACCEPTED AS TO ITEMS NUMBERED	20. AMOUNT	21. ACCOUNTING AND APPROPRIATION

22. AUTHORITY FOR USING OTHER THAN FULL AND OPEN COMPETITION:

☐ 10 U.S.C. 2304(c)( )　　☐ 41 U.S.C. 253(c)( )

23. SUBMIT INVOICES TO ADDRESS SHOWN IN ITEM *(4 copies unless otherwise specified)*	ITEM

24. ADMINISTERED BY *(If other than Item 7)*	CODE	25. PAYMENT WILL BE MADE BY	CODE

26. NAME OF CONTRACTING OFFICER *(Type or print)*	27. UNITED STATES OF AMERICA *(Signature of Contracting Officer)*	28. AWARD DATE

IMPORTANT — Award will be made on this Form, or on Standard Form 26, or by other authorized official written notice.

NSN 7540-01-152-8064
PREVIOUS EDITION NOT USABLE

33-134

STANDARD FORM 33 (REV. 4-85)
Prescribed by GSA
FAR (48 CFR) 53.214(c)

FIGURE 2-1. *(continued)*

REQUEST FOR QUOTATIONS *(THIS IS NOT AN ORDER)*	The Notice of Small Business-Small Purchase Set-Aside on the reverse of this form ☐ is ☐ is not applicable.		PAGE	OF	PAGES
1. REQUEST NO.	2. DATE ISSUED	3. REQUISITION/PURCHASE REQUEST NO.	4. CERT. FOR NAT. DEF. UNDER BDSA REG. 2 AND/OR DMS REG. 1 ▲	RATING	
5A. ISSUED BY			6. DELIVER BY *(Date)*		
			7. DELIVERY		
5B. FOR INFORMATION CALL: *(Name and telephone no.) (No collect calls)*			☐ FOB DESTINATION	☐ OTHER *(See Schedule)*	
8. TO: NAME AND ADDRESS, INCLUDING ZIP CODE			9. DESTINATION *(Consignee and address, including ZIP Code)*		
10. PLEASE FURNISH QUOTATIONS TO THE ISSUING OFFICE ON OR BEFORE CLOSE OF BUSINESS *(Date)*	11. BUSINESS CLASSIFICATION *(Check appropriate boxes)*				
	☐ SMALL ☐ OTHER THAN SMALL ☐ DISADVANTAGED ☐ WOMEN-OWNED				

IMPORTANT: This is a request for information, and quotations furnished are not offers. If you are unable to quote, please so indicate on this form and return it. This request does not commit the Government to pay any costs incurred in the preparation of the submission of this quotation or to contract for supplies or services. Supplies are of domestic origin unless otherwise indicated by quoter. Any representations and/or certifications attached to this Request for Quotations must be completed by the quoter.

FIGURE 2–2.   Request for quotation

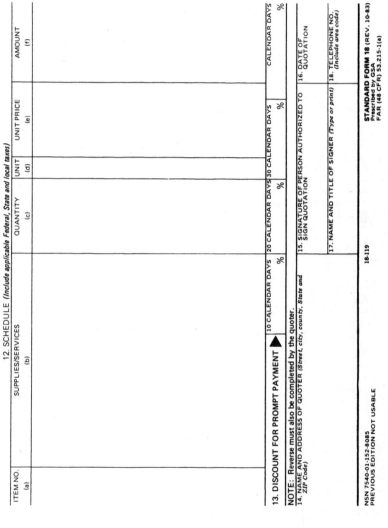

FIGURE 2-2. *(continued)*

STANDARD FORM 147, JUNE 1964—FED PROC REG (41 CFR) 1-3.605

ORDER FOR SUPPLIES OR SERVICES

PAGE 1 OF _ _ _

MARK ALL PACKAGES AND PAPERS WITH ORDER AND/OR CONTRACT NUMBERS ▼

ISSUING OFFICE

General Services Administration
18th & F Streets, NW
Washington, DC 20405

DATE OF ORDER	CONTRACT NO. (If any)	ORDER NO
2/25/77	03023709(A)	

REQUISITIONING OFFICE

CO-Office of Value Management – PWV

REQUISITION NO./PURCHASE AUTHORITY

ACCOUNTING AND APPROPRIATION DATA

192X75.71.P00I0001.901.25.516

CONTRACTOR (Name and address, including ZIP code)

TO→ Mr. Herman Holtz
1001 Connecticut Avenue, NW
Washington, DC 20036

SHIP TO (Consignee and address, including ZIP code)

Mr. R. Glenn Woodward
GSA-PBS-PWV-Room 6316
18th & F Streets, NW
Washington, DC 20405

VIA

TYPE OF ORDER

PURCHASE ☒ — REFERENCE YOUR Written Proposal of 5/22/75 PLEASE FURNISH THE FOLLOWING ON THE TERMS SPECIFIED ON BOTH SIDES OF THIS ORDER AND ON THE ATTACHED SHEETS, IF ANY, AND IS INDICATED. THIS PURCHASE IS NEGOTIATED UNDER AUTHORITY OF FPR Tempo Req 33 dated 8/6/74 and revised Bill 11/7/75

DELIVERY ☐ — EXCEPT FOR THE BILLING INSTRUCTIONS ON THE REVERSE, THIS DELIVERY ORDER IS SUBJECT TO INSTRUCTIONS CONTAINED ON THIS SIDE ONLY OF THIS FORM AND IS ISSUED SUBJECT TO THE TERMS AND CONDITIONS OF THE ABOVE NUMBERED CONTRACT.

F O B POINT	GOVERNMENT B/L NO	DELIVERY TO F O B POINT ON OR BEFORE	DISCOUNT TERMS

FIGURE 2–3. The purchase order

ITEM NO.	SUPPLIES OR SERVICES	QUANTITY ORDERED	UNIT	UNIT PRICE	AMOUNT	QUANTITY ACCEPTED
	SCHEDULE					
	Amendment No. 1 Delete all present wording and replace as follows:					
1.	Develop and produce a 15-minute storyboard for audiovisual presentation of "Overview of Value Management."					
	Revise, per Government review comments, and deliver final draft version as deliverable end-item.				$1,875.00	—
2.	Prepare a brochure version of storyboard, including artwork, through one revision, per Government review and comments.					
	Deliver final version in typed camera-ready copy, with all illustrations also camera-ready.				625.00	
	No change in costs is requested.					
	Items required to be delivered by May 1 3 1977. PW _____					

SIZE CLASSIFICATION	(Check one)	☒ SMALL BUSINESS	☐ OTHER THAN SMALL BUSINESS			TOTAL FROM CONTINUATION PAGES		(See reverse for minimum)
						GRAND TOTAL	$2,500.00	

SEE BILLING INSTRUCTIONS ON REVERSE

SHIPPING POINT	GROSS SHIPPING WEIGHT	INVOICE NO.

UNITED STATES OF AMERICA

BY _____

NAME (Typed) A. IUDICELLO

TITLE CONTRACTING/ORDERING OFFICER

MAIL INVOICES TO:
Office of Finance, BCFF, 19th & F Sts., NW
Washington, DC 20405   *Include ZIP code

STANDARD FORM 147, JUNE 1964   147-105

FIGURE 2–3. *(continued)*

Obviously, some sort of control over all this spending had to be established, so the Armed Services Procurement Regulations (ASPR) was created. And in time, son of ASPR was born: the Federal Procurement Regulations (FPR), patterned closely on the ASPR but tailored to civilian-agency procurement. A few years later, the National Aeronautics and Space Administration (NASA) mushroomed from a small bureau into a multibillion-dollar operation that marshaled its administrative forces and modified ASPR into NASPR—NASA Procurement Regulations. In addition, the Postal Service, which had been spending $10 billion a year even before inflation became serious, became a government corporation with its own procurement regulations.

Today there is, within the Office of Management and Budget (OMB), an OFPP or Office of Federal Procurement Policy. That entity's Federal Acquisition Regulations (FAR) project labored for several years to combine ASPR, FPR, and DAR (Defense Acquisition Regulations) and make them a uniform set to be known as the Federal Acquisition Regulations or FAR. Despite all the labors of the FAR project team, the changes were not dramatic because the various sets of regulations did not have a great deal of substantive difference among them. Some forms were different. Where military organizations used Form DD 633 for estimating costs, civilian agencies used Form 1141 which was quite similar to the 633. One difference among them was that the military operations had many provisions in ASPR for which there was no parallel application or need in FPR.

The Thickening Alphabet Soup

Until now, I've kept things on a rather simple level. There are two basic kinds of procurement, formally advertised and negotiated; two types of solicitation, information for bid (IFB) and request for proposals (RFP); and two types of contract, fixed-price and cost-reimbursement. The exception is the small purchase, for which purchase orders are issued. There may or may not be a solicitation formally announced for small purchases, but they may be arranged informally and spontaneously between buyer and seller.

But there are variants, hybrids, and combinations that defy definition in these terms. An RFP may result in either a fixed-price or a cost-reimbursement contract. Both fixed-price and cost-reimbursement contracts have several versions. The term "cost-reimbursement," for example, includes all of these:

- CPFF (cost plus fixed fee)
- CPAF (cost plus award fee)
- CPFF/AF (cost plus fixed fee and award fee)
- BOA (basic ordering agreement)
- T&M (time and material)

Even these may have variants such as below-the-line provisions (where certain cost items are billed at actual cost, with no profit) or provisions for a labor-hour contract (which is suspiciously close to a T&M). A fixed-price contract may be for a definite fixed quantity or for an indefinite quantity, in which case it is unit priced! There is also the two-step procurement, which is a hybrid of the negotiated and formally advertised procedures.

Now that your head is reeling with the complexity, let's back up and look at these one at a time.

Cost Plus Fixed Fee

I once won and operated a contract to support the NASA/Goddard Space Flight Center with technical publications and some related engineering services. Our contract was a CPFF/AF because NASA did not know just how much work we would be asked to do through the three years of the contract. In fact, as requirements arose, we were asked to estimate each job and quote a price, based on our contract. That made our contract also a BOA or T&M (which are really the same thing, in this case, and the contract could have been called a labor-hour or a task-type or even a call contract). All this will soon become much clearer.

Because NASA could not predict just how much work we would be asked to do (although they could and did provide a fair estimate), we were required, in bidding, to provide a billing rate (hourly) for each category of labor called for—writers, editors, engineers, illustrators, draftsmen, typists, and so on. Once the contract was in force, we would use these rates in estimating each job—for example, so many hours of writing, so many of editing, and so on.

The contract was a basic ordering agreement that established the conditions under which we would bid each task. Because the primary cost was labor, with supplies a minor item, it was principally a time-and-material or labor-hour contract.

When I say we "bid," I do not mean we bid against other contractors: We had the contract, and only we could bid for each task called for under it. But if the customer did not agree with our estimate, we had to negotiate the terms for that task, so we did not have a license to steal. We had a combination fixed-fee and award-fee arrangement. Our fixed fee was 1 percent of the total costs we had originally estimated the whole contract at (which was, in this case, about $1.6 million). No matter what happened to costs, whether the contract ultimately proved to cost more than $1.6 million or less than that, we would get not 1 percent of the ultimate cost, but 1 percent of $1.6 million. (That could change, under certain circumstances, but usually does not in cost-plus contracts.)

One percent is rather small for a fixed fee. Higher percentages are more usual, especially since the great inflation of recent years. However, NASA is fond of "incentive" contracts and wanted a small fixed fee and a larger award fee. Each quarter, a NASA board would sit and judge the amount of award fee we had earned by our diligence, dependability, cost-reduction suggestions, and so on.

In billing each task, we billed our actual costs. If we had a ceiling rate of $8 an hour for a senior writer, we could not bill more than that. If we paid the writer who worked on that task less than $8, we billed less—we billed what we actually paid the writer, plus overhead.

Variants

Not everyone contracts cost-plus jobs in that exact manner. In some cases, an average hourly rate is established for each labor category, and that is what is billed, regardless of who worked on the job or what his or her actual salary was. In still another variation, once the government accepts the contractor's estimate of the costs of a given task, that becomes the fixed price for that task, and that is what the contractor bills, regardless of what it actually costs.

These are the major variants, although different agencies use different terms to characterize such a contract, and each may add its own small flourishes.

Indefinite Quantity

Similar considerations may apply to contracts for goods. One contract may be for a given amount of something or other, at a fixed price. Another may state "indefinite quantity" and ask for unit prices, stipulating only that the total order will be not less than or more than. Again, orders will be issued throughout the year if it is a term contract rather than a one-shot procurement, and each task will be billed at the established rates.

Where such a contract is for more than one year, whether for services or supplies, the bidder is asked to estimate price increases, recognizing that costs are almost inevitably going to go up. And usually, in contracts for more than one year, the government has options each year, so it may drop an unsatisfactory contractor. (There is a strong tendency to keep the contractor, however; bureaucrats are usually reluctant to admit they made a bad choice originally.)

Annual Supply Contracts

What I have discussed so far are primarily those single contracts for custom goods or services and for needs of the moment. But there are thousands of standard commodities that the government refers to as "common use" items, which most, or at least many, agencies use regularly: cleaning compounds, office supplies, furniture, typewriters, calculators, computers, pipe, cameras, clothing, and many other items. There is a variant of this too: There are many items that many agencies use frequently, but not regularly or predictably. This makes for two different situations.

In the first situation, where most agencies will want typewriters, stamp pads, and ballpoint pens on a predictable, regular basis, the government stocks these items and disburses them as necessary from points. (The Federal Supply Service, for example, maintains 10 warehouses and 75 stores, stocks nearly 5 million items, and spends several billions annually.)

But there is the second case, in which many agencies will want photographic supplies, let's say, or dry cleaning services. The need may not be predictable, and the requirement may vary widely from year to year. Therefore, the Federal Supply Service may not want to stock the item. Yet the item must be readily available to any agency that has a sudden need. In this case, the item may be placed on one of the 300 Federal Supply Schedules or 200 similar purchasing arrangements, to be supplied as needed, at prices agreed upon for the year.

When, as in the case of such services as laundry and dry cleaning, it is not possible to supply the services except on a local basis, the government prefers to enter into annual contracts to ensure a dependable service at negotiated prices. Hence, these too are usually procured as annual supply agreements.

A Few Examples

Each military base must necessarily do some local buying—of milk, bakery products, cleaning services, laundry services, and other such supplies and services. Many federal installations use cleaning rags, and these are generally contracted locally on an annual basis. Moving and hauling, crating household goods, carpets, draperies, valves, and literally thousands of other items are on regular annual supply schedules. However, this does not prevent agencies from buying such items and services independently, with a few exceptions.

Here, again, the matter of agency policy is paramount. There are schedules for graphic arts services in many areas of the country, including Washington, D.C. When an item or service is on a schedule, and a contractor for the item is listed as one of the suppliers on that schedule, that contractor has agreed to a scale of prices for the year. (The schedules are agreements for one year; they are basic ordering agreements with each listed supplier.) Any federal agency (and many local governments) may order from that supplier by writing a purchase order. (Here, the $25,000 limitation does not apply but is governed by the terms of the schedule, which may be more or less than $25,000.) Some contracting officers pooh-pooh the schedules, which are supposed to be more convenient for them. They believe they can write their own purchase order as easily as they can write one under the schedule and see no extra convenience in using the schedule. Other contracting officers have a policy of buying only from suppliers listed on the schedule, when one exists for the item or service in question.

As a small, independent government contractor, I have operated under both situations: Some contracting officers did not care if I was on the schedule or not, and others would not give me the contract unless I was on the schedule.

Some Ground Rules and Case Histories

Ground rules for formally advertised procurements are much more stringent and severe than they are for negotiated procurements. In the case of formally advertised procurements, there are extremely few exceptions to the rule of award to the low bidder, for that's the entire objective of the procedure—to find the lowest bidder. But because cost is only one of several considerations in negotiated procurements, the law allows the agency a great deal of latitude in selecting a winner.

For example, a formally advertised bid must be opened at the exact time and place advertised, unless formally changed by a modification to the solicitation. Bidders may withdraw and/or modify their bids any time up to the time of opening, but not one minute later.

A contracting official will usually allow you to withdraw your bid after that time, but the law does not require him to. He can hold you firmly to that bid. For that reason, such solicitations are usually accompanied by a warning sheet urging you to check and double-check your figures, to be sure to sign your bid, and so on.

Your bid will be rejected and disqualified if you fail to sign it properly. This happened to one of my own bids. I was the low bidder, but my secretary had typed the bid and mailed it without bringing it to me to sign. I had not given it another thought until the contracting official called me to say he most regretfully had to reject the low bid.

There are a few other causes for rejecting bids: failure to respond and provide the information requested, failure to tell the truth in your representations, being on a blacklist. Wrongdoing as a contractor may put you on such a blacklist, as a punishment, either permanently or, in most cases, for some defined period.

But being the low bidder with all your paperwork in order assures you of the contract. If you are so low that the customer believes you have made a mistake and can't possibly deliver at the price quoted, he may so caution you and offer the opportunity to withdraw your bid voluntarily. But should you insist on having the contract, he cannot compel you to withdraw your bid or withhold the contract from you.

Theoretically, he can disqualify your bid on the grounds that you do not demonstrate technical capability to deliver. In practice, that is so difficult to prove that a contracting official will rarely try to proceed with it. Even if he should proceed, you may have other recourse, especially if yours is a small business. (I'll take this matter up again in Chapter 3.)

In some cases, bidders make mistakes in their arithmetic, and there are some ground rules for this, too. For example, suppose your price quotation looks something like that shown in Table 2–1.

TABLE 2–1. Price number of units total

Item	Per Unit	Required	Price
No. 2 pencils	$0.02	2,750	$550.00

The mistake is obvious: .02 × 2,750 is 55, not 550. What will prevail here will be the unit price quoted: $.02, or 2¢ per unit. The contracting official will correct the extension from $550 to $55, but neither he nor you can change the unit price. If you meant to quote $0.20, rather than $0.02, that is unfortunate. You are stuck with $.02 for this bid. If the mistake is a disastrous one, you may be allowed to withdraw the bid—but you may not!

If it is your practice to attend bid openings and record figures quoted, be watchful for possible errors in other people's bids, for the same things apply to all bids. In one case, I found myself the low bidder, as I expected to be, down to the opening of the last bid in the stack. To my dismay, that bid was a bit lower than mine. But in checking the figures, I discovered the bidder had made a mistake in his extensions, and I was, in fact, the low bidder. I pointed this out to the contracting official, but it wasn't necessary. He routinely audits all the figures in the bids before deciding who is the low bidder, for this very reason. In Chapters 5 and 6, I discuss bids in somewhat greater detail and explore the cost strategies you may use.

Negotiated procurements have entirely different and less stringent rules by the very nature of the procedure. Although you cannot arbitrarily elect to change your proposal after the opening date and time, the contracting official can give you such a right if he deems such action to be "in the best interests of the government." And he can do so by inviting you to submit additional or changed information, or he can do it during the course of actual negotiations. If you have failed to provide something or to sign something, he has the power to reject and disqualify your proposal as "nonresponsive," but he is not required to do so. He can permit you to make necessary changes, again if he thinks such is "in the best interests of the government."

This does not mean there are no rules or he may arbitrarily do anything he likes; you still have certain rights as a bidder (or "proposer," as requests for proposal solicitations often refer to bidders). Here are the basic ground rules:

1. The proposal must be submitted, in a sealed condition, before the time and date noted, at or to the place indicated.

2. Technical proposals must not reveal costs. Costs are in a separate document, which may be in the same package but must be separately bound. Some solicitations call for costs to be sealed in their own separate envelope within the package. Almost all RFP solicitations call specifically for two proposals: a technical proposal and a cost proposal.

3. Proposals must be individually evaluated by prescribed criteria, with at least some revelation or indication of those criteria made known to the bidders.

4. Those reviewing and evaluating technical proposals must not see or know the costs before making their evaluation, but must evaluate the proposal on technical merit alone.

5. The proposals are delivered to the contracting or procurement office. The contracting official will separate technical and cost proposals and deliver technical proposals to the evaluation team (often called the "source selection board" or panel).

6. Bidders who do not win have the right to a debriefing, which consists of a review of their proposals, after the award has been made, and an explanation of where and how their proposals fell short or were judged less meritorious than the one that won.

7. Bidders who do not win have a right to appeal, called a *protest,* which can be made directly to the contracting official or to the General Accounting Office. Such protests are often made by losers who believe that the evaluation and decision were unfair to them.

These are the basic rules and the safeguards built into the system. When the system fails to deliver what it is designed to deliver or a bidder receives unfair treatment or wins through influence and partiality, the true fault generally lies in the failure of bidders to pursue the prescribed remedies. The machinery is there to keep the system completely honest and above suspicion. But it is foolish to expect the system to police itself, as foolish as assigning a cat to guard a canary. Only the bidders themselves can police the system properly.

There are a number of other considerations, many of which require detailed explanations, which I present later. However, before leaving this chapter, here's a little tale to illustrate the truth of the preceding paragraph.

Several years ago, NASA held a proposal contest for design and construction of its "ATS" satellite, a $65 million project. The chief contestants were General Electric and Fairchild. The award was given to GE, which had done quite a bit of work for it. Fairchild immediately launched its own investigation and discovered that GE had delivered and NASA had accepted its proposal after the deadline. This was a clear violation of the procedures prescribed. (NASA could have granted an extension of time, but it would have had to offer that extension to everyone.)

I was a witness to the fact that Fairchild had delivered on time (barely) because I had personally bound up its proposal (I had been hired to provide certain assistance) and had sent it out to NASA by special messenger. It was delivered with only minutes to spare.

Fairchild proved its case in protesting the award. The GE contract was voided, and a contract was awarded to Fairchild instead. But without Fairchild's vigilance and protest, an illegal award would have been perpetuated.

CHAPTER 3

Get Help from the
Government to Sell
to the Government

They call it "socioeconomics."

Why the U.S. Government
Wants to Help You Sell to It

There are two reasons for the government's interest in helping you sell your goods and services to the federal agencies:

1. The intent of all procurement policy (in theory, at least) is to maximize competition, which is presumed to result in getting lower bids and better offers from suppliers and contractors.

2. There are numerous laws on the books that require federal agencies to provide ample business opportunity (and, frequently, preferential treatment) for small business generally, for minority- and women-owned businesses especially, and for other special classes and cases, such as those run by the physically handicapped and those located in economically depressed areas, where federal contracts would presumably create a few jobs.

A third reason, never openly admitted, is the knowledge that many who ought to be offering their goods and services to the government are hampered in doing so, or even prevented from doing so, by the lack of information on how to proceed to learn about business opportunities.

There is also the consideration that ours is supposed to be a democratic government, and the public is entitled to know all about the what, where, when, why, and how of government procurement. It's public information by its very nature.

Every federal agency has responsibilities in this respect. Some have comprehensive, well-organized programs of aid; some exist solely to provide such aid; and others give little more than lip service to their obligations to help businesses win government sales. First I consider some of the things all federal agencies are supposed to do.

Small Business Set-Asides

All agencies are supposed to identify those purchases or procurements they plan to make that could be satisfied by small businesses. That is, the agency is supposed to determine whether there is a sufficient number of small businesses that could respond to a given solicitation to assure the agency that satisfactory bids or proposals would result and that there would be ample competition. For example, suppose the air force wants to design an entirely new missile system. No small business can handle such a program. The companies that could and would bid for such a contract would be those such as Fairchild, General Dynamics, Boeing, North American, McDonnell-Douglas, Lockheed, GE, and other major aerospace/defense firms.

However, suppose the requirement is to prepare a set of technical manuals or drawings. Many small firms do such work, and a number of them would respond to an invitation to bid or write proposals for such a contract. Under the law, the agency should have determined this and "set aside" the procurement, which means the procurement is restricted to small business firms; large firms are barred from bidding.

Small Business Defined

The Small Business Administration (SBA) sets the standards by which an agency can determine how small a business must be to qualify as a "small business." They call this, in SBA parlance, a *size standard*.

Size standards are not the same for all industries, but must be established for each one. In many cases, there are several size standards, and the contracting officials must identify the size standard that applies in each case if the procurement is to be set aside for small business. In the case of technical writing and related services, three such size standards have been employed in the past:

1. Not more than $2 million per year in sales, averaged over the last three years
2. Not more than $5 million per year in sales, averaged over the last three years
3. Not more than 500 employees

In general, the law says that a firm must be "not dominant" in its industry to qualify as a small business, and the size standards presumably define the yardstick for determining whether a business is dominant in its industry. That is, "size" is never absolute but is relative to the typical firms in the industry and is established in terms of the industry. In the refining industry, for example, size is determined by number-of-barrels-per-day capacity of the firm's refining capability.

The responsibility for setting such procurements aside, for restricting the bidding to firms qualifying as small businesses under the SBA standards, belongs to the contracting official. Here again, internal policy has a decided effect on how well the program works in a given agency. In some cases, a firm policy will dictate that all procurements of a given type (technical writing and drafting, in certain agencies) are automatically set aside.

Such was the policy in the contracting office at Fort Belvoir, where the U.S. Army Corps of Engineers conducts a great deal of research and development. A few years ago, the Night Vision Laboratory there wanted to procure certain engineering support services. The contracting office's policy dictated that the procurement be set aside, but the "program" managers did not believe the work could be handled satisfactorily by a small business. To solve their dilemma, they arranged to have the procurement handled through the Army Material Command, which is at another site and did not have a policy preventing the program managers from opening the solicitation to all comers. The contract was subsequently awarded to a firm that did not qualify as a small business.

Small Business Subcontracts

Every large contract results in a number of subcontracts. When the U.S. Air Force awards that large, prime contract to General Dynamics or GE, the awardee invariably must look to many suppliers and subcontractors for help; no one does everything. Moreover, if the firm is already quite busy, it often does not have the staff or physical capacity to do the whole job itself. When RCA was awarded over $1 billion for the BMEWS (Ballistic Missile Early Warning System) project in 1958, which was the largest single contract ever awarded up to that time, RCA did approximately one-third of the work in-house and awarded more than 300 subcontracts to handle the remaining two-thirds.

Prime contractors are constantly urged, encouraged, and pressed to award at least some subcontracts to small businesses, minority enterprises, women-owned enterprises, and so on. And since the sixties, legislation has mandated some of this activity. The Department of Defense, because it is such a large purchaser, has an organized system to follow up on these goals, with many employees functioning both in the department and in major defense plants to implement such policies and regulations.

The pressure is increasing today. When Congress had the Economic Development Administration of the Department of Commerce disburse $6 billion in public works grants to state and local governments (to stimulate employment in construction industries), grantees were advised that at least 10 percent of the funds must be used to subcontract with minority-owned enterprises. In addition, NASA decrees that all bids for its large projects must be accompanied by at least a general plan for subcontracting with minorities, and a detailed plan must be submitted and approved before a contract will be finally let.

Many of the larger agencies have their own special publications to advise business people on their general needs, procedures, and special arrangements, if any, for winning some of their business. And many agencies have a special program for contracting with minorities and have issued publications to explain their programs. The Treasury and Interior Departments are two such agencies.

All agencies are supposed to have small business representatives or other people whose principal duties are to aid small business people in finding their way around the agency and learning of business opportunities within it. But there are also agencies whose sole purpose is to provide assistance of various kinds to small businesses, minority-owned businesses, and others the law says are entitled to special aid and preference of some kind in winning government contracts. Perhaps the best known of these, but not the only one, is the Small Business Administration.

The Small Business Administration

The SBA was created by the Small Business Act of 1953 and derives its authority from that and other statutes. It is not a large agency in terms of total number of employees or total budget, yet it maintains well over 80 regional and district offices throughout the United States.

It was originally created to further the interests of small business generally, through a variety of programs offering publications, training, counseling, and help in winning government contracts, in addition to several plans for helping businesses get financial aid. Many of its publications and services are entirely free; others are made available at a small charge.

In recent years, SBA programs have been widened to include aid to minority-owned enterprises under its "8(a)" program. The term derives from clause 8(a) of the Small Business Act, which is interpreted to provide the authority for the activities designated as part of that program. In that program, a firm may be certified as an 8(a) firm and thereby be entitled to be awarded federal contracts without the usual competition. Briefly, the program works as follows.

A federal agency identifies an anticipated procurement as one for which there are minority-owned firms qualified to do the work (or asks the SBA to help it make such a determination). Having thus decided, the agency negotiates a contract for the work with the SBA (which thus becomes the prime contractor). The SBA then negotiates a subcontract with a chosen 8(a) firm, without competition. Because the 8(a) firm cannot compete successfully with established firms (at least, theoretically), the SBA may award the subcontract for a larger price than it negotiated for the prime contract. The SBA has money (business development funds) it may use to make up the difference.

That's how the system is supposed to work. In practice, it does not always happen that way. For one thing, most agencies do not exercise a great deal of initiative in studying procurement needs and identifying those that may be set aside for 8(a) awards. Many of the 8(a) awards result from aggressive marketing efforts on the part of the 8(a) firms and the SBA.

Further, although the SBA in theory may arbitrarily decide what 8(a) firm gets the subcontract, in practice, the awarding agency makes a "recommendation" to the SBA after reviewing several 8(a) firms and their capabilities. The awarding agencies often request technical proposals from the 8(a) firms (but not cost proposals; 8(a) firms must not discuss costs with anyone but the SBA). The SBA almost always accepts the agency's "recommendation," although this is the reverse of how the system is supposed to operate.

There were only about 1,500 to 1,600 8(a) firms certified in the United States in 1992. More than 60 percent of them were black-owned firms; others were owned by Hispanics, American Indians, and Orientals, although 8(a) certification is not confined to these ethnic minorities. In fact, no one automatically qualifies by virtue of belonging to an ethnic minority. The law requires that each case be judged on its individual merits—a black or Hispanic citizen who is not "culturally and socially disadvantaged" should not qualify, under the law. However, many do "qualify," despite being relatively prosperous, well educated, and so on. The law was designed to benefit blacks, American Indians, Aleuts, Eskimos, Spanish-speaking Americans, and Orientals, and they are its chief beneficiaries. But to illustrate the law in practice, there is the case of the woman who owned an R&D firm in Bethesda, Maryland. She is white, and her company had been certified as an 8(a) firm. However, the SBA later decided she did not belong to a minority that was "socially and culturally disadvantaged" and revoked the 8(a) certification. She sued, arguing that, as a woman, white or not, she was in a field historically dominated by males and therefore *was* a minority in that field and suitably disadvantaged. Her 8(a) certification was restored.

Today it has become increasingly difficult to win 8(a) certification, especially if the applicant is in one of the fields already crowded with 8(a) firms. These tend to be service fields because service fields usually require far less capital investment than do manufacturing, wholesaling, or retailing. And among the more popular service fields for those seeking to establish a business base with government contracts are computer data processing and that broad sweep of activities marketed as "management consulting" and "management support." The SBA's attitude recently has been that it will not certify a new firm as 8(a) unless the firm is in a field for which the SBA perceives distinct contracting opportunity, the field is relatively uncrowded, and/or the firm can show evidence that it has federal contracts lined up and merely needs certification to get going. On the other hand, the SBA vows that if a minority-owned firm does do its marketing and finds an agency willing to issue an 8(a) contract to it, the SBA will process the 8(a) certifications swiftly and help the firm take advantage of the contract offer.

The Newest SBA 8(a) Program

Under legislation enacted by the 95th Congress (Public Law 95-507), the SBA was given some heavier weaponry in its battle to help minority firms win government contracts: authority to arbitrarily select projects for 8(a) contracting. The U.S. Army was then designated by the president as the first agency to be involved in this program, to test out the new law. New legislation has also broadened the SBA's programs for supporting women in business, an objective that has received little but oratory.

The SBA's "PASS" Program

Federal agencies have long complained that they are hampered in their efforts to make awards to small businesses or to set aside programs for small businesses by their own difficulties in determining whether small business capability exists for procurements they plan. To combat that problem, the SBA contracted for the development of the Procurement Automated Source System (PASS).

This is a computerized file of small businesses, suitably coded and updated each year, with access terminals in 11 federal agencies, including the SBA. The purpose of the system is to provide a library of small businesses so that any agency can swiftly search the files and determine what small business capability exists. The SBA has solicited all small businesses to apply for listing and will gladly send application forms to any who ask.

Other SBA Programs

The SBA has a variety of other assistance programs for small business, including many free publications, other publications available at a nominal cost, seminars, counseling, financial support (loans and loan guarantees), and advocacy.

The latter has some interesting facets. In Chapter 2, I pointed out that in theory, at least, a contracting official may disqualify your bid on the grounds that you do not exhibit the technical capability to deliver what is called for. If this happens, you may take your case to the SBA. SBA administrators will take action to hold up award of the contract while they check out your capability. If they are satisfied that you can handle the job (remember, they are working in your behalf), they can issue you a certificate of competency, which legally cancels the contracting official's action of disqualifying you.

In a counseling program, the SBA utilizes the services of retired executives, and some not yet retired, who volunteer their time to aid small business people with advice and guidance. That program is called SCORE (Service Corps of Retired Executives).

The SBA also provides some training programs, including seminars, through an SBA training division. In 1992, the SBA was planning to expand its training functions.

Department of Commerce

The U.S. Department of Commerce has a number of divisions, as do most agencies. However, because the Department of Commerce is concerned entirely with American business and industry, many of its activities are relevant to this book and its objectives.

Economic Development Administration (EDA)

The overall mission of the EDA is to create new jobs and save threatened jobs. It focuses especially on geographic areas where unemployment is high, that is, above the national average. Its programs are carried out through grants, loans, and loan guarantees.

For example, Congress voted in two bills to provide a total of $6 billion in grants to state and local governments (local governments, primarily) for local public works. The program was assigned to the EDA for administration, and the EDA awarded grants for approximately 8,000 local public works projects, under which were built roads, schools, water systems, industrial parks, libraries, fire stations, airports, and other such projects. The main objective was to stimulate employment in the various construction trades, which were suffering relatively high unemployment. However, the projects also created many other jobs.

Throughout the year, the EDA continually awards grants, under other legislation, to stimulate economies in various communities and so create jobs. Ordinarily, grants are made to nonprofit organizations, usually local governments, but sometimes they are made to institutions of learning, for such projects as vocational training, counseling small businesses, studying local economic problems to seek solutions, and so on.

Loans and loan guarantees are generally resorted to when privately owned enterprises require assistance. Again, the rationale is to create new jobs or save threatened ones. The applicant for such assistance must demonstrate that jobs will be created or saved by the financial assistance. In one program, the EDA furnished approximately $20 million to about 20 small organizations in economically depressed areas to establish revolving funds for small business loans. Small businesses can thereby borrow money at relatively low interest rates. The program is experimental and will probably be expanded if it's successful.

A business suffering "foreign import damage" (losing business because of imported goods) may get EDA financial assistance. First, the Labor Department must certify that the company is suffering such damage. However, it is not the company that applies for such certification, but the employees whose jobs are threatened, usually through their unions. Once the certification is granted by the Labor Department, the employer may take the application and the plan for using the money to the EDA.

The EDA has a large number of programs, each with its own enabling legislation. Among them are the following:

EDA Planning Grants for Economic Development
EDA Grants for Public Works and Development Facilities
Business Development Assistance
Technical Assistance
Economic Development Districts

Trade Adjustment Assistance
The Indian Industrial Development Program

Minority Business Development Agency (MBDA)

As its name suggests, the MBDA is a special office in Commerce devoted solely to helping minorities start and succeed in business. Next to the SBA, it is the most comprehensive and active program of its kind, although it has been heavily criticized in Congress for an alleged lack of effectiveness. Funded at approximately $50 million a year, the MBDA devotes virtually its entire budget to training and technical assistance efforts. Translated into action, this means that the MBDA supports approximately 300 organizations throughout the United States, which have agreed to furnish certain assistance functions to minority entrepreneurs. The organizations funded fall into 12 categories:

Business development centers
Business management development (organizations)
Business resource centers
City MBDAs
Construction contractor assistance centers
Contracted support services
Experiment and demonstration (projects)
Local business development organizations
Minority business and trade associations
National business development organizations
Private resource programs
State MBDAs

Many of these organizations receive all their funds from the federal (Commerce Department) MBDA; others are also supported by the SBA, Labor Department, and other funding organizations, both public and private.

The programs vary widely. Some provide direct technical, training, and counseling assistance to the individual entrepreneur; others pursue larger companies to provide business opportunities for minority firms. Some programs are organized solely to apply for MBDA and SBA funding and carry out the programs contracted for; others are existing organizations that have expanded their activities to handle MBDA and SBA assistance programs, for example, trade associations, local chambers of commerce, and so on.

As a whole, MBDA officials take the most pride in their track record in helping minority enterprises get funding (bank loans), and they appear to measure their success primarily by this yardstick.

Overall, MBDA activities are administered by 6 regional and 12 field offices in the United States. Unlike the SBA program, minority entrepreneurs do not have to be certified in any way to participate in and be eligible for MBDA assistance; they merely need to be qualified as owners, with at least 51 percent, of a business enterprise. And minorities are defined as including, "but not exclusively, blacks, Puerto Ricans, Spanish-speaking Americans, American Indians, Eskimos, and Aleuts." What "not exclusively" refers to is not made clear, but Orientals are generally included in minority programs, and, presumably, other minorities could qualify without undue difficulty.

Commerce also offers assistance in importing and exporting, much of it entirely free of charge, some at a special low cost. American business people may, for example, participate in trade shows held by the Department of Commerce in other countries. Commerce also provides a great deal of information about foreign buyers' needs and functions in several ways to bring American suppliers and foreign buyers together. For example, Commerce prints notices almost daily in the *Commerce Business Daily* (described in Chapter 4). A few examples are given in Figure 3–1.

The U.S. State Department operates AID (the Agency for International Development), under which it provides help of many kinds to other nations, especially to the Third World or developing nations. The Department of Commerce also publicizes these, when they provide opportunities to American business, in its *Commerce Business Daily*. Figure 3–2 is an example of one such notice.

FOREIGN TRADE OPPORTUNITIES
DEPARTMENT OF COMMERCE

Many trade opportunities received from U.S. Embassies are not included in the Commerce Business Daily. For information on how you can receive all such Trade Opportunities, contact your local U.S. Department of Commerce District Office, or the Trade Opportunites Program, Room 2014, U.S. Department of Commerce, Washington, D.C. 20230. (202) 377-2091.

The Commodity codes shown are based on the Standard Industrial Classification Manual, 1972, listing.

U.S. firms should be aware that the listing in "Commerce Business Daily" of opportunities to trade in specific commodities and technical data does not necessarily imply approval of their export by the Department of Commerce pursuant to the Department's Export Administration Regulations. Applicable export licensing regulations must be followed.

Every effort is made to include only firms or individuals with good reputations. However, the Department cannot be responsible for any trade relations.

DIRECT SALES

Foreign private firms and government agencies are interested in direct purchases of these products.

38720—WATCHCASES—INDIA - - Rajendra Singh, Managing Director, Western Maharashtra Development Corp. Ltd., Red Cross House, 3rd Fl., Mahatma Gandhi Rd., Poona 411 001, India, Cable: Westdev; Tel. 28146/25710, wishes to locate U.S. firms interested in supplying a reconditioned plant with a capacity to produce one million watch cases annually. WMDC is a government of Maharashtra undertaking, est. in 1970 with the objective of promoting industries in the western Maharashtra region. WMDC in collaboration with Hindustan Machine Tools, Bangalore, have started a watch assembly unit in the Shiroli Industrial Area at Kolhapur and propose to expand the assembly operation into a watch manufacturing complex. The proposed watch case manufacturing plant will be located adjacent to the watch assembly unit. The project initially envisages manufacturing 500,000 cases, and progressively increase production to one million cases/yr. The watch cases are to be manufactured from stainless steel and brass to international specs. Est. total project cost Rs.20 million ($1 - Rs. 8.20 approx.) of which fixed assets would be Rs.15.6 million. Plant and machinery including measuring and inspection equip. has been est. at Rs.8.0 million. WMDC's proposal envisages the importation of a reconditioned watch case plant to manufacture 1.0 million watch cases. The plant will be operated in conjunction with the watch assembly unit which requires 300,000 cases/yr. The remaining cases would be marketed locally as well as abroad. WMDC would be interested in a buy back arrangement for 500,000 unity. It is proposed that the watch case unit will be wholly owned by the corp. Mr. Singh stated that he is willing to negotiate ASAP with interested U.S. firms. (127)

FIGURE 3–1.   Samples of foreign trade opportunities as reported in *Commerce Business Daily*

22810—YARN MILLS—ISRAEL -- Mr. Danon from Tel Aviv will visit New York City 15-25 May 79 to purchase combed cotton yarns, carded cotton yarns, and blended polyester/cotton yarns for the textile industry. Mr. Danon also wants to negotiate an agreement to represent U.S. yarn suppliers as exclusive agent and distributor in Israel. Mr. Danon estimates that he can handle an annual sales potential of 3,000 tons for cotton yarns and 2,000 tons for blended yarns. Est. in 1943, this family owned company employs 5 and reportedly imported $5 million in yarns from Italy and Spain last year. Interested U.S. suppliers may call or write Mr. Corfitzen, USDOC, Washington D.C. 20230; Tel 202/377-3265. (110)

35590—SPECIAL INDUSTRY MACHINERY—EGYPT -- Mr. Reda Elias Khalil from Cairo will visit U.S. 30 Apr. He wishes to purchase complete line of equip. for making shoe soles and related articles out of therm-plastic materials. Mr. Khalil is especially interested in 3 injection-molding machines with appropriate attachments each capable of producing 40 pairs of soles per hour. He estimates the value of the required machinery at approx. $200,000, and is ready to immediately open a letter of credit. For additional info. contact Jane Puse, Foreign Buyer Program, Rm. 2015-B USDOC, Washington DC 20230, 202/377-3265, ref. Cairo 7287/Khalil. (110)

33160—STEEL SHEETS—PAKISTAN -- Mr. Ghauri from Lahore will visit New York City, Cleveland, Baltimore, and San Francisco in Jul to purchase ferrous and non-ferrous scrap. Specifically, buyer wants to purchase: A) iron and steel items of secondary quality such as galvanized plain steel sheets, soft commercial quality, bright spangled, thickness 20 gauge to30 gauge; B) CRCA sheets, soft commercial quality, thickness 16 gauge to 28 gauge; C) Hot rolled mild steel sheets coils. soft, thickness 9 gauge to 16 gauge; D) Stainless steel sheets Type 384/392, 2B/2D/PA finish, thickness 20 gauge to 26 gauge; E) Non-ferrous scrap such as aluminum scraps, brass scrap and copper scrap of any description; and F) Ferrous scrap such as Isis Code No. 200 Hms 1 and Isis Code No. 210/211 shredded scrap. U.S. suppliers interested in contacting Mr. Ghauri may call or write Bill Corfitzen, Rm. 2015-B, U.S.D.C, Washington DC 20230; Tel 202/377-3265. (127)

11110—ANTHRACITE—UNITED KINGDOM -- High grade Anthracite sizes 1½ to 2" & 2 to 3" for domestic use. Smokeless mfrd. solid fuels especially hard ovoids approx. 2" long. Firm is recently formed small buying agency with 2 employees. Owner is also involved in solid fuel retail firm. E.A. March & Sons, Andover, Est. 1868. Claimed local production insufficient to meet current demand for above fuels which are now being imported from various overseas sources. Quotations Requested. REF-MIDLAND Bank Ltd., Andover, Hampshire. This is a free notice. Your account is not charged. Reply to: D. March, Derrick

FIGURE 3–1. *(continued)*

DEPARTMENT OF STATE
AID FINANCED

Suppliers of goods and services are advised that the Agency for International Development has a policy of obtaining maximum possible competiton for projects that it finances. All qualified contractors are encouraged to participate. A.I.D. will not finance any procurement in which boycott or other restrictive trade practices are applied.

EGYPT: PLANNING AND PRE-FEASIBILITY STUDIES FOR DEVELOPMENT OF THE SINAI. Phase I of the studies will consist of the identification of technically, financially and economically attractive projects in the western section of the penninsula to which access will soon be available. Potential projects to be identified in course of study may include, but not be limited to, agricultural, industrial, mining, (exclusive of petroleum), energy and transportation infrastructure and new settlements. The consultant will establish the overall regional context for such projects by development of a preliminary planning strategy for the entire peninsula. Selected projects will be developed to pre-feasibility levels, for subsequent feasibility study by specialized consultants. The purpose of phase I work is to provide the initial impetus to sound development of the Sinai within a rational, long range strategy. It is anticipated that phase I studies will require twelve months for completion. For information, phase II studies, not a part of this proposed contract, will, tentatively, consist of expansion of pahse I studies into other areas of the Sinai Peninsula as access becomes available, and the development of a 25-year economic and regional plan for the Sinai and detailed master plans for selected areas of the Sinai. It is estimated that phase II studies will require approximately three years to complete. Dollar costs for these professional services will be financed by aid. Local costs will be paid in Egyptian pounds by the Ministry. A cost-plus-fixed-fee contract for the above services is contemplated. Pre-qualification information must indicate the firm's or joint venture's experience and expertise in studies of similar nature. Submittals must include completed standard forms 254 and 255 (Architect-engineer questionnaires) which can be obtained by calling the near east office of project development (202)632-9815. Data indicating firm's financial status must also be submitted. Interested firm's brochures and annual reports may also be of value in presenting qualifications. Joint ventures seeking prequalification must supply full information on all firms in venture. Prequalifying data must be received by Dr. Hassan Marie, chairman, Advisory Committee for Reconstructin, Ministry of Development and New Communities, 1 Ismail Abaza Street, Cairo, A.R.E., by May 31, 1979. One information copy each should also be sent to: (1) NE/PD,, Room 4716, Attn: T.A. Sterner, AID, Washington, D.C. 20523, and (2) USAID, Attn: P.S. Lewis, American Embassy, Box 10, FPO New York, 09527. After evaluation of qualifying information, the ministry will establish a short-list of prequalified firms to whom request for technical proposals will be issued. Firms thus selected who wish to submit technical proposals will be required to attend a pre-proposal conference in Egypt. The firm finally selected may, upon satisfactory completion of the phase I study, and at the option of the ministry, be requested to provide, under a contract amendment or new contract, subsequent services relative to performance of phase II of the study. (120)

FIGURE 3–2. Trade and purchasing opportunities

Also published in the *Commerce Business Daily,* as a service to American business and individuals (although private individuals would rarely see the *Commerce Business Daily*), are notices of government surplus property for sale. For an example, see Figure 3–3. The government-owned surplus property for sale varies widely in both type and condition. Some is quite old and worn, having only salvage value in many cases. Some is quite serviceable. And some is brand-new, still in its original packing.

The property may be raw materials, timber, real estate, equipment, furniture, or almost anything else, including strategic materials no longer needed. In most cases, surplus property is disposed of by the Defense Department or the General Services Administration. (Instructions for getting on mailing lists to bid for surplus are supplied in Appendix 6.) Usually, such bids are sealed, and where it is appropriate, notice is given of where and when the property offered may be inspected.

Other Types of Aid

There are other ways the U.S. government helps business generally, especially in winning federal contracts. One of these is a provision that authorizes government agencies to lend government-owned property to contractors. It is expected, of course, that the loan of government-owned property to a contractor will result in some lowering of the contractor's price (although it does not appear always to have that result). In the free-swinging days of huge cost-plus contracts for military goods, military agencies often bought property especially for the purpose of lending it to contractors! However, it is not uncommon today to furnish a facility with government-owned desks, typewriters, and so on, especially for cost-plus contracts.

Another variation of this, again usually for cost-plus contracts, is to authorize the contractor to buy from GSA stores, which usually means a somewhat lower price for supplies. In some cases, the saving is considerable. In one case that comes to memory, toner for

SURPLUS PROPERTY SALES

FORMER U.S. ARMY RESERVE CENTER Short Cut Rd., Cottrellville Township, MI; 18.89 acres of land, improved with 11 misc. structures, located approx 4 miles southwest of Marine City.—Sealed Bid sale, D-MICH-697, will be opened 25 May 79. (113)

    GSA, Region 5, Business Service Center, Rm 3670, Fed. Bldg., 230 S. Dearborn St., Chicago, IL 60604, Tel: 312/353-5383

VACANT U.S. POSTAL SITE at Fifth St. and Banning Ave., White Bear Lake, MN: 0.57 acre of vacant land, ideal commercial or office site.—Minimum acceptable bid price is $60,000.—IFB P-MINN-524.—Sealed Bid opening 23 May 79.—(113)

    GSA, Region 5, Business Service Center, Rm 3670, Fed. Bldg., 230 S. Dearborn St., Chicago IL 60604

ELECTRONIC MEASURING/TESTING EQUIP Air Purification Equip, Analog Control System, Misc Electronic Components, Misc Hardware, Special Test and Hydraulic Equip, and Project Tooling, condition ranges from Unused Excellent to Poor, Repairs Required. U.S. Navy-owned Research and Development Material of Commercial and Specialized type; 19 lots——Acq Cost $447,391.86—Sealed Bid Sales Case S-4014—Bid Opening 15 May 79—Property Location: 227 Curtis Ave., Milpitas, CA. (113)

    Lockheed Missiles & Space Co., Inc., PO Box 504, Sunnyvale CA 94086, Attn: John Vincent, Org. 41-50, Bldg. 514, Tel: 408/743-0226

VEHICLES: AMC, Ford, Plymouth, Oldsmobile, Cadillac, Buick, Pontiac sedans, station wagons, sedan deliveries, panel trucks, and eight four-wheel drive vehicles: used, 114 lots—Auction Sale, 5DPS-79-46—to be conducted at the GSA Personal Property Center, 4100 W. 76th St., Chicago, IL 60652—3 May 79.—Inspect between 8:30 a.m. and 4 p.m., 1-2 May; and 8:30 until 10 a.m. 3 May. (113)

    GSA, Sales Branch, Personal Property Div, 230 S. Dearborn St., Chicago IL 60604. Tel: 312/353-6061

FIGURE 3–3. Notices of surplus property sales

duplicating machines that cost $40 on the open market was available from the GSA for $8.

Other Types of Financial Aid for Small Business

Any contractor may specify a need for financial assistance when undertaking a contract. Usually, this is specified as "progress payments," although other types of financial aid are possible, including advance payments. The latter, however, are the exception rather than the rule. For example, the Department of Defense may authorize an advance payment, under 10 USC 2700, if the need satisfies the conditions under which advance payments may be made. But advance payments are a last resort, to be used when no other means of financing is feasible and when the agency believes it to be "in the best interests of the government" to consummate a contract with the bidding organization. Ordinarily, the ability to finance a contract is a required qualification for being awarded a contract.

However, a contractor is always justified in requesting progress payments as a contract performance goes forward, and a small business is legally *entitled* to progress payments; that is, the agency cannot deny them that right.

Usually, a long-term contract carries with it a provision for progress payments, often in the form of monthly billings for work accomplished or tasks completed. However, my own experience has been that most contracting officials are willing, especially for small businesses, to accept billings as frequently as every two weeks, although monthly billings are more common.

Assistance in Winning Subcontracts

All the military organizations have small business representatives at major military procurement centers and/or industrial plants engaged in major contracts with the military. Their main function is to see that a fair percentage of subcontracts let is awarded to small business firms.

However, there is an organization known as the Defense Contract Administrative Services, which performs several functions for the military agencies. For one, DCAS (as it is generally referred to) is responsible for "facility clearance." That is the function of awarding security clearances to establishments doing secret work and policing those facilities by inspections. Another function is to represent the agency in inspecting products in cases where it is not expedient for agency officials to do this themselves. A third function is to support small business programs in military procurement. DCAS offices, of which there are a number throughout the United States, have small business representatives.

All these resources may be used by small businesses in seeking subcontracts in military procurements. To report in detail on all the programs referred to in this chapter would be all but impossible, unless I am to produce an encyclopedia-sized book. However, each agency produces its own literature—brochures, manuals, news releases, memoranda, and even newsletters, most of them free to the public. (And even those publications for which the Government Printing Office charges may often be gotten free, as I explain in Chapter 9.) Requests to the various agencies for information on any of the programs referred to here will bring back armloads of literature on each subject. (Some of the specific titles of relevant government publications appear in Chapter 9 and in Appendix 5.)

CHAPTER 4

Finding Out About

Government Needs

It takes legwork.

The *Commerce Business Daily*

The nameplate and part of the first page of a copy of the *Commerce Business Daily* (CBD) is shown in Figure 4–1. It is published five days a week by the Department of Commerce and printed by the Government Printing Office in Chicago. Its main purpose is to advise everyone interested in government requirements where and how to order a copy of the solicitation package (or "bid set," as many bidders refer to it). However, the publication is also utilized to make other information and announcements known to readers:

- Contract awards made: nature and size of contract, agency, awardee
- Trade leads: notices of opportunities for foreign sales, such as shown in Figures 3–1 and 3–2
- Notices of government surplus for sale (see Figure 3–3)
- Research and development sources sought: advance notices of anticipated procurements, with invitation to apply for inclusion on bidders list
- Business news: notices of government-sponsored seminars on federal procurement, trade shows, conferences, conventions, and other such activities of interest to government contractors

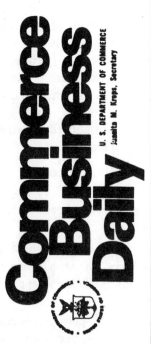

FIGURE 4–1. Front page of *Commerce Business Daily*

A typical issue lists hundreds of solicitations and other notices, such as those shown in Figure 4–1. Solicitations and awards are divided into two broad groups: services and supplies, equipment and materials. Each of these is subdivided into a number of subcategories, amounting to over 100 in all.

See the lists following for the goods and services under which solicitation notices are listed in the CBD. Despite the length of this list, there is a "Miscellaneous" category for both goods and services, for those items that do not appear to fit into any of the categories. However, each category is sufficiently broad to accommodate a wide range of goods and/or services. The heading "Maintenance and Repair of Equipment," for example, may fit any kind of equipment, from ships to typewriters, and "maintenance" may range from minor service work to major overhaul.

Goods and Services Listed in the Commerce Business Daily

Services

A Experimental, developmental, test, and research work

H Expert and consultant services

J Maintenance and repair of equipment

K Modification, alteration, and rebuilding of equipment

L Technical representative services

M Operation and maintenance of government-owned facility

N Installation of equipment

O Funeral and chaplain services

P Salvage services

Q Medical services

R Architect-engineer services

S Housekeeping services

T Photographic, mapping, printing, and publication services

U Training services

V Transportation services

W Lease or rental, except transportation equipment

X Miscellaneous (services)

Y Construction (various)

Z Maintenance, repair, and alteration of real property

Supplies, Equipment, and Material

10 Weapons

11 Nuclear ordnance

12 Fire control equipment

13 Ammunition and explosives

14 Guided missiles

15 Aircraft and airframe structural components

16 Aircraft components and accessories

17 Aircraft launching, landing, and ground-handling equipment

18 Space vehicles

19 Ships, small craft, pontoons, and floating docks

20 Ship and marine equipment

22 Railway equipment

23 Motor vehicles, trailers, and cycles

24 Tractors

25 Vehicular equipment components

26 Tires and tubes

28 Engines, turbines, and components

29 Engine accessories

30 Mechanical power transmission equipment

31 Bearings

32 Woodworking machinery and equipment

34 Metalworking machinery

35 Service and trade equipment

36 Special industry machinery

37 Agricultural machinery and equipment

38 Construction, mining, excavating, and highway maintenance equipment

39 Materials handling equipment

40 Rope, cable, chain, and fittings

41 Refrigeration and air-conditioning equipment

42 Fire-fighting, rescue, and safety equipment

43 Pumps and compressors

44 Furnace, steam plant, and drying equipment; nuclear reactors

45 Plumbing, heating, and sanitation equipment

46 Water purification and sewage treatment equipment

47 Pipe, tubing, hose, and fittings

48 Valves

49 Maintenance and repair shop equipment

51 Hand tools

52 Measuring tools

53 Hardware and abrasives

54 Prefabricated structures and scaffolding

55 Lumber, millwork, plywood, and veneer

56 Construction and building materials

58 Communications equipment

59 Electrical and electronic equipment

61 Electric wire; power and distribution equipment

62 Lighting fixtures and lamps

63 Alarm and signal systems

65 Medical, dental, and veterinary equipment and supplies

66 Instruments and laboratory equipment

67 Photographic equipment

68 Chemicals and chemical products

69 Training aids and devices

70 General purpose ADP equipment; software, supplies, and support equipment

71 Furniture

72 Household and commercial furnishings and appliances

73 Food preparation and serving equipment

74 Office machines, visible record equipment

75 Office supplies and devices

76 Books, maps, and other publications

78 Recreational and athletic equipment

79 Cleaning equipment and supplies

80 Brushes, paints, sealers, and supplies

81 Containers, packaging, and packing supplies

83 Textiles, leather, furs, apparel and shoe findings, tents and flags

84 Clothing, individual equipment, and insignia

85 Toiletries

87 Agricultural supplies

89 Subsistence

91 Fuels, lubricants, oils, and waxes

93 Nonmetallic fabricated materials

94 Nonmetallic crude	96 Ores, minerals, and
materials	their primary
95 Metal bars, sheets,	97 Miscellaneous
and shapes	

The CBD is virtually a "bible" for government contractors, especially those seeking custom service work. However, daily reading of the CBD will not keep you posted on all or even most of the current requirements. The CBD listings probably reflect not more than about 10 percent of the requirements, at best.

A number of factors explain why the CBD reflects probably not more than a fraction of all federal procurement, whereas the total procurement is most definitely well in excess of $200 billion. One reason is that a large percentage of federal buying is done under special arrangements, such as chemical products by using the Federal Supply Schedules. Another is that, under the law, agencies are required to list in the CBD only those procurements expected to be in excess of $25,000. Still another reason is that the agencies are habitually remiss in their obligations to list procurements and often do not list even rather large ones.

In any case, valuable though the CBD is (and, used properly, it is quite valuable to the marketer), other means must also be used to stay on top of the market. Fortunately, there are other ways to learn of government requirements and buying intentions, and alert marketers utilize all of them.

Reading the CBD

The CBD is an "in" publication. Anyone reading it for the first time is almost inevitably thoroughly confused, partially by the trade jargon and partially by the abundance of categories. Here, for example, are a few of the commonly used phrases and abbreviations:

Term	Means
RFP	Request for proposal (proposal required; contract will be negotiated)

IFB	Information for bid (sealed bids, with public opening; sometimes called "formally advertised" procurement; low bid will win)
Indef qty	Indefinite quantity (will call for unit prices, to be ordered as needed, possibly for entire year)
FOB	Free on board (contractor will include shipping costs in price)
B/L	Bill of lading (usually used when government will pay for shipping by providing a B/L shipping document)
RFQ	Request for quotation (not binding on either party, but may be the basis for issuing a government purchase order)
IAW	In accordance with (usually followed by a part or a specification number)
P/N	Part number
o/a	On or about (followed by date)
COB	Close of business (followed by date)
Multiple award	More than one contract will be issued (several suppliers desired)
NSN	National stock number
FSC	Federal stock code
IG	Industrial group

These are by no means all the abbreviations and designators used, but are a sampling. (See Appendix 8 for a more complete list.)

Despite the many categories in the CBD, or perhaps because of them, many items are misfiled. Category 69 is for training aids and devices, for example, meaning training equipment of various sorts. Yet requirements for training manuals may often be found here, although they ought properly to appear under T or U. And sometimes such a requirement may be found under category H, or even "Miscellaneous." It is wise, therefore, to read every possible category every day, or you are almost certain to miss an occasional opportunity.

And those often turn out to be the best opportunities because many other people have missed them, and the competition may be rather light!

Using the CBD

Using the CBD is not the same thing as reading the CBD. In some ways, it's even more important than reading the CBD. A great deal of market research may be done every morning by using the CBD as one information source.

First, there is that special category in the CBD almost every day: "Research and Development Sources Sought." These are advance notices from various federal agencies of anticipated procurements. The purpose of the notice is to develop a list of qualified bidders. The notice describes the kind of technical and professional capabilities sought and requests that anyone interested in becoming a bidder furnish a "statement of capabilities."

The capabilities statement may be a regular, printed brochure, but usually it is developed especially for the purpose. Only those whose capabilities statements satisfy the agency that the organization is technically qualified will be invited to submit a proposal later, when the solicitation package is ready for distribution.

Periodically, the CBD also carries advance notices of military procurements anticipated for the future. And occasionally, a notice will advise readers that they can write to an agency, for example, the U.S. Navy, and get a complete brochure on some of its procurement plans.

The front page of the CBD is used to announce conferences, seminars, symposia, and other events that should interest contractors under the general heading "Business News." Such conferences are held regularly at various places throughout the United States, frequently under the sponsorship of your own congressional representative. At these meetings, you often get the opportunity to hear procurement specialists from various government agencies counsel listeners on future procurements, methods of selling to federal agencies, and related matters. In other cases, the meeting is a professional conference, at which you may be able to gain useful information about trends, both business and technical.

And finally, daily reading of the CBD will eventually reveal certain patterns of procurement. You'll begin to perceive which agencies are buying these days and what they are buying. That is, you'll see some agencies buying certain classes of supplies or services on a regular basis, rather than intermittently, and that should set off an "alert signal," causing you to visit the agency and investigate the reasons behind the surge of buying. It will help you identify which agency or program represents a long-term source for a flow of business, as distinct from the target-of-opportunity source. Such a prospect merits placing that agency on a must-call-on list, just as you would a commercial prospect for business. And reading the awards section of the CBD every day will help you analyze your competition even more readily than you can in the commercial markets because you can learn exactly what they sold, to whom, and for how much!

Bidders Lists

Agencies that buy with any regularity maintain bidders lists—plural for two reasons:

1. In many cases, the agency buys with such diversity that different kinds of suppliers are required; hence, many different bidders lists must be maintained.
2. In some cases, so many bidders apply for inclusion on the lists that several lists are maintained and the bidders are "rotated"; that is, any given list may be used only for every third or every fourth procurement.

On the other hand, many agencies have difficulty establishing and maintaining bidders lists because their requirements are always custom requirements and are almost always unique needs, so they are never certain which of those listed are right for the procurement. In such cases, it is often necessary for the agency to go to the effort of establishing a bidders list for each procurement. That's one function of the CBD—to help agencies find bidders for their needs.

How Solicitations Originate

People who initiate requests for procurements, often referred to as "program people," are not the same as "procurement people" or "contracts people." Their interests and their desires are different, and it is helpful to bidders to understand and appreciate those differences.

Program managers often do not have all the help they need on their own staff to carry out their programs. They must therefore look to outside, contracted services to help them get their jobs done. Let's take a typical case to show how the mechanism works generally and what the various roles are in the process.

Branch Chief Jones has been charged with developing a training program in occupational safety and health. She studies the project, develops a generalized outline of what should be contained in such a program, and searches around her branch for someone to write and produce the program.

She soon discovers that she either does not have enough help available to do the job or that she does not have a staff with the right knowledge and skills to produce the program. She is now forced to consider alternatives, which usually means "contracting out"—seeking contract assistance. First, she must be sure she has the money and can get an okay to spend it (or has the authority herself to spend it). But before she can do that, she must get a pretty good idea of what the job will cost.

There are several ways she can get a fix on probable price. She might call in some suppliers she knows or who have been calling on her and leaving their cards. A little discussion and they will "ballpark" the price for her. She could go out with an RFQ (request for quotation) and solicit prices. Or she could inquire within government circles— call offices in other agencies that have bought similar products and services—and ask them to provide estimates.

In any case, she will eventually come up with an in-house estimate or projected budget for the job. She is now ready to ask for the money, to make a purchase request or sit down with the boss. Or she may be able to earmark the money, if it is hers to spend on her own authority. She will have to decide whether this is to be a formally advertised procurement or a negotiated one, although in this case, it will almost certainly be negotiated.

To actually announce the requirement and invite proposals, she has to turn the package over to the contracting officer who is going to handle the procurement. But before she can do that, she will have to write a statement of work (SOW), in which she describes to bidders (proposers) what she wants and what they are to propose. Once she has that prepared, she will probably consult with the contracting officer about related matters: who will evaluate the proposals, how long she will allow for preparation of proposals, who is to be invited to bid (she can suggest bidders to the contracting officer and may even be invited to do so), and many other details. But at this point, the contracting people take over.

The program people are interested in getting a good contractor, one who will turn out a fine job for them, meet all deadlines, and be easy to get along with. Writing an SOW, reading and evaluating proposals, negotiating, and all the other tasks connected with awarding a contract competitively are extra work that the program people would rather not have to do. But it is just that kind of work that the contracting people are responsible for; that's the reason their jobs exist. The program people are interested only in getting the help they need to get the job done; the contracting people are interested in doing things by the book; so the interests of the two groups do not always coincide.

It's no accident that most contracting officials are either lawyers or accountants and frequently both. Their two areas of greatest concern are the law (procurement regulations) and the "numbers" (costs, accounts, and so on). To look at this another way, the contracting official's goal is to get the best job done or best product delivered, in the shortest possible time, at the lowest possible price. That should be the program manager's objective, too. But procurement is not his occupation; it's just a necessary evil. As far as he's concerned, the time he devotes to that is lost time. Therefore, he is often less concerned with getting the lowest price than with other matters, such as speeding up and simplifying the procurement procedures. Given his "druthers," he might very well elect to avoid a competitive procurement entirely and simply select a contractor with whom to conduct negotiations. In fact, many do exactly that whenever they can.

One way to get the best possible price, and perhaps the best possible job done in the shortest possible time, is to maximize the competition—get as many bids or proposals as possible. Contracting officers therefore usually welcome your bids and are happy to have as many names as possible on bidders lists. Keep this attitude of the contracting officer in mind. It will help you understand contracting procedures. At the same time, remember that contracting officers are human beings, too, and as variable as the rest of the race: jovial, dour, easygoing, hard-driving, and so on. The contracting official's personal characteristics are often a factor in selecting awardees for contracts.

How to Get on a Bidders List

Getting on bidders lists simply requires filling out Standard Form 129 (Figure 4–2). It's a simple form, and all agencies use it or one closely resembling it. However, agencies that do a great deal of procurement, such as NASA, often have their bidders lists entered into their computers, and they ask you to submit another form, which lists a great many services and products.

A Standard Form 129 must be filed with each contracting office in which you are interested and with which you hope to do business. Agencies rarely utilize the bidders lists of other agencies. There are thousands of "buying activities" scattered throughout the United States. Therefore, once you make up your Standard Form 129, you'll want to make enough copies to distribute to all contracting offices that interest you.

Notice that you must file with all contracting offices, not all agencies, of interest because many agencies have more than one contracting office. For example, a multidivision agency may have a contracting office in each division and may even have a contracting office in each of its locations in the United States. That accounts for the reported 15,000 contracting offices. (It takes a lot of people, offices, and organizations to spend over $200 billion a year!)

What Being on a Bidders List Means to You

Reading the CBD every day does not bring all procurement solicitations to your attention, and neither does filing Form 129, even if you file 15,000 of them. There are at least two reasons for this:

1. Where there are a large number of names on the bidders list, the names are "rotated." If a bidders list contains 300 names, and the contracting officer believes that 50 solicitations are enough (he is most unlikely to send out as many as 300), he will select the next 50, then rotate to the following 50 for the next solicitation, and so on. So you will be sent only one out of every six solicitations and miss the other five if you simply file Form 129 and then wait for bid sets to arrive automatically in the morning mail.

2. When custom services are required, the contracting people are trying to interpret your Form 129 to see whether you are likely to be interested in or qualified for the solicitation in question. Suppose, for example, you have listed in block 8 (goods and/or services you wish to bid for) your interest in writing training manuals, and a solicitation comes up for an audiovisual training program. You might wish to bid that contract, but the contracting officer may not (and probably will not) make the connection. He is likely to sigh, decide this one is not for you, and pass you over.

I was once editorial director of a firm manufacturing a "teaching machine," whose materials were recorded on 35mm film and projected onto a screen of normal page size. Learning too late that we had not been invited to bid for a "per program" (printed text) by a

SOLICITATION MAILING LIST APPLICATION

1. TYPE OF APPLICATION		2. DATE	FORM APPROVED OMB NO. 3090-0009
☐ INITIAL	☐ REVISION		

NOTE—Please complete all items on this form. Insert N/A in items not applicable. See reverse for Instructions.

3. NAME AND ADDRESS OF FEDERAL AGENCY TO WHICH FORM IS SUBMITTED *(Include ZIP code)*

4. NAME AND ADDRESS OF APPLICANT *(Include county and ZIP code)*

5. TYPE OF ORGANIZATION *(Check one)*

☐ INDIVIDUAL

☐ NON-PROFIT ORGANIZATION

☐ PARTNERSHIP

☐ CORPORATION, INCORPORATED UNDER THE LAWS OF THE STATE OF:

6. ADDRESS TO WHICH SOLICITATIONS ARE TO BE MAILED *(If different than Item 4)*

7. NAMES OF OFFICERS, OWNERS, OR PARTNERS

A. PRESIDENT	B. VICE PRESIDENT	C. SECRETARY
D. TREASURER	E. OWNERS OR PARTNERS	

8. AFFILIATES OF APPLICANT *(Names, locations and nature of affiliation. See definition on reverse.)*

9. PERSONS AUTHORIZED TO SIGN OFFERS AND CONTRACTS IN YOUR NAME *(Indicate if agent)*

NAME	OFFICIAL CAPACITY	TELE. NO. *(Include area code)*

FIGURE 4–2.   Standard Form 129

10. IDENTIFY EQUIPMENT, SUPPLIES, AND/OR SERVICES ON WHICH YOU DESIRE TO MAKE AN OFFER *(See attached Federal agency's supplemental listing and instructions, if any)*

11A. SIZE OF BUSINESS *(See definitions on reverse)*	11B. AVERAGE NUMBER OF EMPLOYEES *(Including affiliates)* FOR FOUR PRECEDING CALENDAR QUARTERS	11C. AVERAGE ANNUAL SALES OR RECEIPTS FOR PRECEDING THREE FISCAL YEARS
☐ SMALL BUSINESS *(If checked, complete items 11B and 11C)* ☐ OTHER THAN SMALL BUSINESS		$

12. TYPE OF OWNERSHIP *(See definitions on reverse). (Not applicable for other than small businesses)*	13. TYPE OF BUSINESS *(See definitions on reverse)*	
☐ DISADVANTAGED BUSINESS ☐ WOMAN-OWNED BUSINESS	☐ MANUFACTURER OR PRODUCER ☐ REGULAR DEALER *(Type 1)*	☐ CONSTRUCTION CONCERN ☐ SURPLUS DEALER
	☐ SERVICE ESTABLISHMENT ☐ REGULAR DEALER *(Type 2)*	☐ RESEARCH AND DEVELOPMENT

14. DUNS NO. *(If available)*

15. HOW LONG IN PRESENT BUSINESS?

16. FLOOR SPACE *(Square feet)*		17. NET WORTH	
A. MANUFACTURING	B. WAREHOUSE	A. DATE	B. AMOUNT $

18. SECURITY CLEARANCE *(If applicable, check highest clearance authorized)*

FOR	TOP SECRET	SECRET	CONFIDENTIAL	C. NAMES OF AGENCIES WHICH GRANTED SECURITY CLEARANCES *(Include dates)*
A. KEY PERSONNEL				
B. PLANT ONLY				

CERTIFICATION — I certify that information supplied herein *(including all pages attached)* is correct and that neither the applicant nor any person *(Or concern)* in any connection with the applicant as a principal or officer, so far as is known, is now debarred or otherwise declared ineligible by any agency of the Federal Government from making offers for furnishing materials, supplies, or services to the Government or any agency thereof.

19. NAME AND TITLE OF PERSON AUTHORIZED TO SIGN *(Type or print)*	20. SIGNATURE	21. DATE SIGNED

NSN 7540-01-152-8086
PREVIOUS EDITIONS UNUSABLE

129-106

STANDARD FORM 129 (REV. 10-83)
Prescribed by GSA
FAR (48 CFR) 53.214(c)

FIGURE 4–2. *(continued)*

good customer, we asked why. To our horror, the customer was surprised to learn we did not confine ourselves to 35mm film.

Therefore, filing copies of your Form 129 and getting on bidders lists is one of your marketing tools, just as reading the CBD is one such tool. Both are important, but neither is sufficient to cover the market adequately. Nor are the two together enough, if you want to be made aware of most bid opportunities.

Actually responding to a solicitation by submitting a bid or proposal was far more effective at getting me on a bidders list than filing Form 129 was. For some reason, even after filing Form 129, you may not be getting bid sets from the agency. However, once you have submitted a bid or proposal, you are likely to see many bid sets from them.

But in the meanwhile, try to learn of requirements by any and all means possible and request all solicitations you believe will be of interest, whether or not you have filed Form 129 with the agency.

Bid Rooms and Bid Boards

Every contracting office must keep a file or display of outstanding requirements (solicitations) available for public inspection. A busy contracting office (one that buys almost continuously) usually maintains a bid room and bid board. On the wall of that room, you will find a large bulletin board on which are pinned many bid sets. In some cases, they are even arranged in categories such as equipment, services, and so on.

The public is welcome to drop into the bid room at any time during normal office hours and inspect the bid sets posted. And if you do so and find one that interests you, you are welcome to request a set for yourself. Because many contracting offices require that requests for bid sets be in writing, it's a good idea to carry some noteheads or letterheads with you so you can submit a written request there and then!

In smaller purchasing offices, there may not be a special bid room. But the outstanding solicitations are still available for your examination, although they may be simply bound in a folder. You are entitled, however, to inquire and to see them.

How often you should visit contracting offices and bid rooms depends on the amount of purchasing they do. In some cases, it may be advisable to drop by every week; in others, it may not be necessary to visit more often than once a month.

It's a good idea to get to know the contracting official and his or her staff in any agency where you believe you will be able to do business. This helps them remember you when they have solicitations to send out, and it also often results in friendly tips that may mean business for you. (In many respects, doing business with the government is not much different from doing business anywhere else. You need to establish and maintain productive contacts to stay in business.)

In agencies where I did business fairly often, I found the contracting officer and others tipping me off in advance of new requirements coming up. And I made it my business to keep in touch with the program people as well as with the contracts people.

Making "Cold" Calls

As in doing business in the private sector, business can sometimes be generated by standard marketing tactics: "making the calls." Here's an example: An acquaintance gave me the name of an individual in charge of writing standards for OSHA, and I made it my business to drop in and look the gentleman up at the first opportunity. We had a friendly chat, after I introduced myself, but it turned out he had nothing to offer me at the time. However, I asked him if he could suggest another prospect in the office. He took me to meet someone else in another office. The result was the same, but I again asked for a suggestion.

In this manner, I was introduced to five people in the course of about two hours. But the fifth was pay dirt! He had a need, and I looked like the right guy to handle it. It turned into a $2,400 job, which was followed by a $2,500 job, which was followed by a $23,000 job. He also recommended me to another agency, where I did quite a bit of business, and it in turn recommended me to still another agency.

Those two hours were responsible for some $65,000 worth of business over the next two years! Of course, I had the slight advantage of a name and a mutual acquaintance. But the advantage was only slight. Anyone can walk into a federal agency and seek business. There are many ways to go about it and several places to start.

If you are a small business (the Small Business Administration can tell you whether or not you are, if you are in doubt), try finding the agency's small business representative. Most agencies have one, and that person can help you find your way around and meet the right people.

You can call on the contracting officer to discuss your business needs. Many contracting officers I've known are sincere and sometimes even jovial people who will try to help you.

You can visit the agency's library and have a look at the organization charts to see who's who. The agency's librarian can often be very helpful.

Most agencies also have a public information office of some sort (not necessarily called that, however), and the staff there may be able to offer some guidance. That's part of their function.

Most agencies have their own personnel office or personnel function, a publications function, and a training or education function. I say "function" because some agencies have an office set up for each of these; in others, the functions are combined. So you may or may not find a "training office," but the training function will exist (possibly under the personnel office).

In any case, among the things you should want to know are (1) how the agency is organized, (2) who's who, in terms of what you may wish to offer, and (3) what the agency normally buys or happens to be in the market for at the moment.

Market Research

A large corporation for which I worked some years ago had an automation division housed in the same building as the division for which I was editorial director. They built automation systems to order, and one of their orders was for an automatic candy-packing machine for a large candy company in Canada. After many months of intensive labor, they developed the machine, which cost on the order of one-half million dollars. While the machine was being developed, an inspired salesman on the staff sold a second one to another candy company and still another to a third candy company. Galvanized by this promising new business, the marketing vice-president ordered two extra units made up for stock and mounted a brisk marketing attack on the automatic candy-packing market.

Months later, with the two spare machines gathering dust in the warehouse, the vice-president of marketing began to grow uneasy at the lack of success in selling these two machines and began to research the candy market. To his horror, he discovered there were only six candy companies in the entire world large enough even to consider a capital investment of $500,000 for packing candy, and the company had already captured half that market. It was a bitter lesson in the need for market research *before* investing time and money. (The two machines, worth $1 million, were eventually sold off for their salvage value.)

Many make the same mistake in pursuing government business. When the Department of Transportation was organized in 1986, a firm engaged in technical support, primarily technical writing and related services, invested heavily in marketing to the new agency. The basis for this decision was the large operating budget of the new DOT, which inspired the belief that there would be lots of "contracting out."

The company was mistaken in its belief. There was relatively little contract work suitable for it. Most of the contracts at that time were for demonstration "people-mover" systems, such as high-speed electric cars, and for studies of transportation problems, such as those of the railroads. The company, ignoring the advice of its marketing director (who knew better), succeeded finally in winning one subcontract to assist another contractor who had won a people-mover contract. They never did win a direct contract with the DOT.

The mistake they made was to see only the new department's overall budget, without regard to its programs and missions—*how* it would spend the money. In fact, a great deal of the agency's money was earmarked for subsidies to state and local governments, and relatively little was spent for contracted services or goods. Market research into government markets must consider more than the overall budget: It must consider the agencies' missions and programs, their buying history, any new enabling legislation, and any other factors that indicate how each agency will spend its budget and what it will buy.

There are many ways to do this. Information is abundant, although much of it is not organized. The Office of Federal Procurement Policy (OFPP), which is an organization in the Office of Management and Budget (OMB), operates the Federal Procurement Data System. It provides useful information for marketers to the government, as well as for others. However, this is not the only source of information for marketing to the agencies; there are other sources and methods that can help you arrive at reasonable estimates.

In earlier years, it was just a bit laborious to develop estimates. One of the most readily available sources was the *Commerce Business Daily,* introduced earlier, which lists contract awards, as well as requirements, as Figure 4–3 shows. It was a relatively simple matter to review several months' issues and arrive at a reasonable estimate of total purchasing in any given category.

For example, asked to estimate the amount of furniture (in dollars) that the government buys, I resorted to this method. After only about two hours' work with my filed copies of the CBD and a small calculator, I estimated that federal agencies were buying at least $170 million a year in furniture. That was in 1977. About a year later, the new commissioner of the Federal Supply Service mentioned, in a public statement, that the government was buying about $225 million worth of furniture a year. Obviously, my "ballpark" estimate was close enough for market-research purposes. (Allowing for inflationary effects, my brief study came up with a figure within 10 percent of the government's figures.) This is a fairly reliable method for estimating the government's annual buy of commodities because

CONTRACT AWARDS

It is the Government's policy to publish information on unclassified contract awards exceeding $25,000 in value for civil agencies and $50,000 for military agencies.

The letter or number preceding each item is the service or supplies classification code.

Supplies Equipment and Material

61 Electric Wire, and Power Distribution Equipment.

61 -- AMPLIFIER, ELECTRONIC CONTROL, P/O Antenna, Type #AS-2199 and P/O Receiver-Transmitter, Radar, Type #RT-899/APS-94D, NSN: 6110-00-449-5112 and 6110-00-239-5990. Contract DAAB07-79-C-0821, 31 May 79 $91,997 (No RFP) Canadian Commercial Corp, Ottawa, Ontario, Canada.

61 -- POWER SUPPLY, PP6224, 220 Each, NSN: 6130-00-133-5879 (DAAB07-79-R-1909). Contract DAAB07-77-C-2664, P00012 31 May 79 #689,436, Saratoga Industries P.O. Box 422, Saratoga Springs, NY.

61 -- POWER SUPPLY (18A1A), 240 Each, NSN: 6130-00-466-0158 (DAAB07-79-B-1922). Contract DAAB07-79-C-1952, 31 May 79 $80,320 Wire-Pro, Inc., P.O. Box 211, Bridgeport, NJ.

61 -- BATTERY, DRY BA-4386/PRC-25, NSN: 6135-00-926-8322, 92,016. Contract DAAB07-78-D-6344, D.O. 0004, 31 May 79 $778,842 (No RFP) ESB, Inc., 101 E. Washington Ave., Madison, WI.

61 -,-BA-1568/U BATTERY, Dry, NSN: 6135-00-838-0706, 13,770 ea. Contract DAAB07-79-D-6714 25 May .79 $90,606 D.O. 0001 (No RFP) PR Mallory & Co., Inc., South Broadway, Tarrytown, NY.

61 -- BATTERY, STORAGE CELL, Type BB-600 A/A, NSN: 6140-00-881-6887. Contract DAAB07-78-D-6325 D.O. 0008, 25 May 79 $579,576 (No RFP) PR Mallory &-Co., Inc, South Broadway, Tarrytown, NY.

61 -- BATTERY, STORAGE CELL, Type BB-600 A/A, NSN: 6140-00-881-6887. Contract DAAB07-78-D-6325 D.O. 0008, 25 May 79 $579,576 (No RFP) Marathon Battery Co., 8301 Imperial Dr., Waco, TX.

U.S. Army Communications and Electronics Material Readiness Command, Fort Monmouth NJ 07703

61 -- CIRCUIT ASSEMBLY, NSC 6110-NONE, Contract DLA400-79-C-2174, 31 May 79 (RFP DLA400-78-R-2105) 241 ea $127,741 Leland Electrosystems Inc., 740 E. National Rd., Vandalia, OH 45377.

Defense General Supply Center, Richmond, VA 23297, Tel: 804/275-3350

61 -- SILVERCEL BATTERIES—$79,993—Yardney Electric Division, Pawcatuck, CT. Contr NAS5-24611, 7 May 79.

NASA/GSFC, Greenbelt, MD, Code 242.1

62 Lighting Fixtures and Lamps.

62 -- FIXTURE, LIGHTING, NSN 6210-00-548-0222, Contract DLA400-79-C-2175, 31 May 79 (RFP DLA400-79-R-1177) 8677 ea $309,254 The L. C. Doane Co., 10 New City St., Essex, CT 06426.

Defense General Supply Center, Richmond, VA 23297, Tel: 804/275-3350

65 Medical, Dental, and Veterinary Equipment and Supplies.

65 -- APPLICATORS, DISPOSABLE (M1-94-79) contract V797P-1070g $66,960 Hardwood Products Co., School St., Guilford ME 04443.

66 -- CELL, SALINITY INDIC. P/N ICCN853, CEL-261, NSN 1H6630-00-983-2577, Contract N00104-79-C-3345 (RFP-N00104-78-R-6085) dtd 21 May 79, 554 ea. $65,649. McNab, Inc., 20 North MacQuesten Parkway, Mount Vernon, New York 10550.

Navy Ships Parts Control Center, Mechanicsburg, PA 17055

67 Photographic Equipment.

67 -- PRINTER, Projection Photographic (2RH6740-00-069-5462), Contract F42600-79-C-0498 dated 24 May 79 (RFP F42600-79-R-0170) 45 each. $97,785 Berkey Photo Inc, 25-15 50th St., Woodside NY 11377.

67 -- RECEIVER (6720-01-039-3324), Power Supply (6760-01-039-0504), Infrared Performance Analyzer (6720-01-038-4972), Handling Plate Assembly (6760-01-043-6140), Card Assembly for Anti-Hump Clamp and Air Timing Generator (6720-01-046-3630), Card Assembly for Anti-Hump Clamp and AGC Waveform Generator, Appl AN/AAD-5, Contract F42600-79-C-0396 29 May 79, 12 line items. $304,296. Honeywell Inc, 2 Forbes Rd., Lexington MA 02173.

Directorate of Procurement & Production (PPE-1), Ogden ALC, Hill AFB, UT 84406, Tel 801/777-4759

67 -- SPARE PARTS FOR KG-29A CAMERA and LG-15B Magazine, Contract F42600-79-C-0584, 4 Jun 79 (RFP F42600-79-R-0695) 1 SE $84,654 Recon/Optical Inc, 550 West Northwest Hwy, Barrington IL 60010.

Directorate of Procurement & Production (PPE-1), Ogden ALC, Hill AFB, UT 84406, Tel 801/777-4759

67 -- MEDIUM STREAK AND FRAMING CAMERA Imacon 790/S20—Contr. N00014-79-C-0176, 31 May 79—$85,501—Marco Scientific Inc, 1031-H E. Duane Ave., Sunnyvale, CA 94086.

Naval Research Laboratory, Washington DC 20375

69 Training Aids and Devices.

69 -- COUPLER UNIT PANEL (6920-01-003-7805), and Drawer (6920-00-107-0685), appl AN/GSP-T34, Contract F04606-76-A-0072-QPU3 21 May 79 $164,000 Rockwell International Corp, 3370 Miraloma Ave., Anaheim CA 92803.

69 -- DESIGN, FABRICATE AND INSTALL A PROTOTYPE MODIFICATION KIT for A/F37A-T33 (A-7D; F11 Sim (6930K4309315A; and follow-on production kits, installation, technical and engineering data, initial spare parts provisioning and technical manuals, Contract F34601-76-A-2175-QP54 dated 24 May 79. $360,000 McDonnell Douglas Corp, PO Box 426, St Charles MO 63301.

Directorate of Procurement & Production (PPE-1), Ogden ALC, Hill AFB, UT 84406, Tel 801/777-4759

70 General Purpose ADP Equipment Software, Supplies and Support Equipment.

70 -- REFURBISH AND INSTALL FIELD CHANGES on two Model CP642B Computers originally manufactured by Sperry Univac. N00024-77-A-7150, Order WQ3J—$70,400, Sperry Univac, PO Box 3525, St. Paul MN 55165.

70 -- REFURBISH AND INSTALL FIELD CHANGES on two each Model CP642B Computers; one originally manufactured by Sperry Univac and one by Sylvania. N00024-77-A-7150, Order WQ3N, $75,700, Sperry Univac, Univac Park, PO Box 3525, St. Paul, MN 55165.

DCASMA Twin Cities, Federal Building, Fort Snelling Twin Cities MN 55111

FIGURE 4–3. Contract awards listed in *Commerce Business Daily*

virtually all such procurements are listed in the CBD. However, the CBD does not list everything bought by federal agencies, especially in custom services.

Another way to reach an estimate of annual volume of an item of supply is to query the Federal Supply Service, which is part of the General Services Administration. That organization can usually give you a good idea of the volume in any given category.

The Small Business Administration can help, too, in many cases, with at least estimates of the market among federal agencies for given items of goods and services.

In some cases, the Department of Commerce is an even better source of information along these lines than is the Small Business Administration because Commerce takes an interest in business between the federal agencies and the private sector.

If you are interested in a particular agency, queries to its contracting office will often produce good estimates of what the agency buys, or at least what it has bought in the year previous.

All of this is helpful, but today it is much easier to get the information by two other methods: One is to study the reports issued by the OFPP, whose computers do many kinds of analysis for you. The other is to use a public data base version of the *Commerce Business Daily,* CBD ONLINE. This data base is accessible from a number of information services, such as DIALOG. The service will search the data base for you to find at least the recent volume in any given product or service. Using that facility, I satisfied a client's request to learn the volume of government purchase of steel shelters in less than an hour.

Even Government Markets Change

All markets change, and the federal government markets are not an exception. In fact, in many respects, the government markets are even more subject to change, including sudden and abrupt change, than are those in the commercial and industrial communities. There are various causes for such change.

When the Post Office Department was abolished and the U.S. Postal Service, a government corporation, was established to replace it, the formerly close congressional control and political influence over the post office were eliminated. The new managers of the Postal Service gained a semiautonomy, and many things happened as a result.

First, the new department announced a plan to establish ten training centers at university sites, primarily to train postal employees in technical trades and automation, which the new Postal Service planned to install to modernize the establishment and its handling of mail. Second, the Postal Management Institute was established in Bethesda, Maryland, a Washington suburb. At the same time, a Postal Service Technical Institute was established on the University of Oklahoma campus, at Norman. (The remaining training centers were never established.) Simultaneously, the Postal Service began buying a great deal of automation equipment, vehicles, and real estate to house 21 new bulk-mail centers.

With a $10 billion annual gross at the time, the Postal Service invested a great deal of its money in these new activities and let a great many contracts for equipment, much of it custom designed, and for training programs and services. At one time, many contractors (myself included) were doing business regularly with the Postal Service.

Postal Service contracts for these new activities began to slow down by the mid-1970s; and, as postal deficits mounted, they came to an almost complete halt by 1977. The Postal Service came under heavy criticism from Congress, which threatened to take it over and once again make it an integral element in the bureaucracy, where it would be under closer control. Today, the Postal Service still lets many contracts for real estate, transportation services, and supplies, but little for training and custom-designed equipment. Many small companies for which the Postal Service had been almost the sole support were suddenly in straits, and not all survived.

During 1964 and 1965, the Office of Economic Opportunity's Job Corps was a similar bonanza for many, and other elements of the OEO, such as Head Start and VISTA, soon added their own requirements for millions of dollars in services. That, too, dried up eventually as the OEO was all but disbanded and its programs dispersed to older agencies.

New legislation often creates new markets in government. Organization of the Federal Energy Administration and Energy Research and Development Administration (now the Department of Energy) led to many new contract opportunities. But not every new agency becomes a major business opportunity. For example, the new Consumer Product Safety Commission and the new Pension Benefit Guaranty Corporation produced some new contract opportunities, after a year or more of their existence, but neither ever turned into a major market.

Sometimes legislation creates a new market within an existing agency, rather than a new agency. The Occupational Safety and Health Administration (OSHA), for example, was assigned to the Labor Department, and its related agency, the National Institute of Occupational Safety and Health (NIOSH), was assigned to HEW (now HHS). Both have required some assistance from private industry, of course, and have been a source of contracts.

Those who prosper most from new organizations are usually those who get in on the ground floor by starting their marketing efforts early in the existence of a new agency. The energy field is a good example of this. Prior to 1974, no one thought of themselves as "energy experts," although there were organizations expert in petroleum, natural gas, coal, and so on. But the government's programs and needs soon created energy experts, many of them seizing the opportunity early, although they had never worked in the field before! Congress sometimes creates entire new professions with its legislative mandates.

Some "Old, Reliable" Government Markets

The markets discussed in this chapter are largely transient targets of opportunity. Most involve custom work in direct support of an agency's mission, and the RFPs and SOWs often cite specific legislation mandating the requirement. The Department of Housing and

Urban Development (HUD) has a legal requirement to do certain surveys and lets contracts to have these done. The Commerce Department is required to conduct a census every ten years through its Bureau of Census. In many cases, however, such requirements are not for work needed on a regular basis, but must be done once only. To work these markets, therefore, it is necessary to market continuously and aggressively, always searching out new opportunities and rarely doing exactly the same job twice.

It is therefore decidedly hazardous to your (business) health ever to sit back and rest on your merits in these markets or to permit your business to become dependent on one or two federal agencies or programs. A single budget cut or congressional change of mind can wipe out your business almost overnight. It is wise to spread your contracts over as many agencies as possible and always to be working on new markets.

But certain government requirements, such as for furniture, are fairly steady, year after year. These exist in services as well as in supplies. There is a rather consistent demand for moving family goods, general hauling, janitorial services, food services, and a number of other such housekeeping and maintenance functions. In fact, for most of these kinds of supplies and services, the government often issues annual contracts to a number of suppliers, calling on them regularly as needs arise. Some of these are known as Federal Supply Schedules, but there are many others, too. If you wish to offer anything falling into one of these categories, it is probably wise to seek one or more annual contracts, many of which are available through the General Services Administration, but many others of which are announced periodically in the CBD. (Additional sources of information on these are listed in Appendix 4.)

CHAPTER 5

How to Make Bids

*Appearing to be the low bidder is as good as
being the low bidder—in fact, it's better.*

Identifying the Low Bidder

Theoretically, it's easy to identify the low bidder in a contract competition; the bid with the smallest number on the bottom line is the
low bidder, to wit:

Bidder A

3 gr widgets @ $7.40/gr = $22.20
2 dz bobbles @ $2.10/dz = $ 4.20
Total $26.40

Bidder B

3 gr widgets @ $7.39/gr = $22.17
2 dz bobbles @ $2.25/dz = $ 4.50
Total $26.67

The list may be, and often is, much longer than this. Individual
prices for individual items are not the significant factors, although a
contracting officer may question any that appear to be seriously out
of line with the market. It's the bottom line—the total—that estab-
lishes who is the low bidder.

That works out all right as long as the bid is for specific quantities
to be delivered under specified conditions. However, there are many
considerations. For one thing, the bottom line may include prompt-
payment discounts.

Figuring in Prompt-Payment Discounts

Let's see how such discounts affect the actual cost to the government, using the example here:

> Bidder A offers 2 percent 10 days, 0.5 percent 20 days, net amount due after.
>
> Bidder B offers 3 percent 10 days, 2 percent 20 days, 1 percent 30 days.

Applying these discounts to the bids, we come up with these final figures for the bottom line of each bid:

	Bidder A	Bidder B
Paid in 10 days	$25.87	$25.87
Paid in 20 days	$26.27	$26.14
Paid in 30 days	$26.40	$26.40
Paid after 30 days	$26.40	$26.67

Bidder B is the actual low bidder and the winner of the contract because he offered a greater prompt-payment discount. For 10-day payment, the two bidders are exactly the same in their quotation. However, this is not a deadlock because the government will not count a 10-day discount, on the assumption that it is all but impossible for the government to process a payment in 10 days. The government will, however, take a discount for 20-day payment or longer into account. So any discounts you offer for 10 days are meaningless even though bid forms provide a blank space for you to record 10-day discounts!

The actual bottom line on these two bids, for evaluation and comparison purposes, is this:

> Bidder A: $26.27
> Bidder B: $26.14

In a close race, therefore, discounts may well make the difference in deciding who is the low bidder. However, this is not the only complicating factor. Many other factors can make it difficult to judge who is the low bidder.

Pricing Indefinite Quantities

For example, many requirements are for indefinite quantities. The government can give you only a rough estimate or range to help you arrive at unit prices. Usually, such contracts are for a long term, probably a year, and the government will order from time to time, as the needs arise, at the prices you have agreed to in your bid. In actuality, the government may order a great many of some items and extremely few of others. The government doesn't know, nor does the bidder, what the year's requirements are going to be.

Frequently, the solicitation package will give you the range by stating that the government will order not less than *n* or more than *nn* number of units. In these cases, at least you know the minimum and maximum size of the contract, although you've no idea of the probable size of individual orders under the contract. This complicates the evaluation of prices enormously because there is no true bottom line. Here's an example of what such a bid might call for:

	Minimum–Maximum	
Item	Quantities	Price per Unit
5 × 7 notepads	150–300 gr	$ _____
Carbon paper	500–1,000 dz sheets	$ _____
No. 2 lead pencils	5,000–10,000 dz	$ _____

Now both the bidder and the government have a problem. The bidder has no idea how to "bid smart" on this, and the government has to devise some sort of irreproachable scheme for deciding who is the low bidder. The difficulty in deciding who will be the lowest-cost supplier, which is the purpose of the bids, arises because of the uncertainty of quantities. To make this clearer, let's look at a few typical bids:

Bidder	Notepads	Carbon Paper	Pencils
A	$15.70/gr	$2.25/dz sheets	$0.72/dz
B	$16.35/gr	$2.19/dz sheets	$0.71/dz
C	$15.22/gr	$2.29/dz sheets	$0.99/dz

It's immediately obvious that none of the bidders is either low or high on everything. Were the contract to be for any single item, there would be no difficulty. But the contract is to be for as-needed supplies of all the items.

The usual method the government uses to determine the low bidder in such cases is a "bench test." A hypothetical order is used to test each bid, to see who would be the lowest-cost supplier. Let's make up a bench test of our own and apply it. We'll assume these will be the quantities for a typical order:

Notepads: 20 gr
Carbon paper: 50 dz sheets
Lead pencils: 100 dz

Now let's price this order for each bidder and see what the order would cost in each case:

Bidder	Notepads	Carbon Paper	Pencils	Total
A	$314.00	$112.50	$72.00	$498.50
B	$327.00	$109.50	$71.00	$507.50
C	$304.40	$114.50	$99.00	$517.90

Bidder A is the low bidder using this bench test. With another bench test, it could turn out differently. If the bench test were applied to the minimum or maximum figure, another bidder might appear to be the low bidder! Suppose maximum figures were given thus:

Notepads: 5,000 gr
Carbon paper: 1,000 dz sheets
Lead pencils: 2,000 dz

Pricing by maximums would produce the following figures:

Bidder	Notepads	Carbon Paper	Pencils	Total
A	$78,500	$2,250	$1,440	$82,190
B	$81,750	$2,190	$1,420	$85,360
C	$76,100	$2,290	$1,980	$80,370

It is therefore the responsibility of the contracting officer to develop an evaluation method that provides a fair comparison.

In the actual case, such office commodities as carbon paper and lead pencils are generally bought by the Federal Supply Service in large quantity and stocked in the 10 warehouses and 75 stores of GSA. However, for many items, in both supplies and services, such bids as the preceding are common.

Example of a Bid Invitation

There are other complicating factors found among the many kinds of bid situations. Many items purchased are capital items of one sort or another, and some of these have repair and maintenance considerations as well as other "cost of ownership" facts to take into account.

Let's take an actual bid invitation as an example of this. Here is Solicitation No. 5-M-FSQS-79, an IFB issued by the U.S. Department of Agriculture (USDA) in Minneapolis. It calls for bids on a "STAMP, Roller Dating," in accordance with specifications provided in the bid set. The public opening is to be held on January 4, 1979, at 2:30 P.M. at the USDA offices in Minneapolis. (See Figure 5–1.)

The specifications follow and include two drawings to make the requirement absolutely clear. The "Special Conditions" section of the solicitation makes it clear that this is a requirements-type contract, to run from date of award (probably late January 1979) to the end of the government's fiscal year (September 30, 1979). This will be, therefore, an indefinite-quantity contract, with orders placed as needed.

The continuation sheet calls for pricing the stamps individually, with an estimate of 120 stamps to be ordered during the term of the contract. However, the bidder is asked also to supply prices for repair parts, and no estimate of probable orders for repair parts is provided. Each of the ordering activities—the various offices that will order stamps—will order repair parts as needed, but we do not know what that means. That is, we do not know whether each office will order repair parts when stamps need repair or whether they will order a

SOLICITATION, OFFER AND AWARD	3 CERTIFIED FOR NATIONAL DEFENSE UNDER BDSA REG 2 AND/OR DMS REG 1 RATING		4 PAGE 1	OF

| 1 CONTRACT (Proc Inst Ident) NO | 2 SOLICITATION NO 5-M-FSQS-79 [X] ADVERTISED (IFB) [ ] NEGOTIATED (RFB) | 5 DATE ISSUED | 6 REQUISITION-PURCHASE REQUEST NO 0457 0564 FAY 4190 FV-6-P |

7 ISSUED BY CODE	8 ADDRESS OFFER TO (if other than block 7)
U.S.Department of Agriculture, FSQS ASD, Program Services Branch 123 East Grant Street Minneapolis, MN 55403	SAME AS BLOCK 7

In advertised procurement 'offer' and 'offeror' shall be construed to mean 'bid' and 'bidder'

SOLICITATION

9. Sealed offers in original and __0__ copies for furnishing the supplies or services in the Schedule will be received at the place specified in block 8, or if handcarried, in the depository located in __See Block 7__ until __1/4//9__ local time __2:30 P.M.__

(Hour)   local time at   (Date)

If this is an advertised solicitation, offers will be publicly opened at that time.   Minneapolis, MN

CAUTION – LATE OFFERS: See pars. 7 and 8 of Solicitation Instructions and Conditions.

All offers are subject to the following

1. The Solicitation Instructions and Conditions, SF 33-A, _____
   edition which is attached or incorporated herein by reference
2. The General Provisions, XXXXXXXXXXXXXXXXXX edition, which is attached or incorporated herein by reference.

3. The Schedule included herein and/or attached hereto.
4. Such other provisions, representations, certifications, and specifications as are attached or incorporated herein by reference.
   (Attachments are listed in schedule.)

FOR INFORMATION CALL (Name & telephone no.) (No collect calls) ▶ Kent E. DesJardien 612-725-2136

SCHEDULE

10 ITEM NO	11 SUPPLIES/SERVICES	12 QUANTITY	13 UNIT	14 UNIT PRICE	15 AMOUNT
	STAMP, Roller Dating, in accordance with the attached Bid Schedule, Delivery Requirements, Service Requirements, Specifications and Special Conditions, for delivery F.O.B. origin for the period from date of award through September 30, 1979. The attached General Provisions, APHIS Form 326, Sections 1, 2 and 6 are made a part of this Solicitation and any resultant contract.				

See continuation of schedule on page 2

OFFER (pages 2 and 3 must also be fully completed by offeror)

In compliance with the above, the undersigned agrees, if this offer is accepted within _____ calendar days (60 calendar days unless a different period is inserted by the offeror) from the date for receipt of offers specified above, to furnish any or all items upon which prices are offered at the price set opposite each item, delivered at the designated point(s), within the time specified in the schedule.

16. DISCOUNT FOR PROMPT PAYMENT (See par 9. SF 33-A)			
% 10 CALENDAR DAYS	% 20 CALENDAR DAYS	% 30 CALENDAR DAYS	% CALENDAR DAYS

17. OFFEROR CODE FACILITY CODE	18 NAME AND TITLE OF PERSON AUTHORIZED TO SIGN OFFER (Type or print)
NAME AND ADDRESS (Street, city, county, State and ZIP code) AREA CODE AND TELEPHONE NO ▶ [ ] Check if remittance address is different from above — enter such address in Schedule	19 SIGNATURE	20 OFFER DATE

AWARD (To be completed by Government)

21. ACCEPTED AS TO ITEMS NUMBERED	22 AMOUNT	23. ACCOUNTING AND APPROPRIATION DATA

24 SUBMIT INVOICES (4 copies unless otherwise specified) TO ADDRESS SHOWN IN BLOCK _____	25 NEGOTIATED PURSUANT TO	10 U S C 2304(a) ( ) 41 U S C 252(c) ( )

26 ADMINISTERED BY (If other than block 7) CODE	27 PAYMENT WILL BE MADE BY CODE

28 NAME OF CONTRACTING OFFICER (Type or print)	29. UNITED STATES OF AMERICA BY (Signature of contracting officer)	30 AWARD DATE

Award will be made on this form, or on Standard Form 26, or by other official written notice

33-130

Standard Form 33 Page 1 (REV. 3-77)
Prescribed by GSA, FPR (41 CFR) 1-16.101

FIGURE 5–1. Sample government solicitation

STANDARD FORM 36, JULY 1966 GENERAL SERVICES ADMINISTRATION FED. PROC. REG. (41 CFR) 1-16.101	**CONTINUATION SHEET**	REF. NO. OF DOC. BEING CONT'D. 5-M-FSQS-79	PAGE 7	OF 8
NAME OF OFFEROR OR CONTRACTOR				

ITEM NO.	SUPPLIES/SERVICES	QUANTITY	UNIT	UNIT PRICE	AMOUNT
	This Solicitation is being issued to establish a source of supply under contract for Roller dating stamps, as may be required by the U.S.Department of Agriculture, Food Safety and Quality Service, Fruit and Vegetable Quality Division, Processed Products Branch for the period from date of award through September 30, 1979.				
	Due to the nature of the program for which the stamps are required, it is impossible to accurately determine in advance or from past experience the number of stamps that will be required during the specified period. However, it is estimated that 120 roller stamps will be required during the period specified above. This estimate of needs is for information only and is not intended to imply that the estimate is an exact indication of the quantity that will be required.				
	It is agreed that the Fruit and Vegetable Quality Division will procure all of their needs during the stated contract period from the successful offeror at the price quoted and accepted by award of contract and that in consideration, therefore, the successful offeror guarantees by submission of his offer in response thereto, to furnish all of the requirements that may be required by the Fruit and Vegetable Quality Division.				
	BID SCHEDULE				
01.	STAMP, Roller Dating, in accordance with the following Delivery Requirements, Service Requirements, Specifications, Special Conditions and Drawings No. 1 and 2.			Price per Stamp	$_____
	DELIVERY REQUIREMENTS				
	Delivery of the stamps is required within thirty (30) calendar days after receipt of an order. Offerors offering later delivery will be considered nonresponsive.				
	OFFERORS are required to state below the percentage of the contract that will be performed in Labor Surplus Areas and the location of such area.				
	Percentage to be performed in Labor Surplus Area:_____.				
	Location of such area:_____.				
	OFFEROR to state number of Permanent Employees:_____.				
	SERVICE REQUIREMENTS				
	The U.S.Department of Agriculture, Food Quality and Safety Service, Fruit and Vegetable Quality Division requires the stamps for dating and identifying officially inspected products.				

36-108   C43—18—79531-1   GPO : 1987 O—361-063

FIGURE 5–1. *(continued)*

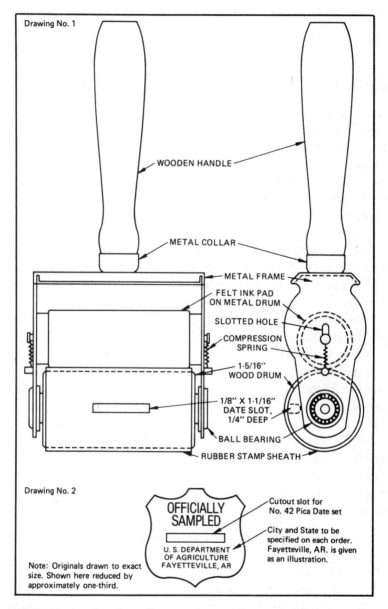

Drawing No. 1

WOODEN HANDLE

METAL COLLAR

METAL FRAME

FELT INK PAD
ON METAL DRUM

SLOTTED HOLE

COMPRESSION
SPRING

1-5/16″
WOOD DRUM

1/8″ X 1-1/16″
DATE SLOT,
1/4″ DEEP

BALL BEARING

RUBBER STAMP SHEATH

Drawing No. 2

OFFICIALLY
SAMPLED

U. S. DEPARTMENT
OF AGRICULTURE
FAYETTEVILLE, AR

Cutout slot for
No. 42 Pica Date set

City and State to be
specified on each order.
Fayetteville, AR. is given
as an illustration.

Note: Originals drawn to exact
size. Shown here reduced by
approximately one-third.

FIGURE 5–1. *(continued)*

supply of spare parts to keep in stock. And that can make quite a difference in how best to bid the job.

Bidding for "Spares"

In military procurement, where spare parts and maintenance are considerations, it is customary for the purchasing agency to make a determination of how many spare parts ("spares," as suppliers to the military often refer to parts) will be ordered and kept in stock. And in many cases, the spare-parts order is more important than the order for the original equipment. In fact, many equipment suppliers follow the example of the razor blade manufacturer who virtually gives the razors away so he can "lock in" customers for his blades. It is not at all uncommon for suppliers of equipment to bid the equipment contract at near the break-even point when they believe they can count on a large order for spare parts, which are usually much more profitable.

In the case of the dating stamp for the USDA, there is no apparent way for the bidder to judge what the spare-parts orders are likely to be. However, the government, the USDA contracting officer, is faced with the same dilemma: How will he determine who is the low bidder? Will he take the prices for repair parts into account, or will he consider only the original cost of the dating stamp? No clues are provided in this particular solicitation. The implication of this is that only the prices for the stamps themselves will be evaluated. But that is by no means certain. One rule the bidder for government contracts should observe scrupulously: Take nothing for granted. Count only on what is specifically stated or specifically provided for under the law and the procurement regulations. In this case, you have three options:

1. Demand to know the basis for determination of the low bidder before you submit your bid.
2. Check on last year's bid to see how it was priced. For a standard commodity such as this, one should be available. Also ask how many repair parts were sold and how many stamps were sold, as a guide.

3. Make your best guess, submit your bid, and attend the opening. If you are dissatisfied with the final determination, lodge a protest on the basis of inadequate information for bidding.

Choosing an Option

If you were a bidder in this competition and you chose the first option, here's what would probably happen: The solicitation would be postponed; the date would be moved back by a week or two to allow the contracting officer to get you the answer you have demanded and have a right to get. But, having either gotten the information or worked out an evaluation plan, the contracting officer would feel obligated to write it up and distribute copies to everyone who had requested an invitation to bid. Your question would therefore have resulted in providing additional information to all prospective bidders, which may mean you helped competitors more than you helped yourself.

You should adopt the second option, no matter what else you do, and as a first step. Under the Freedom of Information Act, you have a right to demand the information, and you should exercise that right. (This is one of the advantages of bidding to the government, as compared with bidding to a private company.)

The third option is always open to you, no matter what else you do, if you believe that the proceeding was less than completely fair or honest.

Usually, asking for information under the Freedom of Information Act does not result in distribution of information to other prospective bidders because getting such information does not confer a special advantage on you, under the law. All the other bidders have equal access to the information (if they are smart enough to ask for it). They could not claim you had information not available to them!

Most government documents are public and available for public scrutiny, on demand. The exceptions are those items of information that affect national security, information that is proprietary (trade secrets), and information that, if released, would be an invasion of privacy. You are therefore entitled to get a copy of any existing or prior contract, although proprietary information may be deleted from your copy. Usually, however, you are not really interested in the entire proposal and/or contract, but only in the "bottom line"—the prices the government is or has been paying.

Should the procurement officer refuse to state a method for identifying the low bid, however, your proper counter is not the Freedom of Information Act, but a protest. Filing a protest will probably force the agency to release such information. However, it will go out to all bidders.

Another Example to Illustrate the Case

The headquarters office of NASA issued a contract every three years for publications-support services, as do many agencies that need services frequently but on an intermittent basis. Typically, it was a basic ordering agreement, under which the contractor agreed to provide services at some specific prices, on an as-needed basis. It was the typical "laundry list" of services, arranged somewhat as follows:

Function	Unit	Estimated Requirement	Price per Unit
Technical writing	hour	1,250 hours	$ _____
Technical editing	hour	800 hours	$ _____
Production editing	hour	300 hours	$ _____
Drafting	hour	400 hours	$ _____
Illustrating	hour	600 hours	$ _____
Typing	page	1,400 pages	$ _____
Proofreading	page	1,400 pages	$ _____
Photography	hour	600 hours	$ _____

This is the typical situation of indefinite quantity requirements. How does the government decide who is the low bidder? And, more important to the bidder, what strategies are possible in bidding this?

It's easy to visualize some sort of bench test being made to determine the relative ranking of the various bids. Although government officials may explain the bench test in general (in fact, they must do so upon demand), they will not tell you exactly what the bench-test quantities are going to be, for obvious reasons.

One Kind of Cost Strategy

You can occasionally win government contracts through chance—the chance that few others have bid or that they have not been smart in their bidding—but you can win them consistently and frequently by using intelligent strategies. The Freedom of Information Act gives you an almost unparalleled opportunity to get the information you need to devise strategies.

To win the contract referred to here, we checked on the history of the contract in past years, learning (1) who the previous years' contractors had been (they would be our competitors), (2) what quantities of each service or function had been ordered in past years, and (3) what the government (NASA headquarters) was paying for each service.

We learned one very interesting fact: NASA headquarters has ample in-house photographic capability and had never ordered any photo services under this contract. The implication is obvious. It is similar to that of the lady who visited her local grocery store to buy bananas. She was outraged to learn that bananas were $.49 a pound, and she protested loudly. The proprietor apologized for the price, explaining that he had no choice in the matter: Bananas were simply high at that time of year.

"But I can get them at Joe's Market for $.29 a pound," she complained.

Gently, the grocer asked why she didn't get them there because they were such a bargain.

"Joe's Market is out of bananas today," she wailed.

The grocer grinned. "Well, I sell them for $.19 a pound when I'm out of them. But they're $.49 a pound when I have them."

Moral: It's easy to give something away when you're out of it—or when there's no call for it. By pricing photographic services at virtually nothing, we made our bid *appear* to be the low bid. It had to.

Why does the solicitation include photographic services when none are needed? For one thing, there is always the possibility they may be needed. But the real reason lies in the nature of the bureaucracy: No one has the initiative to change the bid set, so it remains the same, year after year.

Establishing prices this way is akin to the supermarkets' practice of offering "loss leaders"—items sold at or below actual cost to draw people into the store, where they will buy many other things, more than compensating for the loss on the leader.

A Variation on a Theme

There is another way this same idea can be used to *create* an item for which there will be no demand, enabling the bidder to bid it at a ridiculously low rate and come in the *apparent low* bidder. This plan requires a bit more explanation.

In many of these "laundry list" requirements contracts for general support services, various technical/professional specialties are called for at various levels of proficiency. For example, the customer may perceive a need for engineers of almost an apprentice level for some tasks, but other tasks, they believe, will require engineers with considerable experience. In such cases, the solicitation will describe the various levels, such as number of years of experience following graduation, graduate degrees, fields of specialization, and so on. The cost form might look somewhat as follows:

Category	Unit	Estimated Requirement	Cost per Unit
Engineer I	hour	1,500 hours	$ _____
Engineer II	hour	2,200 hours	$ _____
Engineer III	hour	850 hours	$ _____
Draftsman I	hour	3,000 hours	$ _____
Draftsman II	hour	2,400 hours	$ _____

When the government has awarded a contract, both it and the contractor are bound by the rates agreed upon. However, each time the government orders a task under the contract, the usual procedure is for an official to send a request and a task description to the contractor for an estimate. The contractor—not the customer—decides what levels of personnel are required and for how many hours each. The contractor prepares the estimate, computing costs on the basis of hours for each specialist, and submits the estimate for approval. Once the estimate is approved, the contractor is bound to do three things:

1. Perform the task and deliver a satisfactory result, as stipulated in the task description
2. Charge for each person employed on the task those rates agreed upon (verifiable by audit)
3. Stay within the total price quoted for the task (unless the task is modified by the customer)

The work is performed under contract, and by law, the government may not tell the contractor how to "manage" the project. That means, in practice, that the government may not order the contractor to utilize such and such kinds of personnel or order any specific person to be assigned the task. Therefore—and mark this closely—the contractor is free to assign anyone he chooses to the task, as long as he meets the three conditions noted previously.

If the contractor decides that one of the three levels of engineer, engineer II, perhaps, is really superfluous and need never be actually used on the job, it will cost nothing to bid engineer II at a very low rate—and consequently come out low on the bench test!

As a variant of this, the contractor may bid engineer II on a task estimate but need never actually assign an engineer II to the task. For example, suppose you (as the contractor) receive a request for an estimate on a task. You make a first cut, which looks like this:

Engineer I	60 hours @ $18.00/hour	=	$1,080
Engineer II	240 hours @ $ 6.00/hour	=	$1,440
Engineer III	110 hours @ $ 9.50/hour	=	$1,045
Total			$3,565

You will lose money if you use an engineer II at $6 an hour because you actually pay him more than that. Still, the estimate involves 410 hours of engineering time, which is more than enough for the job, and you should be able to do it for $3,565. And you know the customer will not consider $3,565 an exorbitant price for the job. In fact, you can almost certainly do the job this way:

Engineer I	60 hours @ $18.00/hour =	$1,080
Engineer III	260 hours @ $ 9.50/hour =	$2,470
Total		$3,550

You can estimate the job by the first set of figures, get the customer's approval (he's primarily concerned with the bottom line for the task), obtain a work order, and then go ahead and do the job per the second estimate. You will be able to bill your staff at the rates established for them—profitably—while staying within the total price originally quoted.

You have, in fact, created your own loss leader, but you need never actually suffer the loss! The objective was strictly to *appear* to be the low bidder, without really being low bidder!

The Game of "Changes"

Anyone who has built a house or almost anything on a long-term contract basis knows about "changes." Any change you make, even one that takes something out, costs you more money. That's a general fact of life in the construction business: Changes are almost inevitable, for any of a dozen reasons, and every change costs the owner more money than originally estimated. Rarely do changes result in a lowering of price.

Changes are not confined to construction work, however. Almost any long-term custom requirement is likely to involve changes; there are always circumstances and contingencies no one could have foreseen at the onset or during the planning of the program. Here are just a few of the reasons for changes:

- A material required is in short supply, and something else must be substituted for it.
- A new and superior material becomes available.
- The customer has a change of mind about something.
- An unforeseen problem arises during the course of early work, making a change mandatory.
- The customer does not keep all his commitments to the contractor, requiring the contractor to do more work than originally planned, forcing an expensive slowdown on him, or causing extra costs in some way.

These changes are, of course, not the contractor's fault or the contractor's doing. Therefore, he has a legitimate claim on the customer for amendment of the contract. Changes are especially plentiful in long-term projects involving high technology, such as weapons systems, computers, radar, and the like, owing to the ultrarapid growth of the technologies and the need to react to political and technological developments elsewhere in the world. Rarely is a modern system of any size produced according to the original design configuration. As a system or new equipment is being developed, drawings are made. However, a new piece of equipment almost always needs "debugging" because prototypes rarely perform perfectly until they have been tinkered with at great length. As each change in design is finalized, it is supposed to be made on the drawings. Therefore, an original drawing becomes "revision A," to reflect the first change, "revision B," to reflect the second change, and so on.

Revision letters often go well into the alphabet! In practice, the designers and draftsmen rarely keep up with the actual changes, so for a very large part of the life of a new system, none of the drawings extant is really up to date. The latest drawing available may be revision G, even though 15 changes have actually been made to the equipment!

Now comes the time to solicit bids for work involving the system technical manuals, perhaps, some related equipment, or even contracts for installation; and the bids submitted are based on the drawings, which are part of the solicitation package. That is, the bidders submit prices based on their analysis of the requirement as described in the drawings, which may number into the thousands.

But suppose the drawings are not up to date. Suppose they do not reflect the system as it actually has been finalized. What if the bidders bid on the basis of drawing revision G and are handed drawing revision L when they are about to start work? What if they start working and discover that the actual equipment does not correspond with drawing revision G and that up-to-date drawings are not available?

The "what if?" is easy to answer. The contractor hollers "Foul!" and claims a "change of scope," which the contracting officer can hardly reject. The contracting officer then invites the contractor to "document" the claimed changes and estimate the costs of the changes—how much money should be added to the contract. Ultimately, the amendment(s) to the contract is (are) negotiated, and the contract is amended, which means, usually, that money is added.

There are other situations that result in changes and amendments. A typical one is that in which a contractor has done the research and development (R&D) work to develop a prototype and has (probably deliberately) failed to indicate many key items of information in the drawings delivered with the prototype. An R&D contractor will frequently withhold information in this way if his contract does not have all the "teeth" in it to compel him to make a full disclosure of his work. The following example illustrates why this can be advantageous to a contractor.

It is common practice to issue an R&D contract on a cost-plus basis (because it is almost impossible to predict the costs of R&D) to a firm when a new, improved system is wanted. In the military, the arms race created frequent need for this, as technology continued to explode. Even now many of the technological development initiatives continue, under a momentum of their own. Even without an immediate threat, the military feels compelled to develop capabilities in space, as well as on the ground, often working with NASA in this. As in the case of NASA, military preparation is responsible for a great percentage of our technological development.

Now suppose we develop a high-flying aircraft, such as the U-2, which can fly above most surface-to-air missiles (SAMs). If they catch up and shoot down our U-2, we seek another method, perhaps a satellite that flies even higher or a low-level aircraft that flies under their radar. Or we might see a need for a more flexible or faster radar system. In any case, once our government decides that a new development is (1) needed and (2) possible, officials are likely to invite bids to do the R&D and produce a prototype.

Once the prototype is developed and delivered and the government is satisfied that it works and should be added to the arsenal, a contractor is sought to produce the device in the numbers required. This is a production contract, whereas the original one was a development contract.

The development contract should have called for the developer to deliver a complete set of drawings that make full disclosure: show exactly how the device is built and assembled. There are overall drawings of the device, including views of the assembled end item, detail drawings of each part (or other documentation of parts that may be bought off the shelf, if such is the case), parts lists, and assembly drawings, which show how the various parts are assembled into the final product. The drawings should also show how the various parts are made (whether stamped, pressed, rolled, punched, and so on) and of what materials. In short, if the drawing package is complete, as it should be, any competent firm should be able to build it exactly as it was prototyped.

However, the R&D contractor would like to win the contract to produce the item, too, so he is not going to provide any more information in his drawings than the law and his contract require him to. And unfortunately, sometimes the government fails to "cross all the t's and dot all the i's" in its contracts. So occasionally, an R&D contractor delivers a set of drawings that do not permit another contractor to build the item! This virtually forces the government to give the production contract to the original R&D firm.

However, the government may not know the drawings are deficient and do not make full disclosure and therefore offer them as specifications to back up a solicitation package. Later, having bid on the basis of the drawings, the production contractor discovers the item can't be assembled in the procedure shown or has other problems resulting from deficient information supplied by the government. He then has justification for a change in price.

This happens with such regularity in many fields that it is predictable. It therefore becomes the basis for a popular bidding strategy: If the bidder can be reasonably certain he will have occasions for changes during the course of the contract, he can afford to bid low, sometimes even below anticipated costs, and get his profits out of the changes! This is easily possible because, although he must bid competitively to win the contract, he has no competitive bids to meet in pricing changes. He negotiates these with the customer, and good negotiators can get the right prices when there are no competitive bids to worry about.

This kind of situation is not confined to construction and engineering, although it is almost invariably encountered there. Almost any long-term custom project will run into unexpected difficulties of one sort or another or even meet other kinds of opportunities that will cause a change in scope and a consequent amendment. (A change in a contract that does not affect the price is a "modification." One that does affect the price is an "amendment.") Moreover, only the authorized contracting official can authorize an amendment, and not his "authorized technical representative," by whatever title he is known (for example, contracting officer's representative, contracting officer's technical representative, project manager, and so on).

Procedures for Changes

When a contract is going to be modified or amended, a certain protocol is usually observed. The talks may be initiated unofficially by either the government or the contractor; however, once the change is agreed upon, the usual procedure is to have the contractor write a formal request to the contracting official asking for the change. Here is a typical sequence of events, from an actual experience.

I was the manager of a three-year contract for technical support of a NASA center under a cost-reimbursement contract. The contract listed, among other things, technical writers at three levels of proficiency and established ceiling rates for each class for each year of the contract.

In the third year of the contract, circumstances made it almost impossible to recruit level III writers at the rates contracted for. No one could have foreseen, two years earlier, that a combination of a seller's market and inflation would have led to this situation. Nevertheless, we were bound by a contract that could have forced us to lose money.

After studying the situation to find an escape, I was struck by an idea. I sought out the COTR (contracting officer's technical representative) and pointed out that there had been, in the past two years, an almost quantum leap in the sophistication of the systems about which we were writing manuals. Because we had provided some very talented and capable people in the past, some of the work we were currently being asked to do was a bit beyond that originally envisioned for the project. I suggested we therefore should "modify" the contract to establish a writer IV category, at a slightly higher rate than that of writer III.

I persuaded the COTR to agree with me, and he "suggested" I write a request to the contracting officer, setting forth my arguments. The contracting officer, of course, passed the request to the COTR for comment. When the COTR approved it, the modification was made.

This was a modification, rather than an amendment, because it didn't change the government's commitment on total price for the contract or call for the "obligation" of additional funds, although it did authorize our billing at a higher rate for the new writer IV level.

Ingenuity can also bring about changes, whether or not circumstances compel them!

Rules and Exceptions on Changes

Every contract carries the clear warning that the contractor must not agree to changes calling for more money without the contracting official's approval and authorization. A COTR may request additional work and may promise that a contract amendment will be forthcoming, but it is most hazardous to proceed and incur additional expense on this assurance alone. The COTR does not have the legal authority to obligate the government for more money. Although he may be acting in good faith, he may find out he cannot back up his promise. Also, COTRs are often replaced during the course of a contract, and a new COTR is not likely to feel compelled to honor the pledge of his predecessor, especially when the pledge is not in writing and is not legally binding in any case.

Even when a contracting official agrees to a change and amendment, it is hazardous to proceed before the amendment is formally in writing and legally binding. A contracting official may be replaced by another, too, before the contract is consummated. There are exceptions, however. Here is one such case.

When the Air Pollution Control Office (APCO) of the Public Health Service was in existence (it's now the Environmental Protection Agency), the organization I managed was approached by that agency to help officials produce their four volumes of standards and specifications. The time pressure was great: The four volumes had to be completed, printed and bound, and in the mail, postmarked before January 1, 1970. Our aid was solicited in late November 1969!

Initially, the staff asked for minimal aid such as typing, proofreading, and perhaps some light editing and a few illustrations. When we looked the work over and advised them that we believed they would need more help than that, they assured us they did not. Within a few days, the APCO staff was asking us for more support than we had contracted for. Knowing the hazards of proceeding without the contracting official's okay, we communicated this to the contracting officer. He asked us to draw up a list of changes required and submit it to him, with estimated costs.

While we were doing so, the APCO staff asked for still more support as they began to perceive how far they really were from completing the job. We were compelled to call the contracting officer again. He then authorized us—verbally—to provide whatever the staff asked for and said that if we would keep track, he would settle with us at the end of the job. Under such exceptional circumstances, we agreed to proceed on his verbal assurances.

Ultimately, we amassed a bill of over $35,000 for what started out to be a job contracted for less than $5,000! And even though the customer had been almost supplicating us for help, we anticipated we would have a tough negotiation at the end. (Gratitude vanishes quickly when the crisis is over!) We weren't disappointed: We had to fight hard at the negotiating table to get everything that was coming to us.

In such a case, knowing the pressure to produce a job by a given date and seeing how far the customer was from being ready to meet that deadline without massive help, it did not take a genius to foresee many changes before the job was over.

The Simple Answer

We fallible humans have a great talent for overlooking the obvious. We seek complex answers to simple problems when the simple answer is right in front of us. Nowhere is this more apparent than when we read typical solicitation packages.

The typical solicitation package includes a great deal of boiler-plate material—standard instructions and forms. After a while, the experienced bidder tends to skim by this familiar paper and in so doing often misses information that would, or should, make the difference. He may make telephone calls and visits, and undertake a great deal of unnecessary research, when the information has been on his desk all the while.

In one such case, I had an invitation to bid the U.S. Forest Service for a basic ordering agreement to support their technical publications work. It was a typical laundry list of services that included writing, editing, drafting, illustrating, proofreading, typing, and so on. It was a formally advertised procurement, which meant the contract would go to the low bidder.

As a matter of course, I invoked the Freedom of Information Act and obtained the prices being paid under the then-existing contract. I found them to be highly competitive and was in something of a quandary for a strategy to be or appear to be the low bidder.

Almost in desperation, I leafed slowly through the rather voluminous bid set. But it was only after doing so several times that I made the discovery I should have made on first reading, which proved to be the key to being the low bidder—or apparent low bidder.

One of the items to be priced was, typically, double-spaced draft typing, by the page. The government then used $8 \times 10\frac{1}{2}$ inch paper (this was before the change to the commercial standard of $8\frac{1}{2} \times 11$ inch paper), on which a typical image area (typing area on a page) is approximately $6\frac{1}{2} \times 9$ inches. Typed on an elite (12-pitch) typewriter, a page would be about 27 lines long and 75 characters wide. For a 10-pitch or pica machine, this would be 27 lines, each 65 characters wide.

It occurred to me that I had not seen a definition of whether a "page" of typing was predicated on elite or pica typeface. I therefore began to read all the tiresome boilerplate specifications, to which I had paid little attention before.

I finally came to the specification for a page of typing. To my utter amazement, a typed page was defined as 55 characters wide and 18 lines deep! This represents 990 typewriter strikes (or keystrokes, as many typesetting houses now measure production costs), compared with 2,025 strikes for what I had presumed to be the "standard" page—less than one-half! That meant I could cut the per-page price considerably without running any risks, which enabled us to be the low bidder without cutting any other prices.

Different Strategies for Different Situations

It might be thought that an incumbent, the present contractor on a project coming up for another year's contract, enjoys a decisive advantage over the outsider bidding for the contract. In many cases, this is entirely true, but not in all cases. There is one kind of procurement, in fact, where the incumbent is at a decided disadvantage: the "body" contract.

Under the law, the government may not "hire" people indirectly by contracting for labor to be done on-site (in or on the government's own premises) unless the work cannot be done off-site. If a contractor must manage or operate a government computer or R&D laboratory, he must obviously do so on the government's premises—on-site. If he is writing a manual for the government, he can do that on his own premises and is required to do so.

Work that must be done on-site presents special problems and considerations in bidding for the contract. The pricing competition is quite close for such work because all employers must pay workers approximately the same hourly rates, so the difference among bids is usually rather small, sometimes only pennies per labor hour.

The staff of the incumbent contractor has been working on-site for at least one year, and often for several years. The contractor has tried to keep some continuity of staff by awarding merit increases each year, so most workers are above the starting rate. When the time comes to bid for renewal of the contract, he is compelled to assume that his existing staff will remain in place (the customer would think him a poor contractor if he changed his staff every year) and will continue to get annual merit increases.

The other bidders are under no such restraints or obligations. They can, and do, bid the job at whatever they believe to be starting rates. They are prepared to replace the entire existing staff, if necessary. They cannot be criticized for so doing because they have no obligations to an existing staff and existing customer. In almost every case, such contracts represent a rough, tough game, with rough, tough competitors. Only by hardheaded, realistic bidding can one hope to win these contracts.

The strategies available in competing for formally advertised procurements (sealed-bid types of competition) are all variations on the theme of how to be or appear to be the low bidder. Only the low bidder wins, although the law does not say this explicitly. The law does, in fact, provide for a number of cases where the low bidder does not win. But, as you have already read, in practice, it is rare for the low bidder to be denied the contract, unless he can be persuaded to withdraw his bid voluntarily.

The following case illustrates this clearly: When HUD (the Department of Housing and Urban Development) took over the old FHA mortgages, it inherited a warehouse packed with filing cabinets full of mortgage papers. The documents required a massive updating to reflect the changes occasioned by HUD assuming the mortgages. It was decided to hire a contractor with a crew of clerks to carry out the work.

Bids were invited by IFB (information for bid) and a public opening held. When the bids were opened, the contracting officer and the project manager were shocked by the low bid. It was, in their opinion, unrealistic.

It is not in the interest of the government to have a contractor default on a project. The government gains nothing and loses a great deal of time. Therefore, the contracting officer and the project manager took the low bidder aside and explained that he could not possibly do the job for the figure quoted without losing his shirt. The contracting officer offered to let the man withdraw his bid. The bidder flatly refused. He insisted he knew what he was doing and could and would do the job for the figure quoted.

The officials had no choice but to allow him to try, and they reluctantly awarded him the contract. Within two months, the contractor was in serious trouble and, as predicted, was unable to perform. The officials were compelled to find him in default and cancel the contract. As soon as that was done, they scheduled another competition for the contract.

To their horror, history repeated itself. The same individual again submitted a low bid, claimed he now knew what he had done wrong, and again insisted on having the contract. History continued to repeat itself, and the contractor defaulted a second time, resulting in the contract being canceled a second time.

The contracting officer and the project manager anticipated the possibility that this individual might be bullheaded enough to try even a third time to do the impossible; they headed him off by a simple maneuver: This time they issued an RFP (request for proposal), which results in a negotiated procurement and does not award the contract to the lowest bidder. This is one of several reasons the government often prefers to use negotiated procurement: The low bidder is not always the most desirable or even a qualified contractor.

Negotiated Procurement

In terms of total procurement dollars (not number of procurement contracts), about 85 percent of federal procurement is done through negotiation. The rules for negotiated procurements are different from those for formally advertised procurements in the following ways:

1. Openings are not public.
2. Price is not the only factor and often is negligible. (That is, the government is under no compulsion to make an award to the low bidder.)
3. A technical proposal is required, and an evaluation is made of the proposer's (bidder's) competence or capability, as well as of the general elements of the proposal.
4. Prices may be adjusted after the opening, and bidders may submit additional information and/or changes to their proposals after the opening, if the government wishes to grant them permission to do so.

There are a few points of similarity, too:

1. Everyone bidding (proposing) is entitled to have the same information and access to information. Proposals can be invalidated if one of the proposers is shown to have had an unfair advantage over the others.
2. Price may be the deciding factor.
3. The announced "opening" date is actually the closing date. Proposals delivered after that date may be rejected, and usually are, unless the delay was caused by the U.S. Postal

Service (the proposal having been mailed with such prompt-
ness so that it should have been delivered in time) or due to
other excusable causes, as provided by law.

4. Proposers have the right to know, after award is made, what
others bid and may protest an award if they believe a protest
is justified.

5. A proposal may lead to any type of contract, just as a sealed
bid may. The form of the contract is not affected by the
manner of the competition for it.

In general, the rules and procedures for negotiated procurement
are much freer and more flexible than they are for formally advertised
procurement simply because the contract is to be negotiated, and the
selection of a winner depends on technical as well as on price competition. But to provide as fair and equable an atmosphere as possible,
the agency must establish and use an objective rating scheme to
evaluate all proposals. Further, to ensure that proposals are rated as
objectively as possible on their technical merits, those who evaluate
technical proposals are not permitted to know what costs each proposer has estimated.

Typical Evaluation Criteria

Unfortunately, there is no standard for evaluation schemes. Each
agency, and this can mean an individual "office" or "administration"
within an agency, sets its own criteria and schemes. Therefore, one
solicitation package may describe a heavily detailed and highly sophisticated evaluation scheme; another may present a rather cursory
and general one. Or one solicitation may state some specific number
of evaluation points assigned to each criterion listed; another may
state merely the relative weight of one as compared with another. In
general, however, these are the factors weighed by these schemes:

- The proposer's understanding of the requirement, as shown
by the proposal

- The quality of the plan proposed for satisfying the requirement or solving the problems stated
- The demonstrated ability to anticipate contingencies and cope successfully with them
- The quality of the proposer's plan for managing the work
- The qualifications of the staff proposed for the project, especially its key members, who will be responsible for the critical functions
- The commitment of the organization and/or its parent organization to the project
- The qualifications of the proposer's proposed project manager
- The proposer's financial resources for handling the project
- The proposed schedule for deliveries and accomplishments of milestones

The Source Selection Board

In most cases, proposals are evaluated by a team of three, five, or more members, who award each proposal a technical point score. In some cases, cost is itself a basis for points; in others, cost is considered more generally, with no points awarded specifically for it. No matter how detailed the criteria described in the solicitation are, the evaluation team is working with even more detailed guidance than that described. For example, the solicitation may state that a maximum of 20 points or 20 percent will be awarded for staff qualifications. Internally, in making the actual evaluation, the evaluators will have a breakdown of this under which they will have perhaps 5 points maximum for the individual's formal education, 5 more points for general experience, and 10 points for directly related experience, to make up the 20 points total.

Although a team is usually used, except for the smallest contracts, the head of the team, often the individual who will be the government's project manager, is usually quite influential in making the final decision. The board also usually includes the contracting officer, either directly or indirectly. Although he is probably not a technical expert and can't contribute to the technical evaluation, he is central to the process and can evaluate some of the factors.

Technical Versus Cost Proposal

The solicitation calls for two proposals: technical and cost. That is, the cost presentation is to be bound separately from the technical information. When the proposal package is delivered to the contracting officer, he separates the two and retains the cost proposals under his security while the evaluation team reviews the technical proposals.

After technical review has been made and the proposals have been scored, the review of cost is made. This usually involves conferences between the technical evaluators and the contracting officer. They compare the merits of each proposal with the cost to the government. There are many variations of how the technical and cost considerations are finally reconciled to make a final award decision, but there are three general cases:

1. Cost is assigned a specific point value, which is added to technical points awarded for a final score.
2. A complex scheme is used, wherein each proposal is given a rating based on cost per technical point awarded.
3. Cost is not evaluated on a point basis but is part of a general and final evaluation, usually described as "cost and other factors considered."

The Impact of Cost

As a result of this great variation in how cost affects award decisions, there are several basic situations, which can be summarized as follows:

1. The award goes to the lowest-priced qualified proposer (that is, the lowest priced of those remaining after all technically unacceptable proposals have been rejected).

2. The award goes to that proposer whose final cost-per-technical-point score is lowest.

3. The award goes to that proposer whose proposal has received the highest technical-point score if his price is (or can be brought) within an acceptable range (often referred to as the competitive range).

In the first situation, price becomes an important factor, particularly if a protest or award dispute arises, because it is not at all uncommon for two-thirds or more of the proposals submitted to be rejected on technical grounds. When the government commits itself to such an evaluation scheme, it lessens the importance of achieving the highest possible technical score and places all proposers whose proposals are technically acceptable (within the competitive range) on an equal basis, with price now the determining factor. This places the competition on a basis somewhat similar to that of the two-step procurement (discussed later in this chapter). But it also lessens the effects of the evaluators' subjective judgments and gives the protester a "place to stand" if and when he chooses to dispute the award decision. It has become a matter of record which proposals are technically acceptable and which of those is lowest priced. It is by far the most objective rating scheme offered.

The second approach to evaluating costs is also reasonably objective, but it is affected far more by technical scores, which are inevitably subjective. The usual approach is to select the proposal with the highest technical rating and use that proposer's costs as the baseline or reference standard by which to evaluate the others' cost-per-technical-point rating. Here is an example of how such a method usually works:

The highest scoring proposal receives 97 points (out of a possible 100).

The price offered by this proposer (A) is $240,000.

Baseline is $240,000 ÷ 97 = $2,474.23/technical point.

Proposer B is awarded 93 points and has offered a price of $237,000.

$237,000 ÷ 93 = $2,548.39.

Proposer C is awarded 90 points and offers a price of $278,000. $278,000 ÷ 90 = $3,088.89.

Proposer D is awarded 88 points and offers a price of $216,000. $216,000 ÷ 88 = $2,454.55.

Therefore, comparative costs per technical point are as follows:

Proposer A: $2,474.23
Proposer B: $2,548.39
Proposer C: $3,088.89
Proposer D: $2,454.55

Although not the highest scoring proposer, D's price is lowest in terms of cost per technical point. This is interpreted as representing the best value to the government.

Variants of this basic approach are often used, some of them relatively complex but all based on the same general idea.

The third approach is the least objective because the customer evaluates prices subjectively to determine which represents the best value to the government. He will score all the technical proposals, rejecting those that do not meet his minimum requirements, and then decide which one he believes to be "in the best interests of the government," which may easily mean which contractor he likes best or feels most comfortable with.

Of course, an in-house estimate was made before the solicitation was issued; the requester could not have gotten approval for the funds without some kind of estimate. Ordinarily, no proposal will be acceptable if the cost exceeds that estimate, which has now become the preliminary budget for the project. Presumably, the competitive range is established by identifying the limits of prices quoted by most acceptable proposals. However, in many cases, the customer may accept any quote that does not exceed the budget as being in the competitive range.

However, because this is a negotiated procurement, the price submitted by a proposer is not engraved in stone; it is still subject to negotiation. Therefore, the government may elect to negotiate with the highest-scoring proposers to try to bring their prices down within the range established as acceptable. Typically, the solicitation package states that officials may select a proposal and proceed to make an award without further discussion. The government reserves that right, which is an inducement to the proposer to offer his best terms in the initial submittal. In the case of small contracts, especially when there is an urgency to consummate a contract before some deadline (such as the end of the fiscal year), awards are often made "without further discussion." However, large contracts are almost always negotiated before an award is made.

The Nature of Negotiations

Negotiations can take any of several forms, which may or may not resemble negotiations as practiced in private industry. The proposals have been evaluated, the prices for each have been noted, the contracting officer has discussed the evaluations and gotten the opinions of the evaluators and the program executive requesting the contract, and the proposals have been rank-ordered.

If an acceptable proposal has been priced so high as to preclude, in the contracting officer's opinion, the possibility of negotiating the price down to an acceptable range, no effort may be made to negotiate with that proposer and usually is not. Barring that, any of the following approaches may be pursued:

1. Negotiations are opened with the top-ranking (preferred) proposer only. If successful, no other contracts will be negotiated. If not successful, the next-ranking proposer will be invited to negotiate.

2. The top three or more proposers are each invited to make a formal presentation, answer questions, conduct discussions, and submit any additional technical and cost estimates (or modify original ones).

3. All proposers whose original submittals were acceptable are invited to make presentations, and so on, and submit "best and final offers," as in item 2.

The Contracting Officer's Influence

Much depends on the personality and policies of the contracting officer, who is the agent's authority on contract law and procurement regulations. (Most contracting officers are lawyers or accountants, and many are both.) Many contracting officers will fight hard for the lowest-priced proposal, just as many program executives will fight hard for their own selection, irrespective of price. In some agencies, a contracting officer will demand that the source selection board submit a written justification for the selection of any but the lowest-priced qualified offeror. Because this is not always an easy thing to justify when much of the judgment has been subjective, it often has the effect of directing the award to the lowest-priced qualified bidder, even though the evaluation system was not designed to achieve that result.

The goal of a dedicated contracting officer is to get, for the government, the best product (result) in the shortest possible time (shortest schedule) at the lowest possible cost. He is usually dependent on the program people, as technical specialists, to select the proposal that promises the best product or result, but he can see for himself who offers the best schedule and lowest price.

Policies Versus Regulations

Internal agency procurement policies are as important as the procurement regulations. The regulations are intended to stipulate what is permissible and what is taboo, under the laws enacted by Congress, and to lay down the basic procurement procedures. The regulations are, however, subject to interpretation by the agencies' contracting officials and executive heads. (In some cases, the chief executive of the agency is the designated contracting officer.) Policy may also restrict the application of the law.

For example, the law (Small Purchases Act) provides that small purchase procedures may be used for procurements under $25,000.

This means a limited and informal competition, using a purchase order as the contractual instrument, rather than a formal contract. However, there are agencies whose contracting officials permit small purchase procedures for procurements under $5,000 only. In some agencies, best-and-final procedures are used for only large contracts; in others, they are used in all procurements over $25,000. And so on. This applies even to profit figures. The National Cancer Institute, for example, permits a fee of up to 9 percent in a cost-reimbursement contract; other agencies may restrict fees to lower percentages.

The Hybrid "Two-Step" Procurement

The two-step procurement embodies the characteristics of both the formally advertised and negotiated procurement methods and may well come into greater use, under present trends in government procurement and OFPP policies. Basically, it is a system in which technical proposals only (no cost information) are invited as a first step. After evaluation, those proposers whose technical proposals are considered acceptable are solicited to submit cost proposals. Step 1 is accomplished by RFP, step 2 by IFB.

This means that the second step is accomplished under the rules of formally advertised procurement, with sealed bids and the award going to the low bidder. But the bidders are restricted to those who have submitted acceptable technical proposals, (presumably) eliminating the hazard of awarding the contract to someone who cannot perform. It is therefore a form of prequalifying bidders and screening out those who do not appear to be truly capable of carrying out the work satisfactorily. Ordinarily, this method is used only for large procurements and is still not in widespread use.

Strategy Defined

Given the enormous number of variants and possible permutations among them, what is decisive in one case is of little consequence in another. For example, it may be critically important to be the low bidder to win one contract, but totally unimportant for another. It may be necessary to win an extremely high technical-point score in one case, but in another case, the effort to score above the acceptable threshold may be wasted.

But there are other factors. In most cases, some single factor is uppermost in the customer's mind, although that may not have been communicated in the statement of work and general information package. He may, for example, be definitely seeking something innovative, a totally new and different approach to his project. Or he may be utterly opposed to innovation and want what he considers to be the safe and sound, tried and true, classical approach. Here are some other considerations that are often critical:

The quality of the proposed staff. In many cases, the success of a proposal hinges almost entirely on the customer's reaction to the resumes in the proposal.

The technical plan for the project. The customer must be convinced the plan is sound and has an excellent chance for being entirely successful.

The plan for management of the proposed project. In many cases, the customer considers project management at least as important as the technical aspects of the program and scrutinizes the proposed management plan especially closely.

Corporate commitment. Proposals are frequently submitted by a division or department of a larger organization. The customer may be especially watchful for evidence that the parent corporation is cognizant of and dedicated to success in the proposed project.

Organization experience. Even with well-qualified staff members proposed, the customer requires, usually, that the organization have relevant experience. The organization that has done related but not similar work in the past may not be credible enough to justify the risk of a large project.

Strategy is the conceptual approach for winning. In its simplest form, it involves two elements:

1. Identifying the factor(s) that is (are) most critically important in the customer's mind (or can be made so) and that is (are) key to winning
2. Structuring the proposal so as to persuade the customer that the proposer represents the best prospect for realizing or effecting the objective(s) represented by the critical factor(s)

That is, strategy consists of correctly identifying what the customer wants most and then persuading the customer that the proposer can and will deliver it.

An alternative to this is to help the customer identify the most important factors and then sell the proposer's ability to deliver those things. That is, a successful proposal is often one in which the proposer has demonstrated that some factor(s) is (are) critical to overall program success and then has gone on to present a plan and set of credentials specific to the factor(s) highlighted.

Beating the Competition

Proposal writing is a competitive game, except for those specific cases of unsolicited proposals and sole-source or selected-source procurements, which I take up in Chapter 7. It is not far different from competitive selling in the private sector, except that there are certain specific statutes governing federal purchasing, and the wise marketer becomes fully aware of these and what they provide.

Earlier, I referred to some of the myths about government procurement. One was the myth that only large corporations can win government contracts, and another was that these large corporations usually make arrangements to "fix" the awards. What gives rise to such myths? Part of the reason is that too many contracts are won by large companies that have submitted mediocre proposals. However, they are being competed against by other proposals that are no better.

That is, far too often a contract is awarded to a proposal that is the best of a poor lot.

Given an assortment of proposals, none of which is particularly meritorious, the customer often opts for the proposal submitted by the best-known or largest company. The reasoning is that because none of the proposals is very good, the best chance for a successful project is with the biggest or best-known company! Again and again, a good proposal from a small and little-known organization has beaten a mediocre proposal from even the largest and best-known company.

There is no use pretending that all contracts offered for competitive proposals and bids enjoy completely free competition. Indeed, many have been "wired" for a favored contractor. But even these can often be unwired by someone offering a truly superior proposal. Wiring offers one contractor great advantages over competitors, but it does not—cannot—guarantee the award. The entire process is open to public scrutiny and subject to appeals protests. In that environment, it is simply not possible to make the wiring process foolproof. In Chapter 2, you read of a case where an energetic and aggressive bidder forced an agency to award a contract to another bidder than the one for whom it had been intended. (In fact, the case involving the question about what constituted a typed page was one such.)

In general, beating the competition usually means being a bit smarter and working a lot harder. It is always a mistake to underestimate the competition. You should expect others to know their business and to prepare at least acceptable proposals. But it is equally mistaken to overrate the competition. The biggest and best-entrenched government contractors find themselves being beaten by small newcomers who have worked hard to gather reliable market information and design a superior proposal.

CHAPTER 6

What About Costs?

*To train a dog, the trainer must
be smarter than the dog.*

The Importance of Costs

Every profession tends to shroud its workings in a protective cloak of mysterious jargon that is totally unintelligible to outsiders. Doctors and lawyers do it by using little-known Latin; insurance people say "premium" when they mean "payment"; psychologists build entire careers around the special meanings they ascribe to such words as "behavior" and "reinforcement." Accountants are no different. They frighten others into total dependence on their wisdom by referring to "debits," "offsets," and the like, which other mortals are assured are beyond their comprehension. They draw up their own cabalistic arrangements in documents that only they can interpret but that are supposed to report the health of the business and predict its future.

In many cases, the accountants are responsible for preparing and submitting a bid or proposal that is doomed to failure from the start. But in fairness to the accountants, it is not their fault that they are asked to do cost analyses and prepare cost estimates without adequate communication with the technical/professional specialists who are responsible for preparing the bid or proposal. The true fault lies in the reluctance of the technical/professional specialists to make themselves familiar with costs and their meaning. Yet, when the jargon is stripped away, costs are easier to comprehend than are the specialties called for in the bid or proposal.

In short, no bid or proposal can be prepared intelligently by two or more people who are not working together in every sense of the

119

word: communicating and establishing complete understanding. Nor can anyone design a program and prepare a proposal properly without understanding costs and what the various aspects of the design do to costs. Anyone preparing a bid or proposal must understand costs at least to the extent of being able to discuss them readily with those who specialize in costs and accounting for them.

Have no fear; I'm not going to try to make an accountant of you (even if I were qualified to do so). But the subject is less complex than most people think, as you will soon see.

The Two Kinds of Costs

In any business, there are two kinds of money flow: outgoing and incoming. Obviously, if the business is to survive, it must take in at least as much as it pays out. Bear that simple fact in mind as we proceed; it's the rationale for almost everything I have to say about costs, no matter in what accounting column they appear or by what names they are called. As a result of all the necessary accounting manipulations and jargon of the profession, we may lose sight of this simple fact. (And losing sight of it, failing fully to grasp this simple relationship, has been the downfall of many businesses.)

Actually, a business must take in a bit more than it spends. The bit more is called profit, which is not a dirty word. It's essential to a healthy business enterprise.

There's one more essential fact, which is really another way of saying that the business must take in at least as much as it pays out: Any cost of doing business, by whatever name we call it, must be recovered before a profit can be realized. One of the problems in modern business, particularly in a complex business enterprise, is that many costs are hidden, which leads to severe problems. For example, if an item costs you $3, you know it represents a $3 cost immediately. But you also have some costs for handling it—rent, heat, light, advertising, sales commissions, and your own salary, at least. Your selling price must cover these, as well as the original $3 cost to you, plus some profit. One of the major functions of the accountants is to help us recognize and identify all the costs so we know what we must do to recover them and show a bit of profit. It is this classifying, categorizing, and identifying costs that is complicated and can get us into trouble. In much government contracting, particularly for the larger, custom contracts, the government will not permit contractors simply to charge some fixed price for their goods and services. They must demonstrate that their cost estimates are valid, conform with standard accounting practices, and are fair and reasonable charges to the government.

The point of this discussion is that there are only two kinds of costs: direct and indirect. These are the two broad and basic categories, although each is subdivided into subcategories. It is necessary, for accounting purposes and sometimes for strategic purposes, to know which is which, just as it is necessary to recover both in the transaction.

In the previous example of buying an item for $3 and reselling it at some profit, the $3 represents direct cost, and the other costs (rent, heat, light, advertising, sales commissions, and your own salary) are usually indirect costs. (Sales commissions could be either direct or indirect costs, depending on how your accounting system is organized.)

This subdivision into direct and indirect is not absolute, but it is somewhat arbitrary and varies from one case to another. There are circumstances in which all your costs might be considered direct, for example, if you sold one item only, and that constituted your entire business. But if you sell a great many items, you will find it impossible to determine exactly what portion of your rent, heat, light, and so on is represented by the sale of that one $3 item. Yet you must somehow recover all those costs in conducting your business. To solve this problem, your accountant organizes your books in such a way as to list both direct and indirect costs.

Types of Indirect Costs

The best-known name for indirect costs is overhead. Almost everyone has heard that term used, whether they fully understand it or not. For many small businesses, overhead is synonymous with indirect costs, which are those costs of doing business that must be allocated or spread among the sale of various goods or services because specific overhead dollars can't be assigned to any single item or service sold. Therefore, a rate or percentage figure must be established as a guide in setting a selling price that returns all costs plus a profit.

Suppose, for example, that your own salary and all the other indirect costs of operating your business come to $3,000 a month. Further suppose that the merchandise you sell every month represents a direct cost to you of $7,500 every month. And further, you have decided that you must realize a profit of 10 percent of direct cost on your sales. That means you must sell that $7,500 worth of merchandise for:

$$\$7,500 \text{ (direct cost)} + \$3,000 \text{ (indirect cost)} + \$750$$
$$(10 \text{ percent profit)} = \$11,250$$
$$\$11,250 - \$7,500 = \$3,750$$
$$\$3,750 \div \$7,500 = 0.50 = 50 \text{ percent}$$
$$0.50 \times 100 = 50 \text{ percent (overhead rate)}$$

That is, you must mark up items 50 percent (one and one-half times your direct cost) to arrive at a selling price. Selling that $3 item at $4.50 will bring back your costs plus a profit if you continue to sell $7,500 worth (at your cost) of merchandise every month.

Your accountant will calculate your overhead *rate* (we already know that the overhead *dollars* equal $3,000 every month) as:

$$\$3,000 \div \$7,500 = 0.40 = 40 \text{ percent}$$

Of course, he won't do so on a monthly basis, but on an annual basis, because your sales figures will probably fluctuate from month to month, and you would never be able to keep up with recalculating all your costs every month and changing your prices to reflect these.

To put this still another way: It costs you $.40 to sell $1 worth of merchandise. Therefore, you must add that $.40 to each dollar of what you paid for that merchandise simply to recover your costs *before profit*.

Now of course you are not free simply to charge whatever you feel like charging if you want to stay in business. You must be competitive with whatever the market is for what you are selling. If you allow your overhead rate to get out of control and to rise to unreasonable heights or if you try to get an exorbitant profit, you won't be able to compete successfully. Overhead must therefore be controlled.

Because indirect costs, whether they are all overhead or are subdivided (as they often are), are a rate or percentage of your sales volume, a larger sales volume should mean a reduced overhead *rate*. This can be a decisive factor.

Here are some of the typical expense items that are usually part of your overhead or other indirect costs:

Basic building or facility costs (rent, heat, light, and so on)
Telephones
Advertising and sales
Salaries of nonproduction people, such as receptionists, clerks, accountants, sales people, drivers, personnel people, officers, and so on
Insurance
Delivery vehicles
Sales commissions
Licenses
Legal fees
Taxes
Fringe benefits (vacations, holidays, sick leave, group insurance)
Expense accounts
Repairs
Depreciation (buildings, equipment, furniture, fixtures)
Interest (on business indebtedness)

On your accountant's ledgers, these various kinds of indirect costs are kept in different accounts or schedules, and even these are broken down further. For more general purposes, all these may be considered overhead costs, and in many cases, all these will make up what accountants may refer to as the "overhead pool." However, in bidding to the U.S. government, it is wise to separate these costs into overhead and "G&A," which stands for general and administrative costs. Companies that do not do business with the government usually find it necessary to have a "G&A pool." Here's why.

Many contracting officials, particularly in the Department of Defense, but not necessarily confined to DOD, will not allow certain types of indirect costs to be reimbursed by the government as overhead. They claim, for example, that marketing and sales costs are not properly overhead items and should not be charged to the government. They admit, however, that these are legitimate costs of doing business, and the contractor is entitled to recover these costs somehow. For that reason, some years ago, the concept of G&A was born, and contracting officials see no problem with paying sales/marketing, officers' salaries, and other related indirect costs as long as they are listed as G&A, rather than overhead. Actually, this works out to the contractor's advantage, as you will see later in this chapter when I review the cost forms.

Indirect costs are therefore broken into two broad classes: overhead and G&A. However, some contractors prefer to segregate those overhead costs incurred in giving employees paid time off (vacations and holidays) and other benefits (group insurance, bonuses, and so on). They break indirect costs into overhead, G&A, and fringe benefits.

Direct Costs and Different Types of Direct Costs

I've mentioned only one example of a direct cost: the purchase price of an item to be resold. For a merchant, someone who buys at wholesale prices and resells at retail or dealer prices, this is usually the main item of direct cost. But other businesses incur other types of direct costs.

Businesses are often referred to as being either capital intensive or labor intensive. A capital-intensive business is one that requires that a relatively large amount of capital be tied up in inventory, equipment, or both. Ordinarily, capital-intensive businesses use relatively little labor. Labor-intensive businesses usually have relatively little capital tied up in merchandise or equipment but depend primarily on what labor produces and must be able to meet payrolls.

In labor-intensive business, the principal cost is labor, direct labor, which the business sells at a profit to customers. If we substitute one hour of direct labor that costs the employer $3 for that $3 item I used as an example earlier and we have the same indirect costs, we must resell that one hour of $3 labor at $4.50 to recover all our costs and realize a profit.

The labor hour is a commodity, just as a physical product is, and the same considerations apply: The business must get back the direct costs of the labor, plus the indirect costs, plus a profit. And, as in the case of the $3 product, the indirect costs are a rate applied to the direct labor. If we have a 40 percent overhead rate, our total cost for that one hour of direct labor at $3 per hour is:

$$\$3 + (\$3 \times 0.40) = \$3 + \$1.20 = \$4.20$$

When we add our $.30 profit, the selling price is $4.50. When we prepare a cost analysis for a government contract bid, that is exactly how we must explain our price.

Ordinarily, we have both direct and indirect labor in custom work. If the government has hired us for field engineering a computer, the field engineer assigned to the work and actually doing it is direct labor. Her time is being applied directly to the job and is specifically what the government is paying for. But the clerk who makes up the bill for that labor and the receptionist who answers the telephones and receives visitors in the lobby are indirect labor. The government is not buying what they do, nor is it possible for us to identify how much time each spends supporting the field engineer (if, in fact, it were desirable to do so). Therefore, they are indirect labor, which costs us money and must be recovered but is recovered by making their cost part of our overhead rate.

There are usually other direct costs that are directly chargeable to the contract and can be clearly identified as costs that would not otherwise be incurred. For example, if we pay the field engineer's travel expenses to the field site, that is another direct cost. If she must use a pay telephone or calls the office collect in connection with what she is doing, that is another direct cost. If the project includes a written report, and that report must be duplicated, we can charge the duplicating cost to the job as another direct cost. Any other costs that can be specifically assigned to that job and would not have otherwise been incurred are "other direct costs" and should be recorded and entered on the books as such.

However—and note this carefully—overhead is that percentage of direct labor dollars, excluding other direct costs and G&A, that we must charge to recover all our costs. That is, the overhead rate is applied to direct labor only and not to other direct costs.

We break down costs, then, into these broad categories, which we must report to the contracting official in making our cost estimates:

Direct labor
Other direct costs
Overhead (to include indirect labor)
G&A

To these we add our fee or profit.

Variations

The previous discussion presents the general case. But like most things, it has exceptions. For one thing, an organization may report more than one overhead! Here is how that may happen: Service organizations, which have labor-intensive characteristics, usually run relatively small overhead rates, from a low of 35–40 percent to a high of 100–150 percent. Capital-intensive operations, especially those engaged in heavy manufacturing, usually run much higher overhead rates—400 percent is not uncommon. The reasons for this are (1) the great expense each year of depreciating the equipment that represents the capital and (2) the great difficulty in identifying direct costs.

Many businesses are both labor-intensive and capital-intensive. Take, for example, a firm developing a new aircraft for the air force. The early months of engineering design, drafting, testing, and otherwise preparing a set of drawings are labor-intensive operations. The later stages of actually building the prototype unit in the company's shops are capital-intensive operations. Therefore, the engineering department and the manufacturing division are each likely to have its own overhead structures. In submitting its bid, the company must separate the two types of work and compute the costs for each in the same set of cost estimates.

A multidivisional company may divide a large project among several divisions, and each may have its own overhead base. Again, the cost estimates will have to report these various overheads.

The government recognizes all these situations and provides cost forms for bidders to accommodate them. The form used by the Department of Defense is DD 633, and most other agencies use a modification of this, Form 1141 (see Figure 6–1). (And there is still another, Form 59, used occasionally.) All use the same general approach, however:

1. Direct material (parts, subcontracts, and so on)
2. Material overhead (if any)
3. Direct labor (by category)
4. Labor overhead (rate and extension in dollars)
5. Special testing
6. Special equipment
7. Travel
8. Consultants
9. Other direct costs
10. Total direct cost and overhead
11. G&A (rate and extension in dollars)
12. Royalties

CONTRACT PRICING PROPOSAL COVER SHEET

1. SOLICITATION/CONTRACT/MODIFICATION NO.	FORM APPROVED OMB NO. 3090-0116

NOTE: This form is used in contract actions if submission of cost or pricing data is required. *(See FAR 15.804-6(b))*

2. NAME AND ADDRESS OF OFFEROR *(Include ZIP Code)*	3A. NAME AND TITLE OF OFFEROR'S POINT OF CONTACT	3B. TELEPHONE NO.

4. TYPE OF CONTRACT ACTION *(Check)*

A. NEW CONTRACT	D. LETTER CONTRACT
B. CHANGE ORDER	E. UNPRICED ORDER
C. PRICE REVISION/ REDETERMINATION	F. OTHER *(Specify)*

6. PROPOSED COST *(A+B=C)*

A. COST	B. PROFIT/FEE	C. TOTAL
$	$	$

5. TYPE OF CONTRACT *(Check)*

FFP	CPFF	CPIF	CPAF
FPI	OTHER *(Specify)*		

7. PLACE(S) AND PERIOD(S) OF PERFORMANCE

8. List and reference the identification, quantity and total price proposed for each contract line item. A line item cost breakdown supporting this recap is required unless otherwise specified by the Contracting Officer. *(Continue on reverse, and then on plain paper, if necessary. Use same headings.)*

A. LINE ITEM NO.	B. IDENTIFICATION	C. QUANTITY	D. TOTAL PRICE	E. REF.

FIGURE 6–1. Form 1141

9. PROVIDE NAME, ADDRESS, AND TELEPHONE NUMBER FOR THE FOLLOWING *(if available)*

A. CONTRACT ADMINISTRATION OFFICE

B. AUDIT OFFICE

10. WILL YOU REQUIRE THE USE OF ANY GOVERNMENT PROPERTY IN THE PERFORMANCE OF THIS WORK? *(If "Yes," identify)*

☐ YES ☐ NO

11A. DO YOU REQUIRE GOVERN-MENT CONTRACT FINANCING TO PERFORM THIS PROPOSED CONTRACT? *(If "Yes," complete Item 11B)*

☐ YES ☐ NO

11B. TYPE OF FINANCING *(√ one)*

☐ ADVANCE PAYMENTS ☐ PROGRESS PAYMENTS

☐ GUARANTEED LOANS

12. HAVE YOU BEEN AWARDED ANY CONTRACTS OR SUBCONTRACTS FOR THE SAME OR SIMILAR ITEMS WITHIN THE PAST 3 YEARS? *(If "Yes," identify item(s), customer(s) and contract number(s))*

☐ YES ☐ NO

13. IS THIS PROPOSAL CONSISTENT WITH YOUR ESTABLISHED ESTI-MATING AND ACCOUNTING PRACTICES AND PROCEDURES AND FAR PART 31 COST PRINCIPLES? *(If "No," explain)*

☐ YES ☐ NO

14. COST ACCOUNTING STANDARDS BOARD (CASB) DATA *(Public Law 91-379 as amended and FAR PART 30)*

A. WILL THIS CONTRACT ACTION BE SUBJECT TO CASB REGULA-TIONS? *(If "No," explain in proposal)*

☐ YES ☐ NO

B. HAVE YOU SUBMITTED A CASB DISCLOSURE STATEMENT *(CASB DS-1 or 2)? (If "Yes," specify in proposal the office to which submitted and if determined to be adequate)*

☐ YES ☐ NO

C. HAVE YOU BEEN NOTIFIED THAT YOU ARE OR MAY BE IN NON-COMPLIANCE WITH YOUR DISCLOSURE STATEMENT OR COST ACCOUNTING STANDARDS? *(If "Yes," explain in proposal)*

☐ YES ☐ NO

D. IS ANY ASPECT OF THIS PROPOSAL INCONSISTENT WITH YOUR DISCLOSED PRACTICES OR APPLICABLE COST ACCOUNTING STANDARDS? *(If "Yes," explain in proposal)*

☐ YES ☐ NO

This proposal is submitted in response to the RFP, contract, modification, etc. in Item 1 and reflects our best estimates and/or actual costs as of this date.

15. NAME AND TITLE *(Type)*

16. NAME OF FIRM

17. SIGNATURE

18. DATE OF SUBMISSION

NSN 7540-01-142-9845

1411-101

☆ U.S. GOVERNMENT PRINTING OFFICE : 1984 O - 421-526 (37)

STANDARD FORM 1411 (10-83)
Prescribed by GSA
FAR (48 CFR) 53.215-2(c)

FIGURE 6-1. *(continued)*

13. Total cost
14. Fee or profit (dollars)
15. Total price to customer

This explains why the G&A works to the contractor's advantage. It's applied, as a rate, to just about everything but royalties: purchased parts and subcontracts, direct and indirect labor, other overhead costs, and other direct costs.

"Below the Line" Costs

On some contracts, the government will stipulate that certain items are to be billed to the government at their actual cost to the contractor—that is, without profit. This is often referred to as putting the items "below the line," meaning below the lines on which overhead and fees or profits are calculated. However, this "contractor's cost" is the actual purchase cost plus G&A.

The rationale is, apparently, that the contractor has not stocked the item, has not had money tied up in inventory on the shelf, but has ordered it for immediate use on a contract and is therefore not entitled to a profit. However, the contractor does incur bookkeeping and administrative costs, and those should be recovered through G&A charges. Ordinarily, when purchased items are to be below the line, they are incidental to the main work of the contract.

The standard cost forms do not make provision for such items specifically, but are readily adaptable to the need by simply listing the items in the appropriate places but not including them in the calculations for overhead and fees.

What the Government Expects in Cost Proposals

The "line" referred to in the expression "below the line" is not the same line referred to in "the bottom line." The bottom line shows the cost to the customer, and it should reflect *all* costs, of whatever kind, plus profit. In short, what difference does it make what we call a cost—direct, indirect, overhead, G&A, other direct, and so on—as long as the bottom line isn't affected? It makes no difference to the customers in ordinary commerce because you don't provide them with a breakdown of your costs. They are interested in the *bottom* line only.

This is not the case with the government contracting official. He is very much interested in what your costs are, how they're generated, and how they're distributed (except when he requires that you supply a selling price only). You'll soon see why he is concerned.

For example, let's hypothesize a $500,000 cost-reimbursement contract, for which you estimate the following costs:

Direct labor:	$200,000
Overhead:	$180,000 (90 percent)
G&A:	$ 80,000
Profit:	$ 40,000
Total:	$500,000

The *bottom* line is $500,000. But a breakdown reveals that overhead includes rent, heat, light, and other facility costs; telephone, receptionists, clerical, typing, and duplicating; and insurance, taxes, paid time off, group insurance, and travel.

Note that the overhead is 90 percent of direct labor, a relatively high rate for a service business. Note, too, that there is no entry for "other direct costs." All costs are either direct labor or indirect costs.

This means that typing, travel, long-distance calls, and duplicating done under this contract will be charged off to the general overhead. This is a great convenience because the staff does not have to keep track of all those kinds of expenses incurred under this contract. But it also means that the overhead rate is pushed up. Suppose the overhead figure includes $30,000 worth of such costs traced directly to the requirements of this contract and hence can be charged to this contract as "other direct costs." What would then happen to the figures?

Direct labor:	$210,000
Overhead:	$150,000 (71 percent)
Other direct costs:	$ 20,000
G&A:	$ 80,000
Profit:	$ 40,000
Total:	$500,000

Note that the bottom line has not changed as a result of charging typing and other support labor to direct labor and other such costs to other direct costs. But something has changed: the overhead. It has been reduced from 90 percent to 71 percent. What difference does that make? A lot.

Taking the easier way out and charging all support work to the general overhead has not one, nor even two, but three undesirable results:

1. It puts "spike values" in your overhead—expenses that are not usually there but are caused by the needs of this single contract. It is therefore a distortion of your normal overhead, which should be kept as constant as possible, as *predictable* as possible, if you are to be able to prepare cost estimates with any degree of reliability.

2. By raising your "historical overhead," you place yourself at a disadvantage for other bids. Perhaps your overhead will settle back to 71 percent after this contract is over, but what overhead figure will you use in the meanwhile? You've lost some of your competitive edge—19 percent of it, to be exact.

3. You may have an unhappy contracting officer. Contracting officers do not like to see high overhead figures.

If a contracting officer were to scan the two sets of figures just discussed, he would see the government getting less for its $500,000 in the first case (at 90 percent overhead) than in the second case (at 71 percent overhead). In the first case, $500,000 is buying only $200,000 worth of direct labor, which is the main objective of the contract. In the second case, for the same $500,000, the government is getting $210,000 worth of labor applied to its needs, plus $20,000 in other direct costs.

The official sees the overhead as the cost of buying the direct labor and/or other direct costs, which is something like seeing interest as the cost of using money. To the government, overhead is not productive cost and doesn't contribute directly to achieving the goal for which the contract was written. (In fact, overhead is often referred to as the "burden" or "burden rate"!)

Overhead, to most contracting officers, is a measure of your efficiency as an organization. The lower your overhead, the more efficient you appear to be. And the more efficient you probably are, if your overhead is controlled carefully, meaning nothing that can be properly recorded as an "other direct cost" is ever charged to overhead. The benefits of keeping your overhead low are well worth the time and effort to keep track of all costs and charge them off properly. The ideal should be true overhead, and true overhead should be only and exclusively costs that it is impossible or impractical to assign and charge to specific projects.

The government expects contractors to maintain a reasonably low overhead and judges them to a large extent by that standard.

Projecting Overhead

Overhead is not an absolute constant. Every business has certain fixed expenses (rent, basic telephone service, loan payments, and so on) and certain variable expenses (payroll, light, heat, printing). If you double your sales and activities but can still conduct all business in your present facility, you incur no increase in rent and relatively small increases in telephone, power, and certain other variable expenses. That is, some indirect costs, such as taxes and fringe benefits, will increase in direct proportion to increases in the payroll, but others will not. You probably will not need to expand your accounting department because you have increased sales and payroll, for example.

For this reason, while overhead *dollars* will increase with expansion, the overhead *rate* ought to go down as you spread overhead dollars over a larger labor base or sales base. Because you cannot tell with any great certainty exactly what your overhead rate is at any given moment, the usual practice is to use either your historical rate (that your accountants reported when they completed your most recent year's books) or a provisional rate.

A provisional overhead rate is a projected rate, an estimated one, and it is a fairly common practice to use a provisional rate for large contracts, particularly those that will be subject to audit. (Most contracts over $100,000 are subject to audit; that does not necessarily mean they will be audited.) The usual requirement to do this is to include such schedules of expense pools as to support the projected rate, that is, show how the rate is arrived at.

If the contract is large, and especially if it is a cost-reimbursement contract, using a provisional rate means the books will probably be audited at the end of the year to verify the rate. Adjustments are then made, with the contractor receiving extra money from the government if the rate was higher than that projected or refunding money to the government if the actual rate was lower than what the government was charged.

There are, of course, limits placed on provisional rates. You might project an overhead rate of 60 percent with a ceiling of 70 percent. If, upon audit, your actual overhead rate for the year was 67 percent, you will be entitled to bill the government for the extra 7 percent you have not been charging. But if your actual rate is higher than the ceiling, say, 72 percent, you will be able to bill only up to the ceiling.

Using a provisional rate offers you certain competitive advantages if you are bidding for a contract whose size will make a fairly large increase in your total year's sales or labor base. Here's why: Suppose you have been doing $1 million a year, with a labor base of $600,000, an overhead of $330,000, and a profit of $70,000 (neglecting G&A, for simplicity). Your historical overhead rate is $330,000 ÷ 600,000 = 0.55 = 55 percent. Your profit is $70,000 ÷ $600,000 + $330,000 = 0.0752 = 7.5 percent.

Let's consider a large, new contract, to be *added* to that base, in which you calculate about $300,000 worth of direct labor. Your existing labor base is $600,000. With $300,000 added, you will have a labor base of $900,000. If we cost estimate the new job at the existing rates, we get the following figures:

Direct labor: $300,000
Overhead @ 55 percent: $165,000
Profit @ 7.5 percent: $ 34,875
Total: $499,875

This set of figures assumes that 55 percent is the correct overhead rate. But it neglects the effects of increasing the labor base by one and one-half times, from $600,000 to $900,000. That increase is bound to have a substantial effect on the overhead rate. In fact, it should drive it down to at least 45 percent. Your accountants will have to do the calculations, but let's assume, to illustrate the point, that your projected overhead rate, with that new business in the house, does go down to 45 percent. Let's estimate the job now:

Direct labor: $300,000
Overhead @ 45 percent: $135,000
Profit @ 7.5 percent: $ 32,625
Total: $467,625

This reduces your estimate by $32,250, a substantial reduction that may very well mean the difference between winning the contract and not winning it. And there are no risks involved, if you are confident of keeping that original $600,000 base intact for the term of the new contract, because you have made that lower overhead provisional on winning this new contract. If you don't win it, you have sacrificed nothing. If you do win it, you will be that much more competitive, with 45 percent overhead, for everything else you go after!

Other Methods for Cutting Costs

Costs are always a consideration. Anything you can do to reduce them cannot but help increase your chances of winning. One way of reducing costs is this: Don't reinvent the wheel. It is truly surprising how often contractors develop things in-house that they could have bought more cheaply off the shelf—or even have gotten for nothing! Here are a few examples to illustrate this.

Writing a large bid proposal for a Job Corps center (which turned out to be worth some $25 million of business) called for a great deal of work, including planning six complete vocational training programs and an academic curriculum. The work resulted in a three-volume, 1,000-page proposal, which astonished the customer, who firmly believed we had spent at least $50,000 (in 1964!). In fact, we had spent about $12,000. Here's how:

1. To develop the six vocational programs, which had to be detailed down to a description of and objectives for each hour of instruction, we sent out to the nearest public library and gathered up armfuls of how-to books on the trades we were interested in. We sorted through them and selected one for each of the vocations of interest. An individual was then assigned to draw up a detailed outline of each book, which was then broken down by a training specialist into one-hour increments, and objectives were written for each. Voila! With relatively little effort, we had designed six vocational training courses.

2. To identify training resources for each, we bought for $3 a government publication that listed 6,000 training films and slide/tape programs. We selected the appropriate ones and listed these as training resources. We did the same with publishers' catalogs to identify texts of interest.

3. We also bought a number of military training manuals for related trades and used them as sources of information and illustrations.

4. When this was all assembled, we wrote the text passages to describe how these programs would be taught and administered, our psychology department designed the "group life plan," and a former schoolteacher wrote up an academic course in the "three R's."

This was a great deal of work, but it would have been almost impossible for an organization of our size had we attempted to design everything from scratch. The result was a program far more impressive than anything we could have developed any other way.

In another case, we were to prepare a training program in automation machine technology. This required many drawings and illustrations of all kinds, including photos of many types of automatic machines and systems. We drew up a form letter requesting copies of texts, manuals, specifications, photos, and/or drawings and asked for permission to use them in a training program to be used by government agencies. We promised to give credit lines that would identify the machines and manufacturers and acknowledge their help. Within less than two weeks, a previously unused desk was piled high with materials we had gotten from some 100 manufacturers, all eager to see their products listed and shown in the program!

I had a requirement to prepare an audiovisual program on the history and culture of the American Indian. The Government Printing Office has an abundance of materials on the subject, but GPO publications have become quite expensive, and I needed many resource books and drawings. I therefore called on the Bureau of Indian Affairs with my problem. They were delighted to help. They gave me, without charge, dozens of excellent books, pamphlets, posters, charts, and the like, in addition to lending me an entire library of slides!

In a $78,000 bid for a training program for the Job Corps, we had estimated our art requirement at $8,000. The customer wanted our program but objected to our price. To reduce it, we again utilized GPO publications, most of which are in the public domain. (There are exceptions, so caution is necessary.) We found almost all the illustrations we needed in easily reproducible line drawings. Our final art cost was $2,000.

There are innumerable such resources available. Virtually everything published by the Government Printing Office, for example, has been printed at the request of some federal agency, which always takes a large quantity for its own use and often makes these available without charge to anyone interested! Nothing is free from the GPO today, but what you need may be available free from the originating agency.

The National Archives is part of the General Services Administration. An enormous store of information is contained there, including many rare photos. Copies of photos and other materials are available at low cost from the National Archives. (The photos can be ordered as slides, also at low cost.)

NASA headquarters showered me with virtual armloads of beautiful, multicolored photos of the space program. I would have had to pay for these at the GPO bookstore, of course, but NASA made no charge for them.

As a result of my activities in writing training programs such as these and in producing newsletters, my name has found its way onto many government mailing lists, and hardly a day passed for years after that I did not receive press releases, government newsletters, government monthly magazines, reports, manuals, and many other useful items. (Even today I get a trickle of these.) Anyone can get on these lists, usually by addressing the Public Information Office that every agency maintains.

The General Accounting Office issues a great many reports throughout the year, some of them "letter reports," some of them thick, bound reports. They issue a monthly guide to reports currently available. It is not difficult to get a single copy of any report free of charge.

Some of this information and material is directly useful in performing under a contract, as explained, but much of it is also invaluable in writing proposals! Anyone bidding seriously to government agencies is well advised to begin a library of such resource materials. Such a library not only results in far better proposals than can be written from scratch, but greatly reduces research time and, therefore, the cost of proposal writing.

Make or Buy?

In business and industry generally, "make-or-buy" decisions must be made regularly. No one makes everything—even the giant automobile manufacturers buy wheels, carburetors, and many other components of their cars. The dictum "Don't reinvent the wheel" is analogous to that: It's the government contractor's make-or-buy decision. It comes down, in the end, to a matter of cost. But often a buying decision carries within it the seeds of costs never anticipated. Here's an example.

In a company where I was the editorial director, we were spending a fair amount of money every year for printing. The president of the company became aware of this, as he pored over the balance sheets and profit and loss statements, and came to me with a bright idea: "Why don't we buy a small printing press? A salesman came in the other day and offered me a factory-reconditioned one for only $800."

I tried to explain tactfully that the $800 would only make us "pregnant." We would have to have an operator, a platemaker, and some sort of binding equipment, at the least. Soon we would wish we had a cutter (paper guillotine), a camera, an automatic stitcher, and a few other things. Even then, we would have to send much of our work out because we wouldn't be equipped for all kinds of printing. What would we do with our press operator when we didn't have printing to do? Where would we house all this?

Sad to report, my arguments were overruled, Mr. President succumbed to the salesman's pitch, and he spent the $800. Only a few months later he sold the machine for as much as he could get, which was considerably less than $800.

In costing your bid, plan to use suppliers for anything not properly part of your business. Get the best prices you can, and have your bidders supply *written* quotations, guaranteed for a suitable period of time.

The Creation of Costs

In many companies, particularly the larger organizations, engineers, psychologists, and other technical/professional specialists write technical proposals and proclaim complete ignorance of and no responsibility for costs. They never get any closer to the accounting function than to question a payroll deduction on their checks, nor are they interested in the mysterious world of costs.

After all the specialists have designed the proposed program and written the technical proposal, the job of costing the project falls to the accountants in these companies. Those hapless individuals spend many weary hours with the technical specialists assigning dollar values to their specifications. Typically, the boss sees the final proposal and hits the ceiling when his eyes fall on the bottom line; his mouth drops open in disbelieving shock. Then follow frantic efforts and gallons of midnight oil to chip away at an obviously overpriced project.

The technical specialists shrug. Costs are not their problem. The accountants shrug. They can only cost out what they've been given. The mechanics of costing are the accountants' domain and responsibility. But costs are the creation of the designers—the proposal writers. Only their own ingenuity can cut the costs and give the organization a competitive advantage over less shrewd competitors.

To show clearly how much impact on the bottom line different approaches to a project can have, I'll take a rather simple project of writing a training manual. Here's a first analysis of what is going to be needed:

- Development of a "book plan," to be reviewed by the customer and approved, that will include a complete outline of content, format, and list of illustrations
- Development of a complete draft, to be reviewed by the customer and returned with comments (20 copies required)
- Revision, per customer comments, to be resubmitted to the customer for final review, final comments, and approval to complete (20 copies required for review)
- Setting of type, inking of illustrations, sizing of final art, printing of 200 copies, and delivery

There are several ways to approach this job. Obviously, the main work will be done in-house, by your own expert staff. But suppose you do not have an artist on staff or an existing in-house typesetting capability. You can rent a typesetting machine for about $150 per month, and a good typist can learn to operate it. Or you can use outside services from subcontractors or vendors. Which is the best way to go? See Tables 6–1 and 6–2 to compare the breakdown of costs.

The difference between the two bottom lines is $1,648, a considerable sum. The saving is effected despite paying an outside contractor a bit more than you would have to pay a staff person because you are saving *overhead:* You don't have to provide the contractor with fringe benefits, a place to work, a telephone, or a desk; pay taxes; and so on. You have also reduced the risks. Suppose your staff artist is unable to complete the work within $2,500 worth of time. A dollar added to direct labor costs affects the bottom line this way:

Direct labor:	$1.00
Overhead:	$ .60
G&A:	$ .11
Profit:	$ .17
Total:	$1.88

Conversely, every dollar that can be cut in direct labor saves $1.88 on the bottom line! Even exchanging a dollar in direct labor

Table 6–1. Cost of project using in-house staff only

Direct Labor		Indirect Costs	
Planning and writing	$15,000	Overhead @ 60%	$12,900
Typing and proofing	3,000	Printing 200 copies	1,100
Staff artist	2,500	Subtotal	35,500
Typesetting	1,000	G&A @ 7%	2,485
Total direct labor	$21,500	Subtotal	37,985
Subcontracted	3,000	Fee @ 10%	3,799
		Total price	$41,784

Table 6–2. Cost of project using both in-house staff and subcontracted services

Direct Labor		Indirect Costs	
Planning and writing	$15,000	Overhead @ 60%	$10,800
Typing and proofing	3,000	Illustrating, typesetting,	
Total direct labor	$18,000	subcontracted	1,200
		Printing 200 copies	1,100
		Subtotal	34,100
		G&A @ 7%	2,387
		Subtotal	36,487
		Fee @ 10%	3,649
		Total price	$40,136

for a dollar's worth of outside services or products eliminates that $.60 in overhead.

Proposal writers should always be aware of every dollar of cost they are creating and what they are cutting on the bottom line by every economy they can effect in their planning and designing.

Once, as an editorial director, I found myself plagued with an enormous oversupply of "light editing." My editors were never finished tinkering with the camera-ready copy. Each time the copy they had corrected was returned to them for review and approval of corrections, they found more corrections to make and provoked still another cycle of changes.

One Friday afternoon I assembled a half-dozen of these extremely conscientious people in my office and seated them before my desk, on which I had piled that week's collection of corrections, a rather large stack of "repro masters." "I have here before me," I announced dramatically, indicating the stack of paper, "the third cycle of changes to the masters for the program. I have spent most of the afternoon going through them. They average about six changes per sheet, and there are over 600 sheets. Most of the changes are to punctuation; a few are minor changes in grammatical construction. I've consulted with the manager of our typing pool on what it costs to make these changes. It works out to about $.50 per change, or about $3 per page. A small amount of money—until we multiply it by the number of pages. Altogether, it will cost us more than $2,000 to make these changes."

I paused for dramatic effect as six pairs of eyes widened apprehensively—perhaps in shock. "Tell me," I then went on, "do you believe that you have worked $2,000 worth of improvement in this program? Would you pay $2,000 more for this program as a result of these changes?"

I never had to say another word about excessive cycles of editing and changes to anyone on that staff. Proposal writers, like editors, must be made to understand the cost of the work they do.

Collecting Your Money from the U.S. Government

There's a myth that the U.S. government takes forever to pay its bills. The myth arises from the fact that it's true—in a few cases. In general, however, the government pays more promptly than do many commercial accounts. Being a giant bureaucracy, the government reacts the way all bureaucracies react. When a small, administrative problem arises, lower-level people do . . . nothing. They simply wait for someone else to do it. Here is how the system is supposed to work: You submit your bill to the contracting office (contracts specify how and to whom the invoice is to be submitted), citing the contract number, and so on. The contracting office sends it on to receiving or the government's project manager to approve (certify that the goods were delivered or services were performed and all is satisfactory). The contracting office, having already checked the contract and past payments, if any, to verify the correctness of the bill, approves the bill and puts it on a schedule for payment by the Treasury Department disbursing office. The bill is then paid, usually, within less than a week. Bills should be paid 20 to 30 days after submittal (some government offices manage to do it in 15 days), especially if you have a 20-day prompt-payment discount. (All contracting officers are under standing orders to take advantage of all discounts.)

Delays are almost always due to either someone's lethargy (your bill is lying on a desk) or carelessness (someone has mislaid your invoice). Here is what you can and should do about delays in payment:

1. Submit your invoice in at least two copies. Otherwise the agency must duplicate, another delay. It doesn't hurt to submit in triplicate; some agencies need three copies.

2. Wait not more than 30 days (but more than 21) unless the agency has advised you otherwise. There are some specific cases in which the normal payment cycle is six weeks, for example. Then assume that something has gone wrong, as it almost certainly has, and take action.

3. Start telephoning and find out exactly where your invoice is (at what stage in the process) and what you can do to move it along. Don't let people simply promise to "get back to you" unless they can deliver on that promise within a day or two. Frequently, that's a stalling tactic. Don't settle for anything less than finding out exactly what the holdup is—why it has occurred.

These measures are usually sufficient to get you paid within days. If they do not do the trick, go up in the hierarchy, to the chief of the Contracts Division, for example, or even to the agency head if necessary.

It is a good idea, when doing business with an agency you have not done business with before, to find out in advance exactly how its system works. (There are specific differences among the various agencies.) This helps you troubleshoot if someone slips up later. However, in many cases, you can *walk* your invoice through the first couple of steps and thereby avoid the most frequent hazards of misplaced paperwork or simple lethargy. For example, sometimes you can start with the government's project manager and have him or her approve your invoice, then hand carry the approved invoice to the contracts office, thereby completing the first two steps immediately and avoiding the cause of the most common slipups.

CHAPTER 7

The Proposal Game

Nothing happens until somebody sells something.

The Proposal Defined

While waiting my turn as a guest lecturer at a seminar one day, I heard several other speakers explain to an audience of proposal novitiates that a proposal is a "contractual document." I listened with growing impatience and some sense of outrage because these speakers were supposedly all proposal experts, and the trusting neophytes listening to them were drinking in every word.

Those speakers were referring to a proposal as a contractual document in order to caution proposal writers that they would be held to what they promised in their proposals. To the extent that the contract will incorporate the proposal, the characterization is true. That is, the government has bought what the proposal offers, and the contract seals the bargain.

However, that characterization is misleading. Strictly speaking, the proposal will *become* a contractual document—if the customer "buys" it. Until then, it is not a contractual document; it is a proposal. To put this another way, it is something the writer *hopes* will become a contractual document. Every word in the proposal should be carefully calculated to maximize the probability that the customer will accept it, and it will become a contractual document.

Until such time as the customer accepts and a contract is executed, the proposal is an offer to do something for a stipulated price. The proposal is a sales presentation, for only as a sales presentation does a proposal make any sense. If it is not an effective sales presentation, you need never have any fears about it becoming a contractual document!

When Proposals Are Required

There are many reasons for requesting potential contractors to submit proposals rather than sealed bids:

1. The work or product required is to be to custom specifications, and the customer wants to evaluate the qualifications of the various aspirants for the contract.

2. The customer wants the freedom to make a choice on qualitative grounds, rather than be compelled to accept the lowest bid.

3. The customer is not absolutely certain of what the problem or need is and is seeking the contractor with the greatest ability to identify it.

4. The customer is not up to date on the relevant technologies and therefore is not absolutely certain of what the possible solutions are. That customer is seeking "state-of-the-art" solutions—those that are possible today, but might not have been possible yesterday.

5. The customer needs identified and/or solved a problem that calls for skills not available to him except by contract with private industry.

6. The customer needs more hands and feet; she simply does not have the in-house staff to get the work done.

7. The customer needs a person with some special qualifications that no one on staff has.

8. The customer needs a facility or resource (such as a laboratory) not available except via contracted services.

9. The customer needs a new product or piece of equipment developed (an R&D job).

10. The customer needs an outside study done to validate a program or funding he or she has requested.

11. The work can be done cheaper by a contractor than it could be done by federal employees.

There are many reasons for needing more hands and feet for a program. The program (and the need) may be temporary, making it impractical to hire more federal employees. Or it may be politically impossible to hire more employees because of "freezes" on federal hiring, which are not rare (they occur at least once during virtually every new administration).

A great deal of controversy exists over whether a project can be handled more efficiently (that is, at lower cost) by contract than by federal employees. The federal employee unions always insist that the work is carried out at lower costs by federal employees, but they are hardly impartial observers. Opponents of using federal employees for all programs point out that few privately employed people get the fringe benefits of federal employees and enjoy as little pressure to get work done.

The Office of Management and Budget long ago took a hand in this and issued OMB Circular A-76, which established policy and guidelines for judging whether to contract out or have a job done in-house. The chief bone of contention has been the allegedly low value assigned to federal retirement benefits. The OMB fixed their value at the time as 20.4 percent of salary.

Under the terms of the circular, a project is to be done by whichever appears to be lower in cost, with this provision: If an existing program can be cost reduced by 10 percent or more, it is to be contracted out if it is being done in-house; it must be done in-house if it is currently being done under contract (that is, whichever achieves the cost-reduction goal). Some $10 billion of work being done in-house was scrutinized as well as about $30 billion then under contract.

Here are some typical procurements that reflect the kinds of needs and problems that are the subject of such scrutiny:

- Many federal computer systems are operated by contract personnel under "facility management" contracts. Contract personnel, in these cases usually working on government premises, operate the computers, write programs for them, and otherwise perform all the services associated with running computer systems.

- Contract personnel are often used for engineering tasks of many kinds, for test and maintenance work, for writing, and for a variety of other technical/professional tasks. In some cases, the experience of the organization and its ability to design and manage programs are the chief considerations, although the evaluators are always interested in the individual qualifications of the staff proposed. But in many other cases, the chief organizational credential desired is evidence that the organization can supply qualified personnel and manage them, under technical direction of the customer's project manager. (To a large degree, the contractor's project manager is a conduit for instructions from the government's project manager, who, by law, cannot give orders directly to the contractor's personnel.)

Ordinarily, "personal services contracts" are strictly verboten. These are contracts in which a contractor (or the contractor's employees) is personally directed by a civil service employee or that state as a requirement that the services of some specifically named individual are required. There are exceptions, however, especially to the second case. In one instance, NASA wanted a book written on celestial mechanics, a specialty in physics dealing with astronomy, the motion of heavenly bodies, and navigation in space. The world's leading authority on the subject was a Japanese physicist who was rather elderly and whose number of remaining years was a matter of conjecture. He was therefore bound under a personal services contract to write the definitive work, which probably no one else in the world could have done nearly as well. At the same time, a contract was let for an American scientist who could edit the physicist's manuscript competently. The latter, however, was not a personal services contract.

When the military services want to take advantage of new technology to design a faster airplane or a more accurate radar, they issue invitations to submit proposals, with the intention of evaluating basic design concepts offered by the proposers as well as their general credentials. In many cases, where the effort calls for design, R&D, or problem solving in general—no matter what the end product is to be—the proposer's approach or initial concept is most critical in the contest. Ordinarily, the chief bidders for such contracts are all experienced firms, with good track records. All are quite competent, technically, but one will put forth a concept or design approach that captures the customer's attention.

There are many cases where the customer could, logically, use an IFB, calling for sealed bids, to get acceptable bids. But, as discussed in Chapter 5, this creates the possible problem of being forced to accept as a contractor someone whose qualifications are doubtful. Theoretically, the customer may disqualify a bidder as not showing the necessary technical competence, but in practice, it will fall on the government to prove the bidder's lack of technical competence, and that can and usually does prove to be nearly impossible—hence the resort to an RFP when such eventualities are feared.

There is still another situation that appears to call for an IFB but that often is handled by soliciting proposals and engaging in negotiated procurement: when the customer expects few bids, perhaps only one, but wants the opportunity to negotiate a price, something that cannot be done with sealed bids. This situation often comes about simply because the item is so painstakingly detailed in its specifications that few suppliers can "meet the spec." In such a case, the supplier usually has a realistic appraisal of the competition, and the asking price may be high—hence the need for negotiation.

Sole-Source Procurements

As our technology advances, we see more and more sole-source procurement taking place. Sole-source procurement, sometimes referred to as selected-source procurement, is buying by negotiated procurement methods from a single, selected source, without inviting bids or proposals from others. The procurement regulations provide for such exceptions to the general rule of competitive procurement, and several possible circumstances justify such bypassing of the normal competitive bidding:

- A single firm may be peculiarly qualified by virtue of having done some predecessor work, which results in its being the only firm that can handle the new requirement efficiently. Any other firm would have to learn a great deal to qualify equally well, which would elevate the costs substantially.
- The selected contractor may have some proprietary knowledge, equipment, or patents that represent the only practicable approach to the program.
- The new contract may be an extension of or modification to an existing contract.
- The sole-source procedure may be based on an unsolicited proposal.

Unsolicited Proposals

An unsolicited proposal is one offered by an individual or organization on his, her, or its own initiative, and concepts are developed by the proposer at the proposer's expense. These are somewhat controversial. An unsolicited proposal results in a noncompetitive award, if it is accepted. The government does not have the right to make the proposer's idea known to others and to solicit proposals from others. The government either accepts the proposal, with or without negotiation, or rejects it.

Many contracting officials are suspicious of any proposal purporting to be unsolicited. They suspect that a government executive may have used the unsolicited-proposal provision as a convenient means to circumvent the normal procedures, which represent a great deal of work and time. A statement of work must be written; solicitation packages must be sent out, with time allowed for recipients to prepare proposals; proposals must be evaluated; and negotiations must be conducted. This normally requires six months or more before a project can actually get under way. But an unsolicited proposal avoids the writing of work statements and the evaluating of proposals.

So there is always the possibility that a government executive has actually suggested to a contractor that he or she offer an unsolicited proposal to do something the government executive wants done!

Therefore, many contracting officials closely examine all proposals purporting to be unsolicited and demand extensive evidence that they are truly unsolicited, prepared entirely at the initiative of the proposer and not prompted by the government.

In 1977, following a study of five government agencies, the General Accounting Office reported that most federal agencies appeared to be abusing the provisions for noncompetitive procurements. This does not appear, however, to have reduced their incidence a bit.

"September Buys"

The U.S. Congress is one cause for at least some of the noncompetitive procurement. Unfortunately, although the government's fiscal year has been changed to end on September 30 instead of on June 30, as in earlier years, Congress still rarely completes all its funding authorizations by the end of the fiscal year. In fact, in many cases, funding is not completed until after the end of the calendar year.

That places the various agencies in the position of not knowing how much money they will have to carry out their programs until well into the new fiscal year. As a result, they have considerably less than 12 months to plan and implement their projects because all funds must be spent before the end of the fiscal year.

When Congress finally completes the funding allotments for a given agency, the funds allocated to it are "authorized." Except for those few cases of "full funding" (programs that have been funded for their anticipated lifetimes rather than year by year, as most programs are funded), the funds are to be used during the fiscal year; they may not be carried over into the next fiscal year. Any funds remaining beyond September 30 must be returned to the Treasury.

This, however, does not mean the funds must be literally "spent" (disbursed). It means they must be "obligated." Obligated funds may be disbursed or spent after the end of the fiscal year. Authorized funds are those the agency has available to spend. Obligated funds are those allocated specifically, for example, by contract, to a given program or cost center. That is, if a new contract for $500,000 is signed on September 30, the $500,000 is obligated and does not have to go back to the Treasury.

Given the constraint of completing all contracting and other program implementation for the entire year in the span of perhaps six months, agencies tend to be under pressure to spend money, especially as the current fiscal year draws to a close. Having money left over is a cardinal sin in government circles. Even the White House gets upset at spending shortfalls and tries frantically to reduce them as the fiscal year approaches its end. Add to this the usually lengthy periods necessary for formal competitive contracting, and many government executives feel bound to seek shortcuts that will enable them to spend their allocations before September 30. Those frantic, last-minute buying efforts are sometimes referred to as "September buys," and in many cases, they are the principal reason officials resort to noncompetitive avenues of procurement.

Multiple Awards

At the opposite end of the spectrum from sole-source awards are multiple awards. These are contract requirements in which a number of awards will be made; that is, this is the exception to the only-one-winner-in-the-contest rule. Situations do arise, from time to time, in which the government believes several contracts are merited, for whatever reason, and this is usually made known to the proposers.

A good example of this was the initiation of the Job Corps some years ago. There were to be seven Urban Job Corps centers plus a then-unspecified number of Rural Job Corps centers. However, the centers were not awarded in seven separate proposal contests; proposals were accepted for center operation, and the Office of Economic Opportunity selected seven contractors, one by one, assigning each one of the centers.

In the case of the NASA headquarters contract for publications support services, for example, it was the practice to award four contracts. The chief rationale for this was, apparently, that many of the requirements were sudden and required a rapid response. Having four contractors available lessened the possibility that the task would not get done on time because contractors had the privilege of passing up a task if they felt they could not meet the schedule requirement. The government could then offer the task to the next contractor on the list. For contracts of that type, requiring sudden, quick-reaction services, it is not unusual to award several contracts.

There are other situations in which multiple awards are considered desirable. One of them is where the products or services are used by many federal agencies throughout the country, and they require a local or nearby source of supply. In such cases, there may be many contractors on a "schedule," with copies of the schedule distributed to the various agencies, with instructions for ordering from their nearest supplier.

Formal Versus Informal Proposals

Most RFPs call for formal proposals, and they usually specify what information must be supplied in them. A case in which the proposal may be informal is usually identified as a "letter proposal"—essentially a letter in which the writer makes an offer, supplying only a cursory proposal. This is most often the case with small purchases. Here is a typical situation that results in a letter proposal.

Several years ago I called on OSHA, spending several hours meeting different executives and discussing their possible needs. I finally met a gentleman who had a problem that was a suitable target for the services I offered. As we discussed his problem, I suggested remedies I could supply. Finally, he became seriously interested and invited me to submit a letter proposal.

A few days later I submitted a two-page letter, in which I reviewed his problem briefly, described the services I would provide and the result I promised, and quoted a price for my services. My description of the problem and services to be provided became the statement of work, which he transcribed to a government purchase order and awarded to me as a contract.

In most cases, however, a full-blown, formal proposal is required, and this may be of almost any size, from 25 to 50 pages for a small job, to many hundreds—even thousands—of pages for a major award.

The Essential Nature of the Proposal

In the beginning of this chapter I stated that a proposal was an offer—a sales presentation. What remains to be explained and defined is a sales presentation. To do this, we must look at salesmanship, its basic nature and principles, for the basic nature of a *successful* proposal is salesmanship.

There are more examples of bad salesmanship than good salesmanship. Far too many writers of what is supposed to be sales copy write testimonials to themselves, rather than sales copy. The single most common error is not giving the customer a reason to buy what they offer.

Volkswagen commercials of a few years ago were a good example of clever, entertaining advertising that didn't sell anything. Likewise, one series of Alka-Seltzer commercials constituted great "advertising art" that succeeded in winning everything but sales.

It isn't cleverness with phrases or even with illustrations that sells. The cleverness that sells is *empathy*—understanding the prospect's viewpoint and catering to the prospect's desires. Consider beer commercials on TV. Do they try to sell beer? Certainly not. They promise good times at the beach or at the local tavern. Dishwasher detergent is sold by promising bright, sparkling dishes that win admiration from friends and family—they sell the admiration, not the detergent.

But what has all this to do with proposals offered to the U.S. government? Just this: The U.S. government is *people*. They are no more objective than other people, and although they buy with the government's money, rather than their own, they are influenced by many personal considerations. After all, their own careers are involved!

Advertising people and sales experts will tell you there are four elements in the process:

A: get Attention
I: arouse Interest
D: generate Desire (to buy)
A: ask for Action (close)

This acronym overlooks a few things and is a bit cryptic, but I can use it as a point of departure to explain why the proposal is not entirely dissimilar from any other sales presentation or advertising campaign (which operates on the same principles of salesmanship).

There is one major difference, however: Asking for action, or closing, means asking for the order and is often considered the most critical part of selling and the most common failure of inexperienced (and even some experienced) salespeople. In proposing to government agencies, we don't have to "ask for action." The government intends to buy and doesn't have to be persuaded to order, but rather to select you as the proposer from whom to order. That brings the acronym, for proposals, down to AID.

However, the government already has a desire to buy. That's why the RFP was issued. The question is only which offer (proposal) to accept. So we might modify generate desire to buy to "generate desire to buy our offer."

The key question, then, for each element—A, I, and D—is how. How shall we get attention (and why?), how shall we arouse interest, how shall we generate the desire to buy from us? It's the "how," as well as the "what," that is the art of effective proposal writing—and the subject of the rest of this chapter.

Elements of the Successful Proposal

The element left out of selling in AIDA, and that is most essential in selling anything, is credibility. The most modest claims will not sell if they are not credible, believable by the prospect, and the most outrageous claims will sell if they are credible. The mistake so many writers make is to fail to furnish evidence of truth, to make the claims believable.

Many sales presentations are good up to the point of credibility. They get attention, offer benefits (reasons to buy), are easy to understand. Then they fall on their faces because they fail to convince. They fail to compel belief that the presenter will deliver as promised.

In TV commercials, actors posing as druggists or laboratory scientists are often used to generate that believability through the "white coat" approach if the product lends itself to the use of such authority figures. Candidate Dwight Eisenhower was a shoo-in for the presidency, although he had few qualifications for the job, because he was believable, an authority figure, a father image.

The chief problem is that so many writers mistakenly believe that *claims* are evidence. Typically, such a writer will say something like, "J. Black and Company is the largest tool manufacturer in our industry," which is obviously a claim, the writer's opinion. The adjective "largest" is the giveaway. Lay off the adjectives and adverbs, and stick to the nouns and verbs: quantify. As the late actor Walter Brennan used to say in one of his TV characterizations, "No brag; just fact."

Let's take that claim of being largest. Suppose we said it this way: "J. Black and Company employs 7,000 workers in 43 plants throughout the United States." That's evidence—no claims, just reporting the facts.

Getting attention has a certain importance, but a successful sales argument has just two objectives:

1. To explain, clearly and unmistakably, what will result (benefits to the buyer) from buying what you offer (the reason for buying)
2. To prove your case, to present the evidence that will enable the prospect to believe you can and will deliver exactly those promised results

It may take hundreds of pages to do this, and it does take a great deal of explanation to demonstrate the many subordinate elements in achieving these two objectives. But except for a few techniques for getting the customer's attention—you can't get your message home if the person is not paying attention—every word and illustration in a proposal is aimed at one or both of these objectives: Give the customer the reasons for buying and the reasons for believing. Anything not contributing to this is superfluous, a distraction that can do no good and may do harm.

The following points should be covered in a good proposal. See if you can relate these to the two objectives just stated:

- A general introduction, briefly stating who the proposer is, why that person is interested in bidding for the contract, and the general qualifications, to be expanded on later
- A general statement or review of the requirement that demonstrates an understanding of it
- A somewhat lengthy and in-depth discussion, exploring various considerations in satisfying the requirement (analysis), that logically arrives at a specific plan that will satisfy the requirement
- A specific plan for implementing the approach arrived at, which is, in fact, the proposal (this is what becomes the contractual document)
- Qualifications (resumes) of the proposed staff
- Qualifications (experience and resources) of the proposing organization

Note the logical flow of this presentation: We are the such-and-such company, with x number of years in the business of satisfying just such needs as you describe. We see your need as being thus and so. There are several ways to address this need, and each has its pros and cons (discussions of methods, analysis of each). Therefore, we believe the approach described to be the best method, offering the fewest problems and the greatest probabilities for complete and unqualified success. Here is exactly how we propose to proceed (detailed plans). We have an excellent staff of well-qualified people, whom we propose for key roles in the project (resumes). We have ample experience and resources to demonstrate both our capability and track record of success (experience and qualifications of the organization).

This takes the reader of your proposal through the entire analytical process by which you have arrived at your plan. This is necessary because you must never assume the customer recognizes the merits of your approach and your plan. He may or may not be an expert; that is, he may be equally, more, or less knowledgeable than you in the field of interest. Therefore, he must be made to *understand* all the elements: the benefits, the methodology, the rationale for the methodology, the rationale for choosing the approach you recommend over other approaches that might have been offered (and may be offered by competitors). You may have to *educate* your reader in order to sell him, just as general advertising often includes material to educate the consumer on the pros and cons of electric refrigerators, automobiles, and cough syrup. It's part of the credibility ammunition.

Common Mistakes in Proposals

A typical solicitation for proposals may bring in 5, 10, 20, or even over 100 proposals to be read and evaluated. But the number of proposals submitted does not reveal the true competition. In all cases, a percentage of the proposals submitted is rejected on first reading, sometimes before being read all the way through. The percentage rejected can vary widely. One government contracting official reveals that in some proposal competitions, as many as *9 out of 10* proposals submitted are rejected summarily. It is safe to say that an average rejection rate is at least 33.33 percent.

This occurs because the proposals are nonresponsive. That term can cover many faults, but the most common one is that the proposal writers appear not to have read the RFP carefully. Evaluators of proposals have been heard to mumble to themselves, "They just don't seem to understand the problem." This concern is often reflected in listed evaluation criteria, where points are awarded for "understanding of the requirement." The customer is sending a message: "Don't start writing your proposal until you have studied the requirement and understand exactly what we seek."

There are many ways a proposal can be nonresponsive to an RFP. One is by simply failing to reflect an understanding of the requirement, that is, by offering something other than what the RFP has called for—perhaps by offering a solution to which there is no problem!

Some organizations have developed pet solutions, perhaps a proprietary package or process, and insist on reading into each RFP a need for their own pet solution. In writing their proposals, members of these organizations consciously or unconsciously insist on distorting the customer's description of the need to make it fit their solution.

There is also the problem that many organizations, lacking enough work or trying desperately to break into new fields without adequate preparation, will simply play roulette. They'll bid for work they really know nothing about, hoping to be struck by the lightning of a contract award.

This situation is readily apparent at openings of sealed bids for specialized work. In a typical situation of this type, the U.S. Forest Service had solicited bids for the preparation of a small programmed-instruction course in office procedures. A proper price range for the job, the prevailing "market" for such work at that time, was approximately $8,000–$10,000. The bids read aloud at the opening ranged as high as $80,000! The $80,000 bidder obviously was completely unfamiliar with the work or had not read the RFP.

In all fairness, however, a typical RFP and work statement do offer many opportunities to be nonresponsive. Some statements of work include lengthy lists of specifications, and failure to respond to even one of these may be construed as nonresponsiveness if the customer chooses to so construe the failure.

An RFP usually sets out certain qualifications and conditions required to warn off unqualified bidders so they do not waste their time and money preparing proposals for work they cannot qualify for.

In that list of qualifications may easily be a few that do not match the characteristics of an otherwise well qualified proposer. Simply to ignore these is to risk being nonresponsive, whereas in many cases, the proposer can persuade the customer he or she is well qualified and should be considered, despite failure to match the customer's ideas exactly. Being nonresponsive does not mean failing to match every particular set forth, but it can mean failure to acknowledge and respond to every point on which information or opinion is solicited by the RFP.

Such failure can apply to any element of the proposal—understanding the requirement, staff resumes, company qualifications, delivery dates, management provisions, physical facilities, and so on.

Cosmetics Versus Content

Some organizations have the notion that the cosmetic niceties of proposals—the type, paper, and bindings—are highly important because they focus attention on those aspects rather than on content. Although a proposal is enhanced by a good physical appearance, no amount of cosmetic surgery or makeup can compensate for weaknesses in content. Proposals that have been carried to the extremes of elaborate typesetting and expensive bindings are rejected as swiftly as are the most simply typed and stapled proposals if their content does not merit further consideration. In fact, most RFPs include a statement emphasizing that elaborate printing and binding are neither desired nor appreciated and may be construed as evidence that the proposer is lacking in suitable cost consciousness! This is not to say that a proposal may not be typeset, printed, and bound suitably. It should be made as attractive as possible without going to extremes.

The Attempted Snow Job

One scathing comment often made by evaluators as they read pompous, overblown phrases is, "Madison Avenue!" The effort to overpower readers by obscure phraseology, purported scholarliness, buzzwords, extravagant and unsupported claims, and other such devices simply does not work. One manager in the Department of Labor reports he is amused by such tactics—but he swiftly goes on to read other proposals, often without even finishing the one that has amused him. He also says he is adversely impressed by careless use of language. He believes that spelling errors, poor grammar, and other such weaknesses are most "unprofessional" and that anyone that unprofessional when preparing a proposal is likely to be equally unprofessional in carrying out a program! Further, this manager told me he has often canceled a procurement entirely because he did not believe any of the proposals submitted merited award.

The Rambling Wreck

Many proposals simply ramble, without apparent plan or direction. Someone seems to have sat down and begun to write, putting words on paper as thoughts presented themselves, with little plan and no concrete objectives in mind. The proposal drifts, expanding into great detail when the author happens across a topic of special interest and in which he or she feels knowledgeable, scampering quickly across the shoals of little-known subjects, and arriving wherever it finally arrives because the current has taken it there.

At least, that's the impression one gets from reading some of these. This may come about because the RFP and statement of work (SOW) are not particularly well organized. Often they are not because the SOW writer lacks discipline. The proposal writer (or writers; the word "writer" is used here to include both the singular and the plural) has perhaps attempted to write a proposal in sequence and synchronism with the SOW. Doing that is usually a mistake. Few SOWs are that well organized. Many ramble badly, offering items of information and instruction completely out of any logical sequence, and are often highly redundant. The fact that the person responsible for the SOW (who is likely to be an evaluator of your proposal) is not a good writer does not necessarily mean he or she can't judge the quality of someone else's writing.

However, there is one major reason for bad writing and bad organization in proposals: Most proposals are written by individuals who are not professional or experienced writers, and they attempt to write well in their first draft! They have not learned that hardly anyone can compose a good first draft or even organize the information well in it. Even the untrained eye can see that a large proportion of the proposals received in government offices are first drafts that should never have been seen by eyes other than those of the organization's writers and editors.

Phases of Proposal Development

The actual act of writing the proposal is the final stage in proposal development. Other phases should have preceded it:

1. Bid/no-bid analysis and decision
2. Requirement analysis
3. Identification of the critical factor(s)
4. Formulation of the approach and technical/program/pricing strategies
5. Formulation of the capture strategy
6. Establishing the theme
7. Planning and outlining
8. Design and presentation strategy
9. Writing

The quality of the proposal and its chances for success will depend even more heavily on these early phases than on writing skills, important though those are. Each of these is a subject in itself and will be examined individually, although I have touched on some of them already.

Bid/No-Bid Analysis and Decision

Proposal development begins with a decision to make the bid, to write the proposal, and this is itself an analytical and decision-making process. However, the information gathered during this analysis is— should be—a first input to the proposal-development process itself.

Many factors must be considered when deciding whether to bid or submit a "no bid" to the customer. Some of these are "constants"— they result from fixed policies or conditions; others are variable, according to the circumstances of the moment. An RFP your organization might have wished to respond to in January may not be attractive in August, as you will soon see when you review the factors to be considered in arriving at a bid/no-bid decision. Here are the types of questions to which you must seek answers in reviewing the RFP:

1. Exactly what is the contractor to do or supply? Is it in our normal field of operation, or would we have to gear up especially for this contract? Is it some field we are eager to enter?

2. What are our strengths for this contract? Our weaknesses? Can we overcome our weaknesses? Will our strengths be adequate to carry the day? In short, how credible can we be?

3. What other bid opportunities do we have at the moment? Are bid opportunities plentiful or scarce? What is our backlog? How badly do we need additional contracts right now? How attractive is this contract compared with others we might pursue? What do our chances for this one appear to be compared with others we can go after?

4. What or who is the competition? How strong are they? How do we compare with them? Do we have any natural advantages? Specific disadvantages?

5. What staff do we have available to write the proposal? How big an effort will it be? What is it likely to cost us in dollars? Is diversion of staff needed elsewhere?

6. What is (are) the most compelling reason(s) for bidding this? Potential profit? Follow-on contracts? Breaking into new fields? What are reasons for not bidding it?

The answers to many of these spawn secondary sets of questions. If, for example, you decide that you lack many of the strengths you need for this proposal, yet you'd like to pursue this contract for one reason or another, you may wish to consider bidding with another firm—co-bidding. Frequently, that can win a contract otherwise probably unattainable. Here's an excellent example of that.

When NASA had issued an RFP for management and operation of its Scientific and Technical Information Facility in College Park, Maryland, there was a persistent rumor that the customer was unhappy with its incumbent contractor and would welcome a new one. The contract ordinarily comes up for renewal every three years, at which time proposals are accepted from all bidders. It's a large facility, which then employed approximately 360 people and was worth approximately $5.5 million per year in billings. The contractor installs his employees and manager on the government's own site in College Park and operates a large complex of computers and printing equipment, turning out a variety of technical documents.

One of the contenders was a relatively new firm, Informatics, an aggressive marketer. At the time, Informatics was simply not large enough, nor did it have all the qualifications needed to be completely credible for the contract. However, Informatics "teamed" with another firm, Computing and Software, which also was not a large corporation but had a good track record with NASA as a supplier of computer programming specialists and manager of on-site computer operations. Together, they formed a third entity, in partnership, Technical Information Systems Company or TISCO, as it soon became known. That alliance won the contract. It is unlikely that either firm could have won it by itself. But together, they showed enough strength to satisfy NASA.

Co-bidding is one way to overcome a weakness. Another is to recruit additional staff whose resumes may be used. These may be individuals to be hired or consultants to be retained for the contract in the event of award. Still another way may be to devise a technical plan or approach somewhat different from that suggested by the RFP, but still a legitimate approach and one you believe you can "sell" to the customer. Here is an example of how that may sometimes be done.

The Post Office Department (before it became the U.S. Postal Service) issued an RFP calling for a basic ordering agreement for computer programming services. The requirement was for a contractor who had on staff and available for assignments on short notice a wide variety of computer specialists with a wide variety of skills. The statement of work listed specialists rated on an ascending scale from the most junior programmer to systems design specialists, with experience in many types of machines and knowledge of a wide variety of computer languages. Taken at face value, the RFP required the contractor to be able to produce, on short notice, any combination of skill level, machine familiarity, and computer-language knowledge. The permutations of these several parameters are, of course, a staggeringly great number.

The successful bidder had relatively few computer programmers on staff. However, he had an exceptionally well developed recruiting capability because that was one of his chief services: supplying specialists, under contract, for long or short periods of time. He therefore turned his weakness into a strength by taking the calculated risk of modifying the requirement somewhat in this manner: He told the customer that the real requirement was not to have this stupendous mix of specialists on staff (and that it was most unlikely anyone did), but rather to be able to produce any specialists required whenever a request was made. He went on to explain his company's great strengths in doing just that, citing case after case of having done it in the past. He won the contract without difficulty.

It is frequently vital to interpret or translate the customer's stated requirement into another set of terms—one for your own benefit. The case just cited is a good example of the customer misstating his own need. It was not required that the contractor actually be the permanent employer of all the specialists called for, but only be able to *supply* those specialists when needed; the customer readily agreed with the proposer's interpretation. This is a rather common condition: The customer does not always explain the need clearly enough, and frequently it is essential that the proposer spend a good bit of effort studying that requirement closely and reaching a better interpretation or definition of the need.

There are times when bid opportunities are plentiful, such as three to six months before the end of the government's fiscal year. Most contractors, at times like these, have far more bid sets on their desks than they can possibly respond to. Therefore, they must classify them in terms of desirability and possibilities of winning in an effort to select those best worth their time and effort. However, the contractor who has not been very successful during the "proposal season" may have a slender backlog and therefore will bid for jobs ordinarily spurned.

In any case, the next phase begins when and if a decision is made to bid. And that should begin where the bid/no-bid decision and analysis process began: with a hard look at the requirement and what it means. Even though some study of that was made in the bid/no-bid analysis, additional effort to refine the interpretation further is almost always a good investment.

Requirement Analysis

The discipline known as "value engineering" (VE) or "value analysis" is excellent preparation for RFP requirements analysis, for the major objective and address of VE is the study of function, especially the main or basic function, as value engineers prefer to describe it. In the case of the Post Office Department contract described a few paragraphs ago, a value engineer would have automatically said, "The basic function is to provide computer specialists, so it can't really matter whether they come from the contractor's own staff or from other sources, as long as they are provided." The value engineer has been trained to regard an item (which may be a physical object, system, person, document, or almost anything else) and seek an answer to the question, "What does it do?" (or "What is it supposed to do?"). That's the first step in identifying or defining a basic function, which is the objective of or the reason for the existence of the item (or requirement).

I said before that one of several basic conditions or needs underlies the customer's request for contract help and that you will be asked, as the contractor, to do one of the following:

Solve a problem.

Provide additional staff to carry out a program.

Provide specialized resources—physical facilities, staff, or know-how—to carry out a program.

As a first step in bid/no-bid analysis, you will have already decided which of these categories the job falls into. Now you want to take a closer look at your earlier judgment. The distinctions are not always as clear-cut as they may appear when stated categorically, as they have been here, and sometimes the customer's statement of work can be misleading. Government people often tend to believe that their requirements are very specialized and have no true counterpart elsewhere in commerce and industry, and they are often right about that. But the uniqueness of their requirement may be due to their own notions of how the job should be done, a misconception of their true problem or need, or a lack of familiarity with how similar problems are handled in the commercial/industrial environment. That is, what is presented as a special or unique problem may be a routine problem that has a well-known solution. Whether you point this out in your proposal or not is a matter to be settled later, when you consider approaches and strategies; for now, you must decide whether such is the case or not. Therefore, you should be analyzing the requirement by another series of questions to which you must seek answers.

- *If stated as a problem to be solved: Is* it truly a *problem,* or something occurring commonly and readily solved? Will it be difficult to solve? Is there any doubt about eventual success? Has the customer a true understanding of the problem? Has he really identified the problem or its symptoms? Has he obscured the true problem with a miasma of trivial and extraneous information? Is he gilding the lily—calling it a problem, knowing well that what he requests and needs are really routine services, in an effort to glorify his own project? Or has he some other reason for such obscurantism?
- *If the requirement appears to be a need for a set of specialized services and/or skills:* How "special" are they? Will they require staff of rare qualifications? How specialized does the

customer appear to think they are (as distinct from what you think)?

- *If the need appears to be simply more hands and feet of one sort or another:* How specialized must the hands and feet be? How well qualified? Will they work as a unit on a single project or be utilized in various ways and locations? Will there be an extensive management requirement?

Once you have answered these questions satisfactorily, or as far as they can be answered, you are ready to proceed to the next step: identification of critical factors. However, this analysis (analyses) is not totally sequential and discrete. Iteration is often necessary, and as you proceed, you may find it necessary to return to an earlier analysis and modify your conclusions drawn there. Therefore, operate on the assumption that every conclusion you draw is tentative and subject to change. You will find that these analyses are all interconnected as one overall analysis. I have separated them here as an illustrative device to help you see some logic and order in the process.

Identification of the Critical Factor(s)

As you begin your search for the critical factor(s), you will begin to grasp the true significance of some of the secondary questions suggested in preceding paragraphs. You will also see where this is leading: to the formulation of approaches and strategies. The latter are based on the answers you develop to these questions, and to formulate them without asking and answering these questions is to stab wildly in the dark, hoping to "strike a nerve."

In most cases, there is some overriding consideration in the customer's mind. It may have been clearly stated in the explanatory text, in the explanation of evaluation criteria and their weights, or in both. Or you may not have been given any idea, overtly, at least, of what is most important to the customer. And frequently there is some critical factor or set of factors upon which success really hinges, sometimes in spite of what the listed evaluation criteria are!

For example, in many cases, the resumes overshadow everything else in importance. Sometimes the resume of the proposed project director is by far the most important of all the resumes. A strong proposed project director may carry the day, even though the other resumes offered are not particularly meritorious, and a weak resume for the proposed project director may scotch the proposal despite strengths everywhere else. The customer justifiably feels that the government is entrusting a great deal of money and a most important program to the contractor's project director and is understandably concerned that he or she be well qualified.

Other things also may concern the customer. She may feel the project requires an especially strong management plan. She may be working on a tight budget and be compelled to accept the best she can get for the price—ergo, price becomes a critical concern. She may want an innovative plan (a state-of-the-art approach), or she may want a conservative approach (the tried-and-true, foolproof method). She may want a take-charge kind of contractor who will require a minimum of attention in running the program, or she may want a contractor who will "touch base" with her almost continuously.

Admittedly, it is not easy to learn all this and usually takes a great deal of detective work. Yet the clues are there in the RFP/SOW, in most cases, and the alert analyst can ferret them out.

However, they are not always obscure. In many cases, they are so obvious that they are overlooked completely! When Secretary of Defense Robert McNamara wanted an airplane that both the air force and the navy could use, only one of the bidders for the job saw clearly that the proposal must trumpet "commonality" throughout to let the secretary know they understood his objective. That bidder won, due in no small measure to that strategy, as well as to a generally sound proposal and capability. Other bidders were more subtle, promising commonality, but never spelling it out distinctly, much less reiterating and reinforcing it frequently.

That critical concern of the customer is the keystone of the entire proposal effort. Understanding what the customer wants and what he says he wants—whether they are the same messages or not—is fundamental to the approach, the strategy, and the theme (which is part of the strategy, of course).

I lost one proposal because I did not understand what the customer really wanted, although the contracting officer had taken me aside and urged me to give him a crackerjack proposal because he wanted me to have the contract. (So much for "fixes" when you don't also write the winning proposal!) It happened this way: There were some unclear points in the statement of work, and I felt we had to ask the customer some questions. Because we knew the officials well, and they were highly receptive to our having the contract—if we gave them a good enough proposal—I sent an assistant over to make inquiries about those points that were unclear to us.

It happened that he talked to the man who would manage the contract for the customer. What we did not know was that the individual sharply disagreed with his superior about the conduct of the project and had written the work statement in his own manner, evidently being deliberately obscure about a few things he wanted to do differently than his superior did. Therefore, he explained his intent to my assistant, and we wrote the proposal accordingly. But his superior rejected our proposal because it didn't agree with *his* idea of what was needed to do the job the way he wanted it done. (We did, however, win the next two contracts for the same work, once we understood the situation.)

Formulation of Approach and Strategies

You will use several types of strategies. There is the technical or program strategy—how you propose to design and carry out the project, how you will manage it, and so on. There are pricing strategies, some of which were discussed in Chapters 5 and 6. And there are presentation strategies, which I discuss presently. Any one or a combination of these may represent your "capture strategy"—the main strategy that you anticipate will sway the customer in your favor for the contract.

Your proposed approach is the key to the technical/program/ pricing strategy. That is why I consider them all in a single discussion. You may devise an approach to suit your strategy or vice versa, but you cannot really consider one seriously without the other.

If, for example, you have judged price to be the critical factor, being a low bidder is your capture strategy, but you must devise an approach and technical/program strategy that permits you to be a low bidder without appearing to sacrifice quality or compromise the prospects for a successful project. Logically, you would begin by considering the various possible approaches, selecting the one that appears to suit your purpose best, and designing a program to match the approach. In practice, you may be so familiar with the work that you grasp almost instantly all the possible alternatives and can go almost directly into program design. However, for the sake of logical progression, let's assume you must ponder this matter at length.

Suppose that, at first glance, the project appears to require the full-time services of six highly qualified specialists, who alone would cost the customer on the order of $200,000–$240,000 per year, with overhead and support services. There are several possible approaches to reduce this cost:

1. Use of fewer specialists, supported by junior staff who will be closely supervised so the end result will be as though six specialists had been used

2. As in item 1 but using up to six specialists part of the time rather than all of it

3. Use of a consultant, who will cost less because of reduced overhead on consultants

The criteria for selecting which of these to use would include (1) the total cost savings that could be realized, (2) the relative risks to project success each alternative entails, and (3) the effect on the customer's judgment of your plan and its suitability.

In any case, no matter which alternative you finally select as the one to be proposed, you will have to sell your approach to the customer. You will have to make him agree that your approach and plan are practicable, do not in any way compromise prospects for a successful project or the quality of the service or products of the project, and are more economical to carry out.

To do this, you will have to make a careful analysis and gather up evidence to prove your point. It is not sufficient simply to assure your customer that you have studied the matter and reached the conclusion that these cost savings can be effected without risk to quality or success; you must prove that by providing enough evidence to convince your customer of that truth.

Any time you promise a markedly better cost saving, an innovation of some sort, or a startlingly greater guarantee of results than your competitors can offer, you automatically strain the customer's credulity, and you must take suitable action to establish the credibility of your proposal. The more you offer or promise, the more evidence you must produce to overcome the instantaneous skepticism.

For example, you may discover an inherent paradox in the RFP, for such paradoxes do occur. One of the many RFPs issued by the Job Corps in its earlier days called for the development of an instructor-based course in electrical appliance repair. The SOW explained that the target population was "functionally illiterate," a phrase commonly used to describe Job Corpsmen, almost all of whom were school dropouts (some of them never reached even high school before dropping out). It was thus an article of faith in dealing with the Job Corps generally that most read at a fifth-grade level, at best, and were almost entirely deficient in arithmetic and other academic basics.

To attain even a minimally acceptable skill in electrical appliance repair, students should certainly be able to work from the maintenance instructions published by the manufacturers and be able to read simple electrical circuit diagrams. They also should be able to order parts and understand the workings of the equipment at least well enough to substitute equivalent parts when original replacements are not available, as is often the case. This, in turn, means understanding a few basic electrical laws, such as Ohm's Law and probably Kirchhoff's Laws (not necessarily in the formal sense of being able to quote and interpret them in language, but to grasp their application to simple electrical equipment, at the least). And this, in turn, calls for a grasp of simple algebra. Whether or not the repairpersons ever actually calculate replacement values for circuit components, they must at least understand the calculations to learn the laws and their significance.

So we come upon a paradox: How can students who can't read acceptably well, much less perform algebraic manipulations, be taught electrical appliance repair? This paradox formed the basis for the approach and strategy of the successful proposal. Having reasoned out these problems, which seemed to indicate that the program should not be undertaken at all, the successful proposer proceeded on the assumption that a method must be found to make the project work despite the problem. The approach proposed was to develop a maximum of nonverbal teaching methods, plus several proposed shortcuts that would minimize the need for algebraic manipulations and calculations, plus a great deal of hands-on work experience—almost an OJT (on-the-job training) environment in the classroom-workshop.

The strategy was to dramatize the problem, which was the paradox of the entire procurement, and then to offer an innovative solution, with the goal of persuading the customer that any other approach proposed was doomed to failure from the beginning (one way to handle competition!). The strategy worked well, for the proposal was priced "out of sight," but it was so enticing that the customer offered to negotiate and settled for a highly satisfactory price, which was still considerably higher than that of competing proposals.

As I proceed to other aspects of proposal development, I'll return to this outstanding example and discuss the evidence offered to support the dramatically different proposal.

Formulation of the Capture Strategy

The capture strategy—that aspect of your entire proposal on which you are depending to bring home the bacon—is rarely a single entity, although it may be, in a few cases. Usually, it is the sum of several strategies and techniques. In the previously cited case, the main strategy was to be different from all other proposals by drawing attention to the paradox and utilizing it. The proposal went about it somewhat along the following lines:

1. After introducing the proposer and establishing his general qualifications as a bidder for the project, the proposal summarized the stated requirement. Then it launched into a brief rationale that pointed out that the skills to be taught entailed certain academic education and ability lacking in the target population, and so on. That section ended with a promise to present sound and reliable methods for coping successfully with this problem.

2. The proposal then went into a lengthier discussion, driving home the arguments summarized in the introductory paragraphs, to prove beyond doubt that conventional teaching approaches could not be expected to work in this situation and that the project must be undertaken on a completely different basis if it was to have any chance at all of succeeding. It went on to discuss the specific areas of training required, the normal problems of teaching those, the special problems the Job Corpsmen could be expected to have, and the nonverbal methods and learning aids available, or which the proposer could devise, such as Ohm's Law calculators, nomograms, simplified diagrams, and picture diagrams.

3. The specific plan to develop these things and produce the entire training package was then offered in detail, with many sample materials, such as an Ohm's Law paper slide rule and simplified, multicolor picture charts.

This reflects a number of strategies, although all are part of the capture strategy. Here they are, as they were intended to operate and as they apparently did operate successfully: First note item 1, which discusses the introductory portion of the proposal. It indicated the inherent problem and probably alarmed the customer thoroughly about the basic soundness of the entire plan. (In so doing, it automatically alerted him to things he should be watchful for in competing proposals: Had the other proposers spotted the problem? If so, were they honest enough to point it out and clever enough to provide a solution?) But after alarming the customer, the proposal went on to assure him that relief was coming, if he would only read on!

If there were lingering doubts as to the proposal's initial claims and allegations, the next section, discussed in item 2, presented much more evidence that the proposer's analysis was sound and dependable and that not seeing this and providing against it was predictive of failure. (Here the proposer is telling the customer what to look for in competing proposals and how to spot their weaknesses, but in a thoroughly objective tone!) That second section of the proposal went on to prove that the proposer was capable of developing and delivering the kind of program he advocated by offering details of the kinds of special learning aids and *job performance aids* he would provide. (Even students who had never learned the basic electrical laws would not be stranded because they could use the job performance aids instead of doing the simple calculations.)

Proof was offered by providing actual samples of some of the devices and aids promised in the section describing the specific program and project proposed.

So supporting strategies included indirect blows at competing offers, dramatic presentations, and solid evidence of actual "for instances."

A capture strategy, however, should not be a helter-skelter assortment of everything and anything you think may help. It should be a carefully designed and constructed chain with a clearly defined main strategy (the main reason the customer should buy your proposal) and subordinate strategies that support, reinforce, and strengthen your main strategy. Capture strategy is, then, *all* the strategies you have conceived, but organized to make the net effect greater than the simple sum of the parts.

Therefore, once you have identified the critical factor(s) and have devised your main strategy and approach, you must develop and design those other, subordinate strategies that will reinforce your main strategy and maximize the probability of it being decisive in the competition. The points to consider are these:

- What does the customer appear to be most concerned about?
- What is most likely to be decisive in the evaluation and in the customer's mind? What is his real need?
- How does the RFP lend itself to the purpose? What inherent problems are there in what the customer wants to do?
- What special advantages can your capability and ideas offer the customer?
- How can you dramatize your presentation?
- How can you be *different*, yet credible?

From these and similar questions, you can construct a capture strategy.

Analytical Methodology

Small proposals are usually written by a single person; large proposals almost always require several people. But even the small proposal often requires discussion and analysis by a group of people before writing begins. Each proposal is an individual, custom effort, usually for a custom job or product. Each therefore requires an individual analysis and study: creative effort.

Brainstorming, invented by Alex Osborne, a New York advertising executive, is often used successfully to synthesize the ideas of several people. A group of people gathers in a room, addresses a clearly defined question or problem, and gives free flow to their ideas. The basic rules for brainstorming are these:

1. A leader manages and controls the process. He or she postulates the question or problem to be addressed, keeps the people from wandering off the subject, and enforces the rules.
2. No judgments are to be made. No one is to cheer, jeer, or otherwise react subjectively to an idea put forth. (This is to

avoid discouraging anyone from articulating ideas for fear of ridicule.)

3. All ideas are recorded by someone present to do just that.
4. Anyone may "piggyback" an idea on another thrown out or project an idea provoked by another one.
5. The session continues until the people have exhausted their ideas on the subject.
6. Now the ideas may be judged. Ideas may be discarded, studied more closely, modified, combined with other ideas, and so on.
7. Final choices are made from the ideas found acceptable.

The advertising industry has used this method for developing advertising approaches, slogans, and copy. But the basic idea has been adapted for other purposes. It has become a standard method for value engineering, for instance. Value engineering, usually conducted by a team, is primarily analysis first, followed by synthesis. Proposal writing also follows that pattern. First there is the analysis of the requirement and the many factors to be considered in developing the proposal, then the synthesis of the approach, strategies, and actual proposal. Brainstorming has therefore proved itself most useful in proposal development and is usually a far more efficient method for the overall process than are the alternatives available.

A method often used when a group of technical/professional specialists is working together on a proposal is to have a general meeting, in which the RFP is discussed and the major requirements are identified. Everyone then goes off to their own office to work on some assigned portion or element of the proposal, usually with little instruction or control. The results are often disastrous. This uncoordinated effort yields an assortment of write-ups from various team members that rarely match each other in style, content, level of detail, or any other characteristic and are hardly suitable even as the roughest of drafts. It's an eminently unsatisfactory technique.

The time frame for most proposals is usually on the order of three to six weeks; it is rarely much longer than that. Time is simply too short for wasted motion. Although I noted earlier that few writers, even the professionals, write good first drafts, there is not enough time to do extensive rewriting. In almost all cases, the bulk of the proposal must be "rewritten" through heavy editing, with only partial actual rewrites, if the proposal is to meet the submittal deadline. To achieve this and still have a reasonably well written and well thought out proposal, a great deal of control over the process is needed. It simply cannot be allowed to happen, but must be made to happen.

Adaptation of the brainstorming technique offers a large part of such control, as well as several other benefits. It is an excellent way of analyzing the RFP/SOW and sorting out the definition of the requirement and the critical factors. It also combines several minds in devising approaches and strategies. In addition, instead of having the discrepancies in ideas surface in written drafts two or three weeks into the actual proposal writing, they can be identified during the brainstorming session and resolved there.

If two minds are better than one, how much better several trained minds must be! In a brainstorming session, a synergism usually emerges, and the group often comes up with far better results than even the most gifted individual would have been able to achieve alone.

Even an individual writing a proposal alone can benefit from the method by discussing the requirement with one or more other people at an early stage. In fact, I've used this method quite often in writing my solo proposals, and it works well. At the very least, it gives me a devil's advocate point of view against which to test my ideas. The other party usually makes more substantial contributions than that and helps greatly in devising strategies, directly or indirectly.

CHAPTER 8

The Roles of
the Computer in
Proposal Writing

*Desktop publishing and graphics generally are
rapidly becoming as popular an application
of computer technology as word processing
has been. But the modern office computer
offers other, related aids also.*

Graphics in Proposal Presentations

A technical-writing organization of a few years ago included in its
application form for aspiring writers a simple test: It asked the applicant to describe in not more than 60 words the procedure for writing
a personal check. Few could do so with that word-length restriction.
But every now and then, an applicant was quick-witted enough to
"psych the test out"—perceive the point—and was thus able to do
the job easily within the prescribed word length, in far fewer than
60 words, in fact. The solution to the problem was simple: Provide
the reader a sketch of a completed check.

The solution is perhaps too simple, which is why it is so often overlooked. Or perhaps many writers operate on an unconscious premise that language is the sole tool of the writer and graphic illustration only an afterthought (if it is ever a thought at all), rather than a primary tool for communication. Or—a likely factor, if not a prime reason—words come more easily for most writers than do graphic illustrations, and so even writers who appreciate the need for and utility of illustrations tend to undervalue their contribution.

The Multiple Functions and Objectives of Graphics

The simple device of providing a sketch of a check, especially one made out to someone, provided several benefits: It simplified the writing, requiring only brief referrals to and explanations of the sketch. It helped the writer wise enough to make a sketch organize his or her own thoughts about the subject and, consequently, the writing of the instruction. And it certainly provided much easier to read and easier to understand how-to instruction.

The principles apply even more profoundly to proposal writing. The use of graphics, that is, graphic illustrations, has three major objectives:

1. Certain kinds of graphics are an enormous aid to analysis and design. They help you understand the client's needs and problems, even when the RFP fails to present completely clear, detailed information. These are graphics used when studying and analyzing the client's statement of his or her problem and requirement and planning the proposal.

   As a consequence of sketching charts to help yourself and others visualize the requirements, the conditions surrounding them, and the work to be done, many excellent graphics are developed in rough draft form. Used initially to help crystallize the problem definitions and aid the analysis and planning, the rough draft drawings or sketches are almost always suitable for later refinement and development into final designs to satisfy the client's needs. Thus, the client receives the benefits of that organized and disciplined planning.

2. That is not the end of their usefulness. The graphics—functional flowcharts and other definitive drawings—simplify the writing itself. It is far easier to write to detailed drawings than to rely on words alone. Much of the content of the proposal is so defined in advance.

3. The graphics help the reader as much as they help you by reducing both the verbiage and the introspective gymnastics required to visualize the proposed programs. They reduce the time and effort required to understand the concept or process presented and thus have far greater impact. (By lessening the burden on the reader, they also comply with an important marketing principle: Make it as easy as possible for the prospect to make a decision in your favor.)

There is a spin-off benefit, too: Graphics have a beneficial psychological effect in that they add credibility. The mind is reassured of validity by graphics and tabulated data. That brings up another subject: tables and matrices, discussed later in this chapter.

The Economy of Graphics

The development of graphics costs money, even with the aid of computers. But writing also costs money; it costs the time of salaried employees, and labor is the highest-cost element in our economy today. The question is sometimes raised as to how much commitment should be made to graphics, in light of the cost.

The answer is not difficult to find, for *good* graphics do not cost any more than writing does and, in many cases, cost far less. A good illustration pays its way by "displacing" at least its "weight" in words. That is, if a page of graphics costs twice as much as a page of text, that page of graphics ought to replace at least two pages of text—convey as much information as two pages of text and make those two pages of text unnecessary.

That idea can be turned around to create a yardstick by which to measure the quality and suitability of graphics. If an illustration requires a great deal of language to explain it, it is almost surely a poor illustration. Truly good illustrations explain themselves, with little more than captions and legends required, except, perhaps, for labels on items illustrated ("callouts," in the jargon of the trade), on certain kinds of drawings. In short, don't illustrate your words and don't explain your illustrations. Use each as an independent means for communicating and presenting ideas.

Some Basic Kinds of Graphics

Strictly speaking, the "graphic arts" include typography and printing, as well as photography, drawing, and painting. But for the moment, I'll confine my discussion to drawings of various kinds, such as you are most likely to use in proposals, depending on your field. They include, but are not restricted to, the following categories:

Organization charts
Functional flowcharts
Milestone charts
Plots
Graphs
Pictorials
Mechanical layouts
Schematic drawings
Critical Path Method and PERT charts
Standard forms
Illustrated parts breakdowns

It was once necessary to employ professional illustrators to get professional-looking graphics and avoid that "homemade" look. For the well-equipped office of today, that is no longer true. With modern desktop publishing (dtp) hardware and software (laser printers and dtp programs), anyone can create graphics of professional quality—

even imaginative typography—but especially line drawings. Even without dtp accessories, using only the facilities of modern word processors and 24-pin dot matrix printers and laser printers, impressive graphics can be created. The organization chart shown as Figure 8–1, for example, was made with WordStar Professional Release 5 and an HP IIP, a popular and relatively inexpensive laser printer. It is a simplified presentation, shown only to illustrate what can be done with rather ordinary computer equipment of today. And it is generic, too; in the actual case, names of individuals would appear in the boxes.

Functional flowcharts are principal among those useful in analyzing an RFP and designing a program in response, especially in complex situations calling for complex solutions. Committing an interpretation of the problem statement—the SOW—to paper as a flowchart reveals things that are rarely apparent in a study of the descriptive verbiage alone.

That is true because the flowchart commits to paper what we try, usually with severely limited success, to envision as a complex of requirements, functions, phases, and interrelationships. A division of the U.S. Navy sought a contractor to help it go from several years of experimental programs in developing and using *Job Performance Aids* to a program to create them "operationally." The requirement called for a three-phase program to review what had been done and developed to date, to assess various models and make final choices among them, and to freeze the final design, in the form of a program for final testing and validation. What was uncertain at this point was whether the navy would award the work to a single contractor or to three contractors, one for each phase, and proposers were asked to construct their proposals so the navy could decide what options to exercise.

The successful contractor translated the SOW into a six-foot flowchart, following the client's descriptions and specifications of what was to be done, with suitable expert interpretations as necessary. This demonstrated quite clearly—inescapably—that an award of three contracts would result in a great deal of redundant effort, with lost time and increased costs.

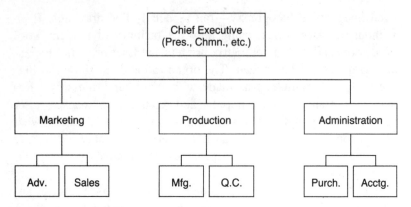

FIGURE 8–1.   A simple organization chart

Until they committed this to paper as a chart showing all the steps necessary and the interrelationships of all the elements, in both phase and functions, the proposer suspected but was neither sure nor could prove to the client the downside of a three-contract approach. With the chart completed, demonstrating the tasks and phases, there was no doubt about it. The functional representation of tasks and phases of work showed clearly that a three-contract effort would inevitably be redundant and wasteful. It won for the proposer a contract for the entire effort.

This kind of result is not unusual. When you use this technique of translating the RFP/SOW into a functional flowchart and refine that into a graphic presentation of your entire plan of action, you often gain greater insight into the client's needs than the client has, and your proposal—especially when it includes that comprehensive display of phases, functions, and relationships—is invariably impressive and often becomes a tour de force.

Figure 8–2 is a small sample of such a flowchart. It is rather technical and reflects only a portion of the project proposed. It is not fully detailed, but it illustrates something of the complexity and the difficulty of presenting a full picture of even this small portion of the effort in words alone. It is often necessary to make overall project charts as foldouts, and it is not at all unusual for them to run to as

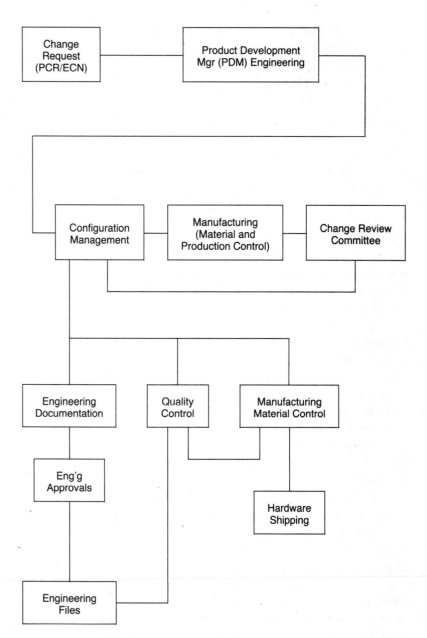

FIGURE 8–2. Functional flowchart example

much as six feet when unfolded and extended. In one proposal, three charts were combined into one six-foot chart, that is, the chart presented three six-foot sequences of functions and phases in three parallel streams. The proposal was one to the U.S. Army Corps of Engineers to help them satisfy a major logistics effort necessary to carry out a multibillion-dollar program requiring shipping huge quantities of a variety of material to Saudi Arabia and receiving it there for storage and distribution. The proposal request mandated continuous monitoring of all activity by computer and a great deal of paperwork, keeping precisely prescribed records and issuing documents of various kinds, most of them standard army forms.

After intensive study of the requirements, the proposal staff decided these many duties and functions—physical handling of the material, computer activity, and documentation—logically constituted three separate and semi-independent series of activities, although with many relationships between them. Initially, it was assumed all would have to be accounted for in a functional flowchart. Then it became apparent, as the main flow of material was being planned on paper, that there was far too much to handle in a single drawing, that it would be impossibly complex. That meant there would be, at a minimum, three functional flowcharts: one to depict and explain each of the three main activities. But as the presentation of the mainstream of physical handling of material developed into the first flowchart, it became apparent that it was a rather straightforward series of sequential events, as were the other two streams of activity. Thus, the idea of combining the drawings in a novel way occurred to the planners.

The proposal effort had begun with collecting all the requirements in lengthy sets of checklists and conducting conferences to discuss and plan the main activity, meanwhile sketching the basic flowchart to reflect the decisions made. This developed into a six-foot display of activities in logical and chronological sequence. The accompanying and related computer activity was also depicted on that chart, in parallel with the functional stream of actual shipping and handling activity. Finally, the trail of documentation was installed on that chart, along the lines of the following overall pattern:

In this manner, the functions and relationships among events in each stream of activity were easily shown, as were the interrelationships among the three sets of activities (for example, an event in the main stream causing the computer to issue a document referred to in the documentation stream). An extraordinarily complex program was thus presented and explained without unusual difficulty. (It also resulted in being declared by the client to be by far the best technical proposal.)

Milestone charts are also commonly used to present schedules. Figure 8–3 is an example of a simple milestone chart and Figure 8–4, a more sophisticated model, both prepared with the same word processor as were the earlier figures. A milestone chart may be combined with a functional flowchart by placing a time line on the flowchart, as in Figure 8–5 on page 189. These are only basic models. There are many different ways to construct these charts and drawings, even with a simple word processor. If you use the special dtp software now available, you can achieve still more artistic and attractive designs.

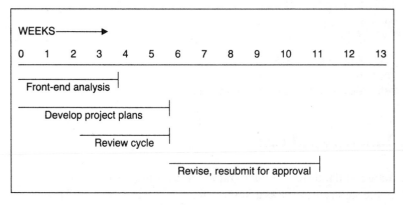

FIGURE 8–3. A simple milestone chart

Time in months: 0	1	2	3	4	5	6	7	8	9	10	11

Task analysis ■ ■ ■ ■ ■
Initial planning ■ ■ ■ ■ ■ ■ ■ ■
Review.................................■ ■ ■ ■ ■ ■
Revision ....■ ■ ■ ■
Field investigation...............■ ■ ■ ■ ■ ■ ■ ■ ■ ■ ■ ■ ■ ■
Interviews ....■ ■ ■ ■ ■ ■ ■ ■ ■ ■ ■ ■ ■
Draft development........................■ ■ ■ ■ ■ ■ ■ ■ ■ ■ ■ ■
Tryouts...■ ■ ■ ■
Final revisions...■ ■ ■ ■ ■ ■ ■ ■

FIGURE 8–4. A more sophisticated milestone chart

    In many fields, plotted curves are used widely to show trends and relationships between two or more related parameters. Figure 8–6 on page 190 is a simple example of such a curve plotted with a word processor. Figure 8–7 on page 190 is another type of chart that can show such relationships; it is a bar or Gantt chart, another widely used type. These are only two types of such charts. You can choose any from among a wide variety of charts or invent new ones. Nor must you start from scratch in doing so. Many dtp software programs include a variety of ready-made charts you can easily adapt to your own needs, with or without modifications.

    But line drawings are not the only shortcuts to greater efficiency via more lucid presentations. There are other useful devices that lighten the burden of writing to show relationships and trends and otherwise explain and sell your ideas.

Tables and Matrices

Tables and matrices are not graphic illustrations, but they serve many of the same purposes as and share many characteristics with graphics, not the least of which is that the use of the computer is a special asset

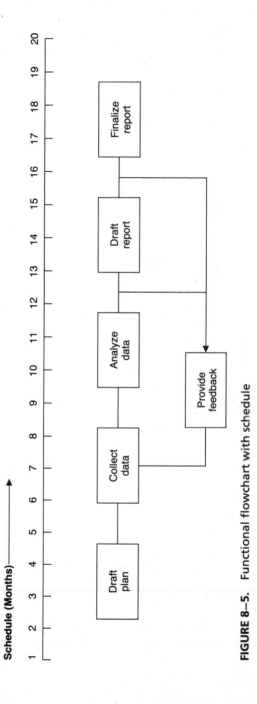

FIGURE 8–5.   Functional flowchart with schedule

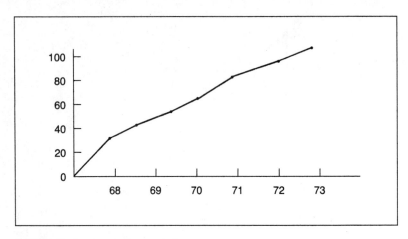

FIGURE 8–6. Typical trend plot

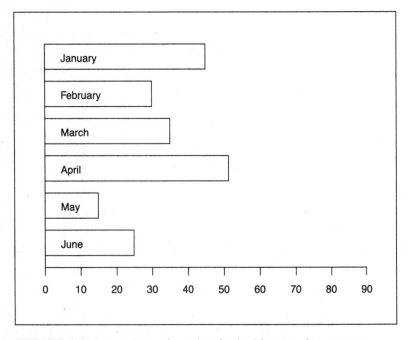

FIGURE 8–7. Bar or Gantt chart sketched with a word processor

for creating tabulated data, furnishing inherent capabilities for collecting, organizing, previewing, and presenting it.

Any means for organizing data for presentation is as useful to you as is the development of sketches to grasp the essentials and plan the presentation. That is, finding the logical relationships among the data is something you must do, and tabulating helps you discover those relationships. Even more significant, a tabular presentation helps the reader perceive relationships, trends, commonalities, variables, or other factors having some logical significance that is more readily apparent or more useful when presented in tabular form.

In the case of proposals, use for future reference is usually not a consideration. Proposals usually have no life after the award. Therefore, using tabulated data in proposals should be considered only as an aid to presentation and understanding, especially if they enhance the credibility of the information presented.

The sample of a proposal response matrix presented earlier is one example of a table commonly used in proposals. A labor-loading chart, used to show details of a proposed effort, is another, and usually takes the approximate form of Figure 8–8.

There are many possible formats for tables. (The *Government Printing Office Style Manual,* revised and reissued periodically, is an excellent source of ideas and models for tabular formats.) They can be as simple as the one shown in Figure 8–9 on page 193.

Many people assume that tables are always compilations of figures. That is not true; many useful tables have nothing but text in each column and cell. Figure 8–10 on page 194 provides a small sample of that.

Hardware and Software Considerations

There are many special considerations of both hardware and software to take into account in buying and adding to your computer system. I discuss only those aspects that bear on the graphics considerations. As far as graphics via computers are concerned, certain things are especially important. RAM is one of them.

Labor-Loading Estimates				
Tasks	Staffing and Hours			
	Proj. Mgr.	Sr. Eng'r.	Jr. Eng'r.	Technician
1. Meeting w/COTR	8	8	16	—
2. Prepare preliminary design specs	24	40	40	40
3. Review w/COTR	16	16	—	—
4. Breadboard circuit	24	40	80	40
5. Test breadboard	—	12	24	24
6. Build prototype	—	12	24	40
7. Test prototype				
a. Lab	—	12	24	24
b. Field	8	8	24	24
Totals:	80	148	232	192

FIGURE 8–8. General format for a labor-loading table

Capital assets:
Land and buildings	$645,000
Fixtures and equipment	325,000
Inventory	88,600
Cash reserves	123,750
Total	**$1,182,350**

FIGURE 8–9. A simple tabulation of assets

Random Access Memory

RAM (commonly referred to simply as *memory*) is important, especially if you use dtp software. Most of the leading dtp programs call for a minimum of 512 or 640KB of memory to run the software satisfactorily. IBM XT and AT models, their many clones, and the newer IBM and other computers are capable of supporting up to 640KB of memory without difficulty. However, the fact that many computers are advertised as 640KB machines does not mean they are supplied with 640KB memory installed. Many are delivered with far less, and you must either specifically request that the system be supplied with 640KB (or more, if available and you want it) or add additional chips after you get the machine. Make sure to be clear about this when you buy the system. You will usually benefit from having a larger memory in your system, if that is an option. RAM is like money: You never have too much, and having more than you need (at the moment, at least) is never inconvenient. You can now buy computers extended to as much as 16MB.

Disk Storage

The lowest-cost systems—XT clones, most commonly—are often offered with a single 5.25-inch floppy disk drive. You can manage with only one disk drive, but you will find it a great inconvenience, even a hardship. Many systems are offered with two floppy disk drives. However, a better and more commonly offered system

Proposed Training System

Learning Objective	Main Medium	Ancillary Medium	Remarks
History of Forest Service	Lectures	Audiotapes and videotapes	Students will be tested
Forest Service missions	Lectures	Field trips	
Organization	Reading	Videotapes	
Typical FS problems	Lectures	Field trips	
Typical FS tasks	Field trips	Audiotapes and slides	Practical tests
Administrative tasks	Guest lecturers	Videotapes	Written tests

FIGURE 8–10. Sample of all-text table

configuration today includes one 5.25-inch disk drive, a 3.5-inch drive, and a 40MB or larger hard disk.

Today's prices for systems and hard disk drives are sufficiently low that it is foolish to use a computer for serious purposes without at least a 40MB hard disk drive. (I have a 65MB hard drive because I bought a system with it. If I were replacing it today, I would get a larger hard disk.)

Backing Up

One problem with hard disks is that they are subject to "crashes," which means everything stored there is wiped out, for all practical purposes. It is easy to make an inadvertent move that will cause the loss of important data; even expert computer users make such mistakes occasionally. Experts can sometimes salvage portions of the data in the crashed disk, but this kind of salvage is not a reliable resource. Because most hard disks eventually fail, from one cause or another, it is essential that they be "backed up"—that copies of all the data on them be stored in some other medium as a safety measure. That means keeping the back-up medium up to date, on a daily basis for busy systems.

However, hard disk space is far too valuable to waste it or use it frivolously. To keep the entire system manageable and efficient, store on your hard disk only those files/that data you need reasonably frequently. Remove and store elsewhere, on tape or disks, data you need to refer to only once in a while. (Preferably, use disk storage; it is easier to get at the data on those rare occasions when you need to, and it is not necessary to transfer it back to hard disk storage.)

Printers

The laser printer, especially for graphics and/or desktop publishing, is often considered a must today. However, despite the outstanding reproduction quality of which a good laser printer is capable, the machine has its cons, as well as its pros. It is relatively fast—probably four or eight pages a minute. The quality is good. Because it uses cut sheets, rather than continuous paper, it can accept frequent and convenient changes of paper and/or forms. However, most laser printers can store only a limited quantity of paper and so cannot be left unattended for long periods. The cartridges of toner are relatively expensive. The machine itself is expensive, although prices have declined in recent years.

The state of the art in dot matrix printers has advanced. Today there are many 24-pin printers that achieve true letter quality in normal text and come reasonably close to laser printers and classical methods in line art, even in relatively complex line art. Moreover, many of these newer 24-pin printers are quite inexpensive, selling at a fraction of the cost of laser printers. And dot matrix printers can use tractor paper and so be loaded with over 3,000 sheets and left unattended for lengthy printing runs.

Software

One of the problems with graphics and dtp software is the agonizingly slow speeds with which many of them function. But many of the tables, charts, and other drawings you will want to use are easy to construct in a good word processor and print as rapidly as ordinary text. The "extended character set" provides via your keyboard all the characters available to those designing dtp and graphics programs. Following are just a few of the graphics characters available:

These characters can be summoned by depressing the *Alt* key and some combination of numbers on the number pad. *Alt 197,* for example, produces ╋, and *Alt 219* produces ▇. *Alt 254* produces ■, and I used a series of these (■■■■■■■■) in constructing the milestone chart of Figure 8–4. (I could have used others in series, such as *Alt 220* (▄▄▄▄▄▄▄▄▄▄▄▄) or *Alt 223* (▀▀▀▀▀▀▀▀▀▀) or even *Alt 205* (═══════════).

It can get somewhat laborious to draw a lengthy line, such as

■■■

using the *Alt 254* combination repeatedly. That is one place a macro-command is handy. Most modern word processors have a built-in capability for creating your own macrocommands, or you can use one of the special programs available for the purpose, such as the venerable and macro-pioneering SmartKey. You establish another key, temporarily or permanently, as *Alt 254,* and then you merely hold it down while it repeats and draws the line for you.

Automating the drawing of vertical lines is a bit more difficult, but it is also possible. A key designated *Alt 179 Enter* will produce a continuous vertical line as long as you hold the key down. (It draws it along the left margin, so change the left margin to wherever you want the line while drawing it.)

The word processor I use has a program called *Box* that produces a small box on screen that I can manipulate, enlarge or reduce, and make multiple copies of. The ten function keys are set up as macros and enable me to draw boxes and lines of my choice, supplying these ten characters:

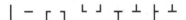

I supplement these with other available characters, using the method described here, to create my own simple but clean and professional looking graphics.

This does not mean graphics and dtp software are not useful and necessary; some types of drawings are beyond the capabilities of the simple devices described and do require special software, such as Ventura or PageMaker. With these programs, you can draw pie charts, CPM (critical path method) and PERT (program evaluation and review technique) charts, and other more sophisticated graphics. Although most good word processors offer more than one type font, the selection is considerably more limited than those offered by the special programs.

CHAPTER 9

Marketing
Intelligence
and Computers

*Modern research and data-gathering methods
increasingly rely on communication via
computers—computer-to-computer
communications, to be technically correct. To
function without this important aid is to be
severely handicapped in marketing today.*

The Critical Importance of
Intelligence in Marketing

Nothing is more vital in any marketing program than marketing intelligence—knowledge of a broad variety of factors that affect your success in the marketplace. If you know that a given procurement is pending long before your competitors do, you have an obvious immediate advantage. If you know more about the procurement—the client's problems, desires, preferences, procurement history, and other factors—you have an even greater advantage. Any relevant information you have is important. Any extra or special information is especially advantageous.

In the case of the federal government, those who pursue government contracts regularly usually subscribe to the *Commerce Business Daily,* wherein the government agencies list their requirements and announce their requests for bids and proposals every day. Now an electronic version is available, and several public data bases carry CBD ONLINE. You gain time with this. The printed copy takes several days to reach you, but the on-line version is available as soon as it is posted.

Most of those who provide CBD ONLINE also do searches of various kinds. When a client wanted to know what uses the federal agencies made of rolled steel, I did a search of prior procurements via a computer-to-computer link with one of those services and got a file, which I edited and printed out for my client, all without leaving my desk! Figure 9–1 illustrates several award announcements from CBD ONLINE as an example of one kind of information that can be gleaned in this manner. Here are others:

Procurements by certain agencies

Procurements of certain classes of goods or services

Awards to given companies

Awards on a regional basis

Awards set aside for small business

Awards made to minority-owned enterprises

Awards made to your competitors

Awards by types of contracts

The public data base services that include CBD ONLINE offer companion services, such as ordering solicitation sets for you when you find something of interest listed and supplying you listings of only those categories of interest to you, rather than the entire content of the CBD.

Desktop computers become more and more important for communication every day. The number of desktop computers in government offices generally is expanding quite rapidly, and

4 — EXPANDABLE SHELTER/CONTAINER, ES/C, Model A, Empty, NSN 5410-00-009-9852 J-55 ea, ES/C, Model A, nondestructive, NSN 5410-00-407-9579EJ-8 ea, ES/C, Model A, life support, NSN 5410-00-140-8963EJ-7 ea and 10 other items with 1st, 2nd, 3rd program year option requirements. Contract F09603-84-C-0015, 23

Mar 84, (Solic 2-53401), $18,588,825, Nordam, Tulsa, OK.<Warner Robins ALC directorate of Contracting and Manufacturing, Robins AFB, GA 31098<

— S-280C/G SHELTER ELECT EQUIP, (No RFP), Contract DAAB07-84-C-B102, Mod 00002, $1,983,400, 8 Jun 84, Gichner Mobile Systems, P.O. Box B, East Locust St, Dallastown, PA. (180)<U.S. Army Electronics Command, Fort Monmouth, NJ 17703<

— MODIFICATION OF MARINE EQUIPMENT SHELTER. Award of Contract No. 14-08-001-20772, Modification No. 4, was made to Woods Hole Oceanographic Institution, Water Street, Woods Hole, MA 02543, in the amount of $68,250.00 on June 8, 1984.<U.S. Dept of Interior, Geological Survey, Eastern Region Management Office, Procurement and Contracts Section, Room 2A233B, 12201 Sunrise Valley Drive, Reston, VA 22092, 703/860-7817<

K — MODIFY GFP SHELTERS for the AN/TRQ-32 mobile, multi-station, ground-based, direction finding and intercept system, Contract DAAK21-82-C-0072, Modification P00016, dtd 22 Jun 84. $163,000, Magnavox Government and Industrial Electronics Co., 1313 Production Rd, Fort Wayne, IN 46808. <Harry Diamond Laboratories, Contracts Branch (Vint Hill), S.H. Wake, DELHD-PR-CV, 703/347-6573, Vint Hill Farms Station, Warrenton, VA 22186<

Y — CONSTRUCTION OF HANDICAPPED ALTERATIONS, Heated Pump Shelters & Improve Heating/Ventilating Systems at Holston AAP, Kingsport, TN, DACA01-84-C-0088, Awarded 12 June 1984, DACA01-84-B-0038, National Geothermal, Inc., Rt. 4, Box 32, Florence, MS 39073, Amount $198,336.00<Mobile District, Corps of Engineers, PO Box 2288, Mobile, AL 36628.<

FIGURE 9–1.   Sample of CBD ONLINE search results

computer-to-computer communication with government agencies will increase. (Already, many of the electronic bulletin boards originate in government offices.) Eventually, you will be able to get solicitation sets in your own offices, without leaving your desk, using computer-to-computer links.

So far, state and local governments have not progressed to anything analogous to the CBD, either on-line or off-line, but usually announce their requests for proposals via classified advertising in their local newspapers, under the heading "Bids and Proposals." But computer-to-computer communication is expanding steadily, along with the growing popularity of FAX transmission and the growing number of FAX machines and FAX circuit boards for computers.

Public Data Bases

The success and swift acceptance of the microcomputer on millions of desktops led directly to the development of public data bases— banks of information available to subscribers at any time, on demand. That is, the information is stored in "host computers," as files; and subscribers can call the host computer, via their own computers, and search out information stored there. They may have that information displayed on the screens of their own computers, copied, stored in their own files, and/or printed out, immediately or later. (It is more economical to print it out later because the cost is in terms of time spent—"connect time"—and printing is relatively slow.)

Some data bases (for example, GEnie and CompuServe) are general, offering information of interest to the general public: airline schedules, hotel listings, stock reports, news, electronic mail service, and other such electronic bulletin board items. But there are thousands of specialized public data bases, offered by hundreds of services (most services have multiple data bases available for your access, and many cross-connect to others), designed to serve specific business and professional interests, such as Westlaw, serving the legal profession, and TRW Information Services, providing credit reports. Here are a few of the many types of information these services offer:

On-line encyclopedias

Summaries of civil suits and court decisions

Chemical sciences and engineering data

Scientific and engineering news items

Accounting and economics

Medical data and diagnostic support

Socioeconomic data

Electronic versions of many newsletters

Labor/industrial relations

Grant programs

Foreign trade information

Abstracts of journal articles in many fields

Abstracts and full-text copies of many newspaper stories

Economic indicators and forecasts

Radio and TV ratings reports

Banking information

Construction industry news and reports

Management information, literature, and conference proceedings

Mathematical research literature

Pharmaceutical abstracts

Catalog of government publications

Press releases of major corporations and government agencies

Mineral processing abstracts

Roper reports on public attitudes vis-à-vis many subjects

These represent a huge source of information for research in developing proposals and support in writing them. But this is not the only source of support and comfort in pursuing contracts; there are many others, similar and yet different.

Private and Public (Government) Data Bases and Bulletin Boards

Many individuals have established their computers as host computers—electronic bulletin boards (known colloquially today as "BBS" systems). These provide many free services, given over largely to chatting about many subjects and disseminating computer software known widely as "shareware."

Many federal agencies have joined this trend and authorized employees to establish quasi-official BBS systems. The Department of Commerce, General Services Administration, U.S. Navy, National Oceanic and Atmospheric Administration, Department of Defense, Department of Veterans Affairs, World Bank, State Department, NASA, Department of Energy, Federal Deposit Insurance Corporation, National Bureau of Standards, and others have such BBS systems operated on behalf of their different divisions.

These BBS systems are valuable for gathering information for and about purchasing and procurement, but they are also a resource for finding and recruiting technical specialists to help write proposals, furnish needed information, and provide their own resumes as available specialists. It is increasingly common to find announcements of job openings and jobs wanted posted on these bulletin boards.

Other sponsors of BBS systems are the many computer clubs that have sprung up around the country—indeed, around the world. One of the most popular is the CPCUG—Capital PC Users Group—centered in Washington, D.C., but with extensions in many places.

Yet another kind of BBS system is that sponsored by and operated for commercial purposes by or in behalf of computer sellers—retailers and manufacturers—and other commercial interests, such as publishers of computer magazines, some of whom operate their own BBS systems for readers. Well-known manufacturer NEC (Nippon Electronic Corporation), for example, operates a BBS system in Boston that furnishes many special NEC printer drivers to users. The publishers of *PC Resource* magazine also operate a BBS system for their readers, supplying the usual BBS system services plus original programs presented textually in the magazine and available without charge to callers.

Computer-to-Computer Communication

What is overlooked or not understood about computer communication is that the intervention of public data bases and electronic bulletin boards is not absolutely necessary to communication between computer owners; *any* individual computer owner equipped for computer communication (that is, with a telephone, modem, and communication software) can communicate directly (computer to computer) with any other individual computer owner similarly equipped, whether the two use the same or different hardware and software. There is almost no compatibility problem in this arena of computer usage: Regardless of your type of computer, operating system, and/or communication software and protocols, you can almost always send and receive English language messages and files of all kinds to and from another computer owner. The text/data files are almost always transmitted as Ascii files, a nearly universal protocol for text transmissions. (However, this is not true for utility files, word processors, and other applications programs; they do have to be compatible—that is, if you send a Macintosh-compatible word processor or data base manager, it will not work on an IBM XT computer.)

Marketing intelligence encompasses many areas of information. The term includes gathering and using many other kinds of information gotten in many other ways. It includes virtually all kinds of information, gathered in or contributed by many different means, such as via special consultants, vendors, and others.

In some cases, you need more than one kind of consultant. For example, a large company bidding a complex "GOCO" (government-owned, contractor-operated) ammunition-manufacturing project to the army called in several vendors and consultants to help with the proposal. One was a specialist in proposal writing per se—in proposal writing as a marketing presentation. Another was a specialist in the technical subject matter or process—ammunition manufacture, in this case. Still another was an expert in army arsenal organizations and their procurement of related services. And there were the representatives of prospective vendors, who acted also as consultants. This required conference facilities and many meetings, with travel and per diem expenses for all borne by the company.

One thing that computer-to-computer communication means or should mean is that you can "telecommute" with associates, vendors, consultants, and others when you co-bid, plan extensive use of subcontractors, and/or retain special help (for example, consultants) to help with the proposal. Usually, in such circumstances, your co-bidders or subcontractors help write the proposal, and this can be a problem when they are many miles away. But that need no longer be a major problem because you can now communicate with each other via your computers and send each other extensive documents. (For large documents, it is usually far more efficient to transmit files via computer-to-computer communication than to FAX the printed documents.)

It is also feasible to conduct spontaneous conferences in this manner, especially with simultaneous voice communication and graphics software that permit freehand drawing on the screens. This opens the door to a far wider array of co-bidding possibilities because it eliminates or greatly minimizes the need for face-to-face meetings and advance planning for these meetings, which often involve unacceptable delays. (Never forget that proposals are almost always prepared under the gun of impossible deadlines and that schedule pressure has in the past often compelled proposers to forgo meetings and conferences they would have liked to conduct.) It is thus a great advantage to you in both your possible roles—as a prospective prime contractor with primary responsibility for the proposal and as a subcontractor or co-bidder with subordinate/support responsibilities. Frequently, neither you nor anyone else is well equipped to qualify as a sole bidder for a program, and it makes sense to aim for less than the whole loaf, if you can increase your win probability thereby. In summary, taken proper advantage of, computer communication can open up many additional sales opportunities and greatly increase your chance of success.

Relevant Software

Among the many kinds of computer programs that can contribute to these factors of design, approach, and rationale are at least the following, mentioned in brief here.

CAD/CAM (Computer-Assisted Design/Computer-Aided Manufacturing) software is becoming more and more popular. If the project is a technological one, programs of this type may be invaluable.

Data base managers (dbm) are so versatile and useful for such a broad array of applications that they are today in almost universal use. Even for such simple needs as my own, I find it useful to maintain a dbm program with a half-dozen files. Those with good search capabilities are especially useful for building your own library of relevant data, to which you will have increasingly frequent access as it grows. For example, you will want to build "swipe files," stores of material that is likely to be useful again and again, either directly or with some modification and adaptation to your latest need. In fact, this kind of software is so important and so useful that Chapter 11 is devoted to it.

Spreadsheet programs are in many ways similar to data base managers and are, in fact, often used instead of them. They have some added capability, especially for making long-term and what-if projections, trial fits, models, and other manipulations that may be useful in many cases.

Outliners or "idea processors" are another kind of software often included with modern word processors. They help people think out ideas by providing facility with outline development and facile manipulation of the outline.

"Findit" software is programs designed for searching among multiple files. Some are designed to find a file by name; others are designed to find any word or information item within a group of files. One such program, for example, which resides among my own utilities, can search my entire hard disk for any file title or portion of a title I can supply. ProFinder, a support program that was supplied with my word processor, can as one of its many capabilities search out a file title, word, or term ("string," in computer tech talk) in all the files in any given subdirectory. These kinds of programs are most often capabilities of larger programs that have multiple capabilities.

Communication software is necessary to manage the communication process at each end, and a wide variety of it is available. The better communication programs do most of the work for you, making it quite easy to send and receive messages (either as mail to be read when the other party can get to it or spontaneously, as in a telephone conversation) and to send and receive complete files, including graphics. You can read your mail on-screen, download it to a disk file, print it out, or do all of these. These are the basic functions, but several refinements make the use of the communication more convenient.

Hardware

Of course, some hardware is necessary. For communication, you need your computer and a modem, a device connected between your telephone and your computer. Your telephone line is plugged into your modem, and your modem is plugged into your computer.

The modem translates the digital signals from your computer into an audible code that is transmitted over the telephone lines to the modem that is connected to the other computer. That modem translates the audible signal back to the digital codes the computer "speaks" and sends it on to the other computer.

The more popular modems today operate at 2,400 *baud,* which means they send and can receive 2,400 *bits* or changes in voltage per second. That, in turn, equates to roughly 200 to 250 words per minute. Older modems operated at 1,200 baud, and we are promised that the day of the 9,600 baud modem is close. In fact, 9,600 baud and even faster modems are a reality, but they are not yet in widespread use for the purposes I describe. The 9,600 baud modems are expensive, and they are useful to an owner only if the other computer has a similar modem, although other, technical reasons have impeded their widespread usage. Most modems can operate at several speeds, so if a

9,600 baud modem communicates with a 2,400 baud modem, both will operate at 2,400 baud, nullifying the advantage of the more expensive modem.

Hardware Compatibility Considerations

When it is not practicable to communicate with vendors, co-bidders, and other associates by computer-to-computer or FAX links, you normally turn to express delivery services, usually of the overnight variety. (Time and schedule pressures are a way of life in proposal work.) And you are often sending and receiving computer disks. But here is where a compatibility problem arises, as the following anecdotes illustrate.

I assisted a San Antonio firm bidding a complex, state-of-the-art project to a U.S. Navy organization. The firm was supported by several co-bidders and suppliers-to-be that were widely dispersed geographically. On one occasion, important data sent us via overnight express from White Sands, New Mexico, arrived on a 5.25-inch floppy that we were unable to read on any of the available computers. We lost many hours before we discovered this was a "quad"— quadruple-density—disk, with data packed at twice the density of the double-density drives that were the only kinds we had available. The solution was to find a local vendor who could translate this data onto double-density disks for us.

On another occasion, I sent software on 5.25-inch disks to an associate, only to find that he had a system using 3.5-inch disks only. Fortunately, we were not hard-pressed for time, and I had the capability to transfer the software to a 3.5-inch disk. We were thus able to solve the problem without outside intervention. But such mismatches of hardware capabilities do cause many problems of incompatibility.

There are so many different disk drives that it is increasingly important to consider disk and drive compatibility problems when sending and receiving disks to and from others. The following disk sizes and capacities are in widespread or increasingly popular use today. (SSSD—single-side, single-density—disks are obsolescent and rarely found today, so I do not include them.)

5.25-inch Disks	3.5-inch Disks
360KB	720KB
720KB	1.44MB
1.2MB	

By far the most widely used size today is the 360KB 5.25-inch floppy, and probably the least popular is the 1.2MB 5.25-inch floppy. That is largely because of the huge success of the IBM PC, XT, and AT models and their many clones, virtually all of which were fitted with 360KB disk drives. But since the newer IBM systems appeared on the market, the 3.5-inch drives and disks have become increasingly popular, and the trend to them appears likely to continue. However, optical drives and disks appear to be gaining favor and are quite likely to be the wave of the future in disk drives.

A 1.44MB drive can usually read 720KB 3.5-inch disks without difficulty, and the 1.2MB drive is alleged to be able to read 360KB disks. But the latter cannot always do so reliably. Reports from many users suggest that even among the same make and model systems, some 1.2MB drives can read the 360KB disks, and some cannot.

When you exchange disks with associates, you must ascertain what kinds of disks the receiving party can utilize. It is helpful if you can read any of the ones listed here, but if you can't or if there is doubt about it, you should determine in advance who, at some nearby location, can translate among all the disks listed.

Data Compatibility

Data may or may not be in compatible form. Textual information prepared on a given word processor (for example, WordStar) is not usually directly compatible with another word processor (for example, WordPerfect), although there are translation programs available for some cases. Even the same word processor may produce a file that is not compatible with an earlier version of the same word processor. One form is virtually universal, however: Ascii, which almost all word processors can generate and read. (At least one leading word processor, XyWrite, prepares all its files in Ascii code. You must specifically order the file in Ascii when using most word processors.)

The Proposal Library

If you write proposals at all frequently, you should establish and maintain a proposal library that includes at least the following classes and kinds of material:

Boilerplate about your own organization
  Resumes of staff
  Descriptions of facilities and resources
  Descriptions of current and past projects
  Organization charts
General reference materials
  Your own past proposals
  Books, reports, memoranda, other documents on relevant subjects
  Your own proposal standards (for example, a manual), if documented
  Your own promotional materials (brochures, news releases, photos, and so forth)
  Brochures and other information about your customers and prospective customers
Competitor materials
  Copies of competitors' proposals
  Copies of competitors' literature
  Intelligence you have gathered about competitors

As much of this information as possible should be in "machinable" form—on disks and/or computer tape. However, whatever form it is in, it should be indexed and accounted for in a data base management program so you can find what you need when you need it without delay. Such a library grows rapidly; somehow, even copies of competitors' proposals fall into your hands. (Using the Freedom of Information Act, you can get copies of competitors' proposals to government agencies with all but clearly proprietary data included.) Before long, it becomes difficult to keep track of the information without computer assistance.

CHAPTER 10

Writing with a

Personal Computer

*The personal computer is the greatest boon
to writing since movable type was invented—
when it is used as a true writer's tool. Every
literate person can become a far better
writer by learning to use the computer
as a true writing tool.*

A General Discussion of Writing

To get a perspective on some of the most important benefits desktop
computers can provide in the actual writing process, it is necessary
to digress first into a general discussion of writing, a subject greatly
misunderstood by those for whom it is a chore and not a calling. But
eventually, I will link writing to proposals and, more important, to
proposal success.

Professional *Attitude* in Writing

Every literate person writes and so is, technically, a writer. But the
way most truly professional writers write is somewhat different than

the way most others write, no matter how literate or how well educated those others are.

The most significant difference is not in size of vocabulary, choice of words, elegance of expression, efficiency, or style; many who are not professional writers and for whom writing may be an unwelcome duty or chore excel in all those areas. The chief difference is in *attitude* toward writing.

Most truly professional writers have learned *and accept* the need for editing, rewriting, and polishing: They accept as fact that few of us—*extremely* few of us, even those with lengthy experience as full-time professional writers—are capable of excellent first-draft writing. Although we may write a good first draft—good as a first draft, that is—we can almost always make major improvements on the first draft of anything we write by editing, rewriting/revising, and polishing that rough copy through at least another draft, and often through several additional drafts. The true writer is, in fact, never really satisfied with his or her final draft and always wishes there were time to go over it and polish it one more time!

Ernest Hemingway, best-selling and highly lauded writer that he was, forced himself to write second drafts. He said he knew he was too lazy to write a second draft if he were not forced to do so, so he forced himself to rewrite by first writing his manuscripts in longhand, knowing no publisher would accept holographic manuscript, even from him. That compelled him then to type a copy of his manuscript, and he was thus able to edit, rewrite, and polish his copy while typing the manuscript!

Editorial Functions Generally

There is another phase of editing, by someone whose entire function is editing and who is not "close" to the manuscript, as the writer is, and is thus able to be far more objective in judging the manuscript and deciding what changes are needed. Truly professional writers cheerfully accept editing; it is usually the tyros who fight it, who think their words are precious gems, never to be altered. Perhaps that is because they regard editors as critics, intent on derogating their literary efforts. But professional writers have a more mature attitude and regard editors as helpers, improving their work. That attitude, that acceptance of the need to improve, and the efforts to improve show up in the writer's work. Those who resist being edited are resisting improvement, with predictable results!

Understanding the Editorial Functions

An editor's most useful and important function is probably to cut the author's verbiage. On the average, about one-third of most authors' verbiage can be slashed, with resulting improvement to the manuscript. Most authors overwrite, consciously or unconsciously padding their manuscripts with philosophical observations, asides, trivia, and numerous other miscellany that does not contribute to the product. The editor's duty is to bring the author back to directly addressing the objective.

Of course, editors do not know everything and sometimes make mistakes. They are well aware of that. That's why they don't always make the changes they suspect are necessary, but initiate queries, asking the author to have a second look at his or her words, answer a specific question, or approve/disapprove a specific suggested change. (I sometimes quarrel with my own editors, but they are most often correct, I must admit.) A good editor is a writer's alter ego and urges, cajoles, persuades, and nags the writer into making the changes that should be made.

Editorial functions, as practiced generally in industry, fall into two broad categories: One is the mechanical or technical area of spelling, grammar, punctuation, and other matters, where there are specific, firm rules, with few exceptions. The other is the more subtle area of meaning—logical argument, organization, rhetoric, imagery, flow, style, tone, and related areas. Here it is most difficult to judge one's own work, but it is also relatively difficult to judge another's work. This is also the more important area, bearing most directly on the effectiveness of the proposal and its ultimate success—or failure.

Discriminating Between
Rewriting and Revising

The terms *rewriting* and *revising* are used rather casually, but they are not totally interchangeable or ought not to be. The similarity and difference between the two terms is subtle, often much more one of degree than of kind. Revising implies an at least relatively extensive change, probably involving some major reorganization and possibly adding or replacing some material. Rewriting implies far lesser change, probably limited to simplifying sentences, searching out and eliminating ambiguities, and clarifying unclear statements. Polishing is a final stage of providing the most communicative rhetoric and purity of style, adding the final fillips to already carefully crafted text.

This is one place the computer and word processor make an enormous difference. With the capabilities for manipulating copy that is still in the form of magnetic bits on disks and illuminated phosphor on a CRT (cathode ray tube) screen (even if a hard copy—paper copy—exists), the writer may easily move sentences, paragraphs, pages, and even whole chapters about to reorganize and revise copy. (For example, my own computer and word processor enabled me recently to do about a 40 percent revision to a 300-page manuscript in five working days. That would have been unthinkable in pre–desktop computer days.)

But there is another side to this, for the computer and its wp (word processor) produce not only greater efficiency in writing; a wp, used properly, produces a better *quality* of writing. It enables those for whom writing is a chore to improve the quality of their writing.

They no longer need to ponder the old question of whether it is worthwhile to make the change. Before when writers believed re-phrasing would be of some help, they had to weigh whether there was time to retype one or more pages and whether the improvement was worth the time and effort to do so, especially when the change would involve retyping many pages. Writers often found it difficult to summon up compelling reasons to make the changes. (I have personally and not infrequently in the past discarded as much as

50 pages of typed copy to start again, so I do know the pain of doing so, even when I know, as a professional writer, that I must do so.) With a wp, one need not hesitate; most changes take minutes and involve relatively little effort, as compared with doing so under the classical conditions of typewritten copy.

Writers who work at the computer/word processor keyboard almost inevitably do much more self-editing, rewriting, revising, and polishing of their copy than those working longhand or at a typewriter keyboard. The result cannot be other than better writing. Writers who are still scribbling their words on lined, yellow pads, to be input by typists cum "word processor operators" (a practice that still prevails in many offices) lose a major set of benefits.

The Problem of Writer's Block

A classic writer's problem is "writer's block": The brain appears to have gone on vacation; the writer is mentally stuck, unable to get started with his or her exposition. It usually appears only at the beginning of the writing session. This affliction is apparently far more common and severe with those who are not professional writers, but professionals are certainly not immune to it. It affects and afflicts almost everyone who writes.

Most writers have their own favorite methods for curing writer's block, although they are not always very effective. Some go back and rewrite the previous few pages, some doodle idly, some stare out the window, and some just start writing anything at all as a method of pump-priming, kick-starting, or jump-starting the brain, shocking it into action.

Some writers have their own very special devices to cope with block. One writer I know of makes it a point to end the day's work in midsentence. His theory is that the mental effort to complete that sentence the next morning will warm up his brain and get it started for another day. Another starts her day by editing and revising her work of the prior day. (I have used this method on occasion and found it useful.) Others do housekeeping chores—sharpening pencils, cleaning typewriter keys, straightening their desks out. (This does not appear to work well, although it has the beneficial effect of getting one's desk and office straightened up a bit!)

Doodling idly with words to get the turgid thought processes flowing again is highly effective for many writers—it works well for me at times—but it is wasteful, especially when working at a typewriter. Most of what is generated in this phase is not directly useful or easily salvaged; it must be discarded. Writers who word-doodle at their typewriters fill up their wastebaskets with such material.

With computers and wp, the situation is different: It is relatively easy to sort things out, discarding the doodles and salvaging the useful words. What is not used is dumped in the "bit bucket," where it is lost forever and does not contribute to the trash overload that afflicts the world today.

For me, at least, one of the major benefits of the word processor is that I do far more revising and rewriting than previously. There is never a question of whether it is worthwhile, and I believe the quality of my writing has improved as a result.

More Pointed Discussion

To produce quality writing, the rewriting or revising must be highly disciplined and directed to certain objectives, both on general principles and as the result of editing, by the writer or by another. Editing should address questions and formulate answers that will translate directly into the objectives to be pursued via rewriting or revising. Here is a list of some of those questions, followed by discussions:

1. Organization. Is the presentation of information logical (that is, progressing in an orderly manner and consistent pattern)?
2. Flow. Does the information flow smoothly, with proper transitions (leads or introductions to each new subject, bridging the gap from a discussion just concluded)?
3. Sentence structure. Are the sentences straightforward— not unnecessarily complex or awkward—and with clear

communication (that is, do they make positive and specific statements)?

4. Rhetoric. Are the words used properly (that is, the most suitable ones for the thought intended)? Are they the most expressive or most accurate ones possible? Are they spelled correctly?

5. Grammar and punctuation. Does the use of the language and the punctuation follow the accepted principles? More important, does it facilitate clear and accurate exposition?

6. Clarity. Ambiguity, although not intended, is a major problem in writing. Its avoidance, detection, and correction should be objectives of writing and editing.

7. Readability. In general, is the text easily read and understood by an average educated individual?

Organization

A presentation can be organized in many different ways—chronological or order of importance, ascending or descending; from the general to the particular or the reverse; or even in other ways. You judge for yourself which organization is most suitable for your presentation. But even more important than choosing the most appropriate organization is using it consistently. Occasionally, a writer mixes different kinds of organization without somehow signaling the reader about the change, thereby bringing about profound confusion.

The need for a change in method of organization may be legitimate (that is, both necessary and unavoidable). But it is never permissible to make such a change abruptly and without warning. For example, if you have been using an order of importance for your presentation and you find a need to shift abruptly to another mode— perhaps chronological—you should first alert the reader to the fact that there is to be a change with words such as "on the other hand" or "however." Then go on to explain the change with an introductory statement. You might say, for example, "However, the forerunner of the Zanzibar security system first appeared some 12 years earlier," if you wish to digress from an order-of-importance organization to shift momentarily to a chronological one.

Sometimes when you get deep into a presentation, you find it is not working well. Even though you thought the matter out carefully and prepared a detailed outline, somehow you begin to run into problems you did not anticipate; the organization you chose does not fit the presentation strategy you decided to use. Obviously, you must make serious changes. This is where computers and word processors are so useful. Instead of discarding many pages of manuscript, you can completely reorganize your presentation without losing much material or time rather than continue with a force fit that does not fit very well.

In short, working with modern systems and being completely at home in their use, you can afford to be totally objective and unemotional about making drastic changes when it is necessary. (Again, a difference between professional writers and others is that they know they must not fall incurably in love with their own words. They must have the discipline to slash away at even a good piece of writing if it is misplaced or not suitable for the need of the moment.)

Flow

The flow of a presentation is a more subtle matter, although it is directly related to organization (the flow can never be smooth if the organization is not logical, orderly, and consistent). But even given that, writing by those who are not professional writers is often ragged because of other factors, of which the principal one is a lack of suitable and appropriate transitions or bridges. Despite the efforts of many of us to resist it, our minds tend to flow in logical patterns, and we thus tend, consciously or unconsciously, to expect information to be presented to us in a manner that flows smoothly along a single train of thought—a unifying theme. The failure to bridge logically from one subject to another, when it is necessary to conclude the discussion of one subject and go on to another, is an abrupt interruption of the train of thought, an aberration, a departure from the theme. Consider, for example, the effect of such an abrupt and unwarranted change in the following two paragraphs:

> The fact is that there are many ways to succeed as a free-lance writer. There are even more ways to succeed than to fail. Most of us do not need instructions in failing! But most of us do need instructions in succeeding.
>
> Although writing is an easy and pleasant way to earn a living for those who have become "names," a recent study revealed that by far the majority of free-lance writers work at their writing only part-time and earn little money at it. That much is well-documented and undisputed fact.

Both paragraphs address the same subject generally, free-lance writing and the financial rewards—or lack of them—available to writers. But the bridge between the thoughts is missing, and the argument is thus badly flawed. The first paragraph leads us to believe we are about to learn how to succeed as free-lance writers. But the next line lets us down and leaves us a bit puzzled. That free-lance writing is an easy and pleasant way to make a living for the "name" writer may or may not be true, but it is not relevant here.

This writer has not explained himself or herself very well. But a few changes to the text may provide a better idea of what the writer meant to say:

> The fact is that there are many ways to succeed as a free-lance writer. There are even more ways to succeed than to fail. Most of us do not need instructions in failing! But most of us do need instructions in succeeding.
>
> One clear bit of evidence of that need is the documented and undisputed fact that most free-lance writers do not make much money, although writing is an easy and pleasant way to earn a living for those who have become "names." But it is not necessary to be celebrated to sell your writing.

The second example illustrates how easily two ideas may be joined to amalgamate them as portions of a mutual theme to achieve the unity that is a necessary aspect of all writing.

Sentence Structure

Sentence structure, like other mechanics of usage, is one of the most basic elements of writing, and yet many have problems in constructing simple sentences—and I emphasize *simple* sentences, for many are better at constructing complex sentences than simple ones.

Actually, the use of complex sentences is not antithetical to the principles of good writing. It is easily possible to create complex sentences that are clear and easily understandable, as it is possible to construct simple sentences that are vague and difficult to fathom. "Complex" and "simple" refer only to the mechanical structure of the sentence, and not to its content. In fact, do not look to my writing for examples of simple sentences, for I am given to writing complex ones with appositives and clauses, but with clear objectives and messages. Unity of thought and clarity of expression are the essence of writing, even if used in structurally complex sentences.

This is a "simple" sentence: You should not rely on the ESCAPE key because use of it subtracts from the main memory available for XYZ-File. This is a "complex" sentence: You should not rely on the ESCAPE key to retreat from errors you make because each use of that key uses a portion of main memory, leaving less memory available to you for the execution of important functions of XYZ-File.

Rhetoric

Rhetoric is partly mechanical—using words correctly—and partly artistic—finding the most appropriate or most eloquent word to use. It involves the mechanical matter of absolute definition—*denotation*—and the more judgmental and artistic matter of nuance or inferred meaning—*connotation*. It involves the difference between using *determined* and using *stubborn* to describe something. But it is not even that simple, for it also involves judging the word to use in the context because *determined* and *stubborn,* as well as their several synonyms, have different connotations in different contexts.

Rhetoric also involves an understanding and judicious use of idioms. And there, too, judgment is involved because many idioms have different meanings for different individuals. In fact, not even the understanding of what constitutes an idiom is universal. To those interested in the development of humankind and other life on earth, the notion of changes in physical characteristics *caused* by environmental changes is a scientific or technical idiom, for example. The layperson may interpret that idea as literal truth, but the student of that science understands it really means that changes in environmental conditions determined what mutations contributed to survival and thus were perpetuated. So the long-term, introspective impression or view may be summarized—idiomatically—as a change in species caused by a change in environment. This points up the need to understand your reader, to have a good view of who and what your reader is.

Grammar and Punctuation

The so-called rules of grammar and punctuation are not rules at all; they are principles. Those reported as rules in even the best textbooks simply reflect what the authorities on the subject believe are good practices. There are even two schools of thought about punctuation: "open punctuation" and "closed punctuation." Those of us who went to school a long time ago tend to install commas and other pauses and stops in our copy quite freely, setting off clauses and phrases cavalierly, whereas younger graduates of our system tend to be more sparing of those symbols, using them only on the basis of perceived need and not to conform to any old-fashioned rules.

In addition, everything changes. Where the split infinitive was once almost a hanging offense, today it is grudgingly accepted, when "necessary." Even the once reprehensible practice of ending a sentence with a preposition is now tolerated occasionally, although not gladly. And during my own lifetime, I have seen many English spellings (for example, "colour" and "humour") vanish from our dictionaries.

Far more important than anyone's rules or principles are precision and clarity—communicating your meaning and your nuances accurately—so your reader *feels,* as well as understands, your message. Try to understand the principles and philosophy underlying the guidelines offered in style manuals, for it is popular and accepted usage, far more than scholarly and pedantic opinion, that is responsible for the state of the language.

Clarity

Ambiguity of meaning, although not intended, is a common problem in writing. It may be the consequence of unclear thinking—writers who were really not quite sure what they meant to say. It may stem from careless use of grammar and punctuation. Or it may be the consequence of other malfunctions. A misplaced comma in legislation covering the importation of certain plants cost the U.S. government a great deal of money by exempting banana plants, which was not the intent of the statute. Carelessness in language leads to many contractual disputes and legal actions and can lead to the loss of a contract that could have been otherwise won.

In reviewing and editing your first draft, ask yourself: Is the meaning absolutely clear here? Can this reasonably be interpreted in more than one way? (If it can be, it will be!) If you can answer "yes" to any such questions, you have a clear signal: Rewrite the passage and work at making its meaning as unambiguous as possible. Make it more difficult to misunderstand it than to understand it.

Readability

Most people assume that people read at the grade level they achieved in their formal education (for example, that a high school graduate reads at the twelfth-grade level). In fact, even most better educated individuals cannot easily understand text rated at the twelfth-grade readability level. You may be surprised to learn the grade-level ratings of the text in several popular periodicals, at least one of which is aimed at and read by well-educated executives and professionals:

Publication	Rated Reading Level
National Enquirer	Sixth grade
People	Seventh grade
Reader's Digest	Ninth grade
Wall Street Journal	Eleventh grade

Readability is a subject well suited for computer application. Several computer enthusiasts have attacked it and produced computer programs that attempt to measure the readability of writing samples.

Many problems militate against achieving accuracy in measuring readability; it is not a characteristic or function that lends itself easily to precise measurement. At their heart, all readability measuring systems are based on the complexity and length of sentences and words, with some also taking into account whether the words have familiar referents. But there are at least some formulas to enable a program to identify syllables, words, and sentences as such, at least approximately, and their accuracy is in some proportion to the size of the sample measured. (Small samples generally offer a lesser degree of accuracy than lengthier samples.)

But readability, as a measure, has little or no relation to the *quality* of the writing—to its validity, accuracy, adequacy, appropriateness, fluency, smoothness of expression, or any other factor normally considered an element contributing to "good" or "poor" writing. Nor does it necessarily have anything to do with whether the writing is interesting or dull. Even bad writing, writing that is tedious and dull, can be highly readable, in a technical sense. And some excellent writing, even classics of our literature, would score poorly on readability. Readability is a measure only of how easy or how difficult it is to *understand* the author's words and sentences, and the common standard of reference is grade level, although the method developed by Dr. Rudolf Flesch utilizes a scale of numbers that do not themselves identify the estimated grade level. For example, one sample measured as 6.6 (between sixth and seventh grades) in one system is graded 70 by another system, using the Flesch method. In another case, using the same systems, a sample is measured as a 6.6 by the first program, but the second program reports a Flesch number 57 for that sample.

In general, readability above the high school or college freshman levels is considered higher than it needs to be for popular consumption, even by executives and professionals. Ideally, many experts agree, most writing for general consumption should be at seventh- to eighth-grade levels.

Overall, readability measures are based on average sentence and word length. This ignores other factors, such as the reader's prior knowledge of the subject, organization, use of tables and illustrations, number of concepts presented, complexity or simplicity of sentence structure, rhetoric, and other factors. It is still an inexact science. Yet it does give us at least a rough standard for measurement, a first requirement for automation, and it has been automated via computer software.

This has a double benefit: There is the direct benefit of improving the writing being measured and revised. And there is the added—and perhaps greater—benefit of creating a consciousness of readability and influencing those who write proposals to develop a simpler style. (Ironically, perhaps, a simple style is almost invariably more forceful and more effective generally than a complex one.)

Putting Theory (and Proposal Writers) to Work

In far too many offices, the computer and word processor are the exclusive domain of the typist, now known as a *word processor operator* and paid as a specialist, and no one except that now exalted typist and the seller of the hardware and the software have benefited or are benefiting. You, as the party responsible for the proposal, gain none of the benefits under this system, where the writer still scrawls his or her prose on lined yellow paper and hands it over to the word processor operator to be turned into magnetic hieroglyphics on disks and printed text on paper.

Most benefits of the systems and resources described materialize only when the proposal writers are fully trained in using computers and word processors and are seated at keyboards, writing words and drawing sketches that appear on the screen and calling up stored materials to be pasted up (electronically, that is), adapted, modified, cited, or otherwise put to work. None of these benefits accrue until the proposal writer is seated at the console (keyboard) writing first drafts, reviewing and revising the drafts, and putting the computer/ word processor magic—for it is magic—to work.

Problems and Hazards

There is one significant difference between writing a small proposal, composed entirely by a single individual, and writing a large proposal, employing more than one writer. That is, there are some potential problems and hazards in having a staff of writers working independently, each at his or her own computer. First, there is the difficulty in coordinating and managing the efforts of several people—*many* people, in some cases—under the pressure that is typical of proposal writing. There is an anomaly in this situation immediately: Overall, the effort is a joint one of several people nominally participating in a cooperative program and yet working alone, for writing is essentially a lonesome task. Some of the problems that arise from this are typical. For those attempting to manage their first proposal, reviewing the copy submitted by a half-dozen or more proposal writers as their first drafts is eye-opening and shocking. The copy developed by a number of writers almost always falls into three general classes: Some writers produce reams of copy, far in excess of need and requiring heavy editing. Some produce far too little copy, totally unsuited to the need. And some, blessedly, produce copy that is acceptable at least as a first draft.

Of course, there are marked differences in styles and, far too often, in understandings of the requirements and objectives of the proposal. There are also hazards in generating revisions as second, third, and sometimes even more drafts. But because of the multiplicity of writers and the varying characteristics of and problems with the copy of each, some copy goes into third and fourth drafts, while other copy is acceptable and becomes final in its second, perhaps even its first, draft version. Before long, unless firm controls are in place and in use, it becomes difficult to know what has been edited, what has been revised, what is to be revised, and what is final copy! In one case I can recall, in which I was attempting to manage the first proposal we had ever done with the aid of computers and word processors, I found myself constantly reading familiar words, only to discover I was reading a long-discarded and superseded earlier draft.

All proposal efforts employing a staff of writers (quite often they are not truly "a staff of writers," but executives, professionals, and others assigned to find or make time to write their proposal contributions between their regular chores) require careful, firm, and directly involved management. Proposals written with the aid of computers require even more such management, and the subject merits a chapter of its own. But a few words about hardware and software needs for writing with a computer are in order first.

Software and Hardware for Word Processing

A word processor is software, not hardware, and there are many available. Unfortunately, computer users tend to treat word processors almost as they treat their political and religious preferences: Many develop fierce loyalties to and firmly resist abandoning their favorite programs.

WordStar was one of the wp pioneers and was for some years by far the most popular and the best seller. Many of us found what was the current version (edition) of WordStar packaged with our first computers. But MicroPro International Corporation, publishers of

WordStar, evidently became complacent, failed to make serious improvements in its main product as the technology advanced, and eventually lost its first-place position to WordPerfect. Later, WordStar finally began to install the improvements in the later versions of the program, but as of this writing, WordPerfect continues to be the favorite. Even today, with the latest WordStar versions offering all or nearly all the advanced features found in other major word processors, the complaint is still heard that WordStar is slow compared with many of its rivals.

Word, a wp published by Microsoft Corporation, is also a major contender in the field, as is Wang, a computer manufacturer publishing its own word processor and prominent in the office market.

XyWrite is in a class of its own. Where most other word processors employ embedded commands, so the files created can be read only by that word processor unless converted, XyWrite produces pure Ascii files, which can be read directly by any word processor or the DOS TYPE command. XyWrite is beloved of many writers and especially enjoys favor in publishing offices.

An array of pros and cons can be established for every word processor. My personal choice is WordStar, and I am using the latest version available at this time. I have tried others, but I am still most comfortable with WordStar. Perhaps that is because I know WordStar, after using it for years, and resist learning another.

These are the features available today in one wp or another, although you probably will not find all of them in any given word processor. Some are inherent in the word processor per se; others are autonomous or semi-autonomous programs that are packaged with the wp and are entirely compatible with it. You may wish to use this as a checklist, if you are shopping for a word processor and want help making comparisons. (Those marked with an asterisk are features I consider especially useful and important, at least for proposal writing.)

Speed: This varies a lot. XyWrite, for example, executes commands much faster than most word processors.

* "WYSIWYG": This acronym (pronounced whiz-ee-wig) stands for "what you see is what you get." It is a characteristic that presents on the screen precisely what your hard copy— printed output—will look like. (It is also known, more formally, as "Page Preview.") I find it a most useful and frequently used feature.

* Searching: Most word processors have a feature that enables you to search the file to find a given term or every occurrence of the term. This feature also enables you to delete or change that term each time it appears.

* Spelling checker: It is a rare word processor that does not have a built-in spelling checker, but spelling checkers vary widely in size, speed, and capability. It is a most important feature, one you will use constantly, and it is wise to check this out when buying a wp.

* Indexing: This is a useful feature for proposal work, especially if you are engaged in developing a major proposal. Indexing is a tedious job, and computer aid in doing it is most welcome.

* Table of contents: Many word processors include a subprogram to help you prepare the table of contents. Like indexing, this is a tedious job, and the help is welcome.

* Footnotes and bibliographies: Many word processors include the capability for developing footnotes and bibliographic notes, which are in the same category of usefulness as the indexing and table of contents capabilities.

* Graphics: The newer versions of word processors have been emerging with at least some graphics capabilities for drawing lines, boxes, charts, and otherwise using the "extended character set" to present mathematical symbols and equations, foreign words, diacritical symbols, and other special marks.

Windows: "Windowing," the capability to present two files at the same time on the screen, is another relatively recent development in word processing. Usually, the windowing feature permits transferring or copying material between files via the windows. However, this is not to be confused with a popular program—even more than a program, but almost an independent system—known as "Windows," which carries the basic idea a great deal further and has changed the way many people use their computers.

Outliner or idea processor: Many word processors include a program for outlining and/or aid in developing your ideas. Most of these follow the same general strategy or pattern because they are largely free-form programs.

Pulldown menus: Most modern word processors offer menus, usually of the pulldown (available when requested) variety as helpful reminders or reference when the user is unsure of a command or a procedure.

Training: Many word processors include tutor programs to help the new user learn the program.

* DOS shell: Most modern word processors permit "shelling" to the command line—DOS, in the case of IBM and IBM clones—without exiting the current file. This is a most useful feature too.

* Macros: This is a key-redefining feature, similar to that function made famous by SmartKey and other pioneering key rede-finers. They are great time-savers and are most useful if you are not already using a separate program for that purpose.

* Miscellaneous: Many word processors include other features, such as general utility programs that facilitate copying, delet-ing, searching across all the files ("global" search), creating menus, and performing other chores for you.

These features are implemented differently in each word pro-cessor, and that can make an important difference to you, as the user. Check on the speed of operation, the difficulty or ease of using, and the convenience of each of the important features.

CHAPTER 11

Writing with a dbm

*Despite the wide popularity and usage of data
base management software—and "data base"
and "data base management" have long been
among the most widely used terms in connection
with computers—the importance of the direct
application of dbm software to proposal
writing has long been overlooked.*

Exploiting dbm Capabilities

We normally think of wp—word processing and the word processor—as the principal tool for writing with a computer, despite the growing influence and capabilities of desktop publishing software. We think of data base managers—dbm software—as tools for more mundane business uses, such as compiling mailing lists, managing inventory, sending out form letters, and other such activity. That is a mistaken notion or at least an underestimate of the power of dbm software in what it can contribute to proposal writing.

Consider, first of all, what a data base is: a body of information, related in some manner. It may be a list of customers. But it may be a list of customers, prospects, vendors, and others, the only common factor or relationship being that all are names and addresses you wish to keep on record. It may, in fact, be all the information you keep in all your files, even if it is not likely that you would lump all your disparate data into one base. Still, you can, and the reason you can do so on a practicable basis is the data base manager software! That means it is time to take a casual look to see what dbm software really is and does.

A dbm program permits you to handle all that information effectively, no matter whether you dump it all into one data base or separate it into many. It is software that provides a tool for handling data—indexing, classifying, sorting, organizing, and reorganizing it so you can retrieve all or specified portions of the entire base, according to how you have indexed it. For example, if you have lumped all names, addresses, and telephone numbers into one massive file (although you would more likely have set up several different files), but have coded the entries properly, the software can search out any single name or set of names you wish. It can, for example, retrieve all customers' names, all names of customers living within a specific range of zip codes, all prospective customers, all vendors of printing services, or any other set—if you have coded the entries with a clear vision of how you might wish to retrieve the information later.

A great deal of writing in general and proposal writing in particular depends on one or more sources for and compilations of raw data—of data bases, that is. The collection, management, and use of such data is a permanent or semipermanent resource to support proposal writing generally. But there is more to it than that, for proposal writing is not writing in the ordinary sense of a narrative that progresses from a beginning to an end. Effective proposal writing involves not only the compilation, organization, and narrative presentation of information, but also the use of the same raw information more than once, often several times, reorganized and reformatted to convey other messages. That is one aspect of proposal writing in which data base management may assume great importance, much more so than anyone appears to have recognized before now. But it is necessary to look first at some basic facts regarding dbm software and discuss the nature of this genre of computer software. However, before doing that, it is necessary to establish one more premise for the discussions.

There are two basic kinds of data base managers, *relational* and *flat file*. The relational dbm is by far the more sophisticated. It derives its name from the fact that the relational dbm permits the user to draw data from several files at the same time and work with establishing relations among data in two or more files. The flat file dbm permits the user to have only one file open at a time—to draw data from only one file at a time.

Which you need depends on the amount and complexity of the data you will use, as well as on the kinds of use you require. For use in proposal writing, a good flat file dbm is probably adequate. Certainly, it is simpler to use, and that alone is a good argument for it if you do not truly need the more complex relational dbm. I discuss dbm usage in proposal writing with reference to a flat file type of dbm.

The "Secret" of Effective dbm Use

In the early days of computers, long before the desktop computer appeared on the scene, there was not very much software available off the shelf. Almost all programs were written to order by programmers, some on the staff of the organization, some working under contract. One major difficulty was that the lay user and the programmer technician did not speak the same language. The customer who wanted a payroll program written, for example, usually knew little of computers, programming, or what could be done with a computer and so did not know what to ask for. He or she relied on the programmer, often a consultant, for advice—even left the decision making to the computer applications expert. Unfortunately, the programmer, who knew all about computers and programming, may or may not have known anything about payroll records or business needs in general and certainly did not know much about the client's specific needs in the payroll-records area. So each operated in ignorance of at least one-half of the situation. That is why so many of the programs were far from what the client should and could have had and why so many programs were revised to improve them or even abandoned and replaced.

Modern software has changed that to a large extent, putting much more control into the hands of the user in many ways, an outstanding one of which is as in the case of the dbm. If there is any secret to the effective use of dbm software, it is in the advance planning, in your own *design* of your own applications. Remember, the purpose of dbm is to enable you, the user, to organize your data in whatever ways are most useful and convenient for you, and it is unlikely that anyone can design a single system equally useful to everyone, for no one knows your needs as well as you. Therefore, the design of the dbm software by the publisher is primarily one that provides a set of *capabilities for you,* rather than furnishing forms or formats for products (although the software publisher may furnish models—sample files—suggesting possible forms and formats). In fact, the publisher of the dbm software really provides a kind of shell, with a set of capabilities; and *you,* the user, develop the program, using those capabilities. Program usefulness therefore largely depends on your ability to foresee your own needs and plan efficiently and effectively for satisfying them through the use of the tools placed in your hands. It is now no longer a job for the computer programmer or software publisher; it is a job for the executive, the office systems manager, the office systems planner, or whoever designs your systems and decides what your needs—your *anticipated* needs—are.

Those observations about your perception of your needs and your planning the means for satisfying them sum up the key to effective design: You should design all systems from the viewpoints of the users and their needs—their *expected* needs—not the viewpoint of the creators. To look more closely at this, let's take first the simple case of compiling a data base as a mailing list.

The software will ask you first to name or identify a data base. Because you do not yet have any data bases—this is your first—you will come up with a short name that you can recall and is a *mnemonic*—memory triggering—name. Let's therefore call this first file "ML," for *mailing list.*

You will be asked to design your fields. (Each item or entry assigned a label of its own is a field.) I chose to design my own mailing list, using the following set of fields:

Name _____

Company _____

Address _____

Address _____

City, St, Zip _____

Tel _____

Notes1 _____

Notes2 _____

That means I cannot search the list by last name, by state, or by zip code. I can search by first name or initial, by company name, by city, by telephone number, or by Notes1 or Notes2. That is, I can search only by the beginning items in one of the fields.

That suits my needs because my mailing list is small, and I know the first names or company names of everyone on it. I can call up all the Davids or Susans on the list and select the right one. But suppose my list were long—had thousands of names. I would have too many Davids and Susans for convenience, with resulting difficulty in finding any particular one. I would probably want to be able to search by last names. To do that, I would have to set my first fields this way:

Last name _____

First name _____

Or suppose I wanted to be able to mail selectively by geographic regions—by city, state, or zip code. I can accomplish that by setting up the address fields this way:

City _____

State _____

Zip code _____

If I needed to use demographic data in my searches, I would set up appropriate fields for age, occupation, income, and so forth so I could sort out a list of engineers, retired individuals, high- or low-income residents, home owners, renters, apartment dwellers, or others by any parameter or combination of parameters for which I had fields and, of course, data to put in the fields. Actually, it can get a bit more sophisticated than that, having more than one field on a line and providing sorts at more than one level, thus:

Street address _____

City _____ State _____ Zip _____

That makes the physical layout more efficient, but the net effect is the same. The simpler example suffices to illustrate the main point: You must anticipate your demands and usage in advance if you are to design the system to serve you well.

For example, there are the matters of checklists and the spinoff products of the checklist, the functional flowchart and the response matrix, at the minimum. With the "manual" methods of writing longhand and with typewriters, there was a great deal of labor involved in all the manipulations, building tables and matrices, and using the raw data over and over, in other formats and other applications. But with a computer and a good dbm, you can have the computer do much of this kind of work for you if you prepare the ground by first compiling the checklist as a data base file, structuring it so it is readily adaptable for use in those other functions—by looking at how you will want to use the information.

You do this by designing, at least in draft form, your planned needs and applications, in addition to providing as much flexibility to the dbm file as you can. For example, you know you will wish to include at least these items in your response matrix:

Identification of each RFP/SOW requirement (for example, section/page/paragraph number)

Summary of requirement

Remarks

Summary/identification of proposal response

You know also that the functional flowchart you will want will include major phases and functions of the program, at least as far as you can identify, extrapolate, or project and predict them from a study of the RFP and SOW. With this in mind, you can construct the data base file, which you name and identify by the RFP number or any code you wish to use:

RFP section _____ Page _____ Par. _____

Prop. req. _____ Proj. req. _____ Qual. req. _____

Major phase _____

Function _____

Worry item _____

Summary1 _____

Summary2 _____

Prop. sec. _____ Page _____ Par. _____

Summary1 _____

Summary2 _____

This record is divided into two fields: the requirement listed in the solicitation and the response offered in the proposal. There is a record for each requirement found in the solicitation. You set up the file and fill in the first section while studying the solicitation, and you complete each record as you develop the proposal. You can then actually print out the response matrix later as a report printout. But first you will wish to print out the initial entries as the checklist of items that must be responded to in the proposal, as well as the section of the proposal that should contain the response. You may not be able to fill in all of the second set of fields in this record until you have begun to write the proposal, although there are at least three phases of the proposal effort during which you will be able to make at least tentative entries:

1. During early study of the RFP
2. During the meetings, conferences, and/or brainstorming sessions
3. While writing the proposal

Of course, you can always fill in your estimates and update or correct them later, as more information accumulates. For example, you may decide you will be best able to present some required evidence of qualification in the chapter or section on company experience but find that you can also support this need in the discussions of approach. You may therefore add that later.

On the other hand, you know in which section your resumes will go, although you do not yet know the page numbers. So you can at least fill in part of that field and complete it later.

The worry item field is very important. The search for "worry items"—special concerns of the client—in connection with developing effective capture strategies begins early in the project, and finding such items or items that are potentially worry items should be a specific objective in this and other phases of the effort. Note here anything that appears to be useful in this regard. Again, this demonstrates rather clearly the usefulness of a data base in supporting many areas of the proposal, if the data base content and structure are planned carefully.

Using the dbm to support development of the functional flowchart is more difficult. The file structure provides a means to note and summarize any major phases and/or functions of work you can identify, even tentatively, when you decide that some item represents such a milestone as a major phase or function—that is, not every record in your file will have entries for those two fields.

There is an alternative: You can eliminate those two fields in this record and set them up independently in a file all their own, perhaps along the following lines, calling the file by a suitable name:

Phase _____

Function _____

Task _____

Subtask _____

The advantage of this latter alternative is that it provides a data base with another application. The identification of tasks and subtasks, as well as of phases and functions, supports both the functional flowchart and the labor-loading chart that should be a key exhibit in the proposal section that presents the specific proposed plan of action and commitments (see Figures 8–5 and 8–8). But you could also add a worry item field to this record and use this added opportunity to search out a strategy; studying the phases and other items to be listed here as fields may alert you to opportunities you had not seen earlier to develop effective win strategies.

The philosophy is applicable to all areas. Consider, for example, the record of current and previous projects relevant to the one being proposed. Let's look at how we might structure the record to build a data base file of this. The file name might be "PROJECTS," a good mnemonic title. And the fields might be along the lines shown here, with enough fields to give you the flexibility to print it out in almost any format suitable for your needs.

Description _____

Size of project _____

Title _____

Client _____

Contact/reference _____

Budget _____ Total end cost _____

Schedule _____ Finish date _____

Remarks1 _____

Remarks2 _____

As in the case of other files, you can have your dbm program prepare this part of your proposal by simply coding the entries and designing the report suitably. However, even if you do not have a field that is just right for your report, you can go through your file, select the items you want, place a special mark at the beginning of one of the fields, and print out just those you have so marked. Or you can add a field labeled "Special" or some other such name, which you can use for coding special reports. The flexibility of a dbm means far less work and far less time required for the job than any other method you might employ.

Importing dbm Files to wp

Although you can design and print out a variety of reports directly from your dbm file, it is far more convenient to have all the material in your word processor files. In most cases, it is easy to "print to disk." A simple command to do so sends the report to a disk file you name. That can be a wp file, and you can then manipulate, edit, rewrite, or otherwise process the report to add it to or integrate it with other material in your growing proposal manuscript. This takes advantage of the power of the dbm to manipulate the information for you, whereas it would be awkward drudgery to do many of the manipulations in a word processor.

An Idea Bank of Titles, Headlines, and Captions

One important principle is that of using titles, headlines, and captions frequently and writing them so they make specific statements rather than vague or general allusions. "Understanding the Requirement" is more specific and thus better than "The Requirement" or "About the Requirement," but "Understanding the True Need" is far better than any of those because it is not only more specific, but it says something important to the reader, conveying an attention-commanding *message*. Most important, it is a *selling* message; it compels the reader to pay attention and read carefully.

One other attribute of the suggested headline is that it alludes directly to a worry item or, at least, an item about which the client should be worried if, in your opinion, the SOW masks the true need.

Writing such headlines is not always easy. In fact, headline writing is something of a special skill or art, and some writers become quite good at it. Others always find the right headline elusive and spend a great deal of time trying to find it.

Headlines are usually written after the fact, that is, after the text has been written and it appears that (1) there are not enough headlines guiding the reader's thoughts and understanding and (2) the headlines and captions that have been used are rather ineffectual and weak, the typically vague "Introduction" and the like. This is a subject for a swipe file, a bank of powerful headlines and captions. When good ones occur and appear broad enough to fit more than one case, as "The True Need" would, they should go into a dbm file for retrieval on another occasion to help write another powerful proposal.

Of course, the titles, headlines, and captions you use must be exactly right for the proposal in which you use them, and the ones you have stored are often close, but not right for the use. However, having a file of good models to help you is a great asset as an idea bank, from which you can select good candidates and modify them to fit the exact need. With good models to emulate, the task is much easier.

Powerful headlines and the ideas upon which they are based may themselves provide you a basis for effective strategies. For example, that one mentioned earlier, "Understanding the True Need," bears within it the seeds of a possible strategy. Certainly, if it has not occurred to you before, scanning a headline such as that in your data base files of reports should cause you to consider the question of whether the client understands the true problem or need and, if not, just how serious that failure is and how much capital you might be able to get out of it.

The chief difficulty is classifying headlines and captions for sorting and retrieving the most appropriate ones, for once the data bank is begun, it will soon grow large enough to require some kind of indexing scheme to be useful. Again, the judicious choice of fields for sorting is the key to success in this. Among the possible ways to key the list (that is, characterize the items) are the following. (There are, of course, many other possibilities.) First the suggested field appears, and following it, indented, are a few of the possible entries.

Chapter/section titles
    Chapter I: Introduction
    Chapter II: Discussion

Chapter III: Proposed Program
Chapter IV: Company Qualifications
Executive Summary
Subject matter
Technical discussion
Understanding of requirement
Introduction
Approach
Management
Project organization
Resources offered

Many items will fit in more than one field and should be indexed so they can be retrieved suitably. "Technical discussion," for example, might be a title or headline for a chapter, paragraph, or discussion and so should be retrieved under any of those categories. Retrieval has more than one meaning. It can refer to the individual record appearing on the screen for observation or editing, but it can also mean being made part of a report that may be directed to appear on the screen, be printed out, or be printed to disk. The latter means the report can appear as a separate file or be added to some file, perhaps in your word processor and directly in the proposal file.

The same philosophy should be applied to a storehouse of titles and captions for figures and tables. Many of the figures and tables are virtually mandatory, or at least useful for and used in virtually all proposals, including the following examples:

Functional flowcharts
Organization charts
Milestone charts
Delivery schedules
Labor-loading tables
Tables of current and past projects
Resource lists

Financial data

Response matrices

PERT and CPM charts

Equipment lists

These are all merely beginning ideas, and they should seed your imagination and provoke a spinoff of many other, better ideas. One more file in your idea bank is a file of ideas for strategies. Strategies have been mentioned frequently throughout the earlier chapters and discussed in some depth in Chapter 2, where I pointed out that there are several kinds of proposal strategies, including technical or program (design) strategy, cost strategy, competitor strategy, presentation strategy, and win or capture strategy, which is usually a combination of the several strategies but focuses primarily on one, most often technical or cost. But there are several approaches to each kind of strategy. For example, a winning cost strategy does not necessarily mean offering the lowest cost! It may mean a strategic method of presenting or explaining the costs. Suppose your cost discussion begins with a title such as "Understanding the True Costs of the Program," and the discussion goes on to demonstrate why your cost quotation is actually the lowest cost, although it may not quote the smallest number of dollars.

The same principle applies to all other kinds of strategy. Although a given successful strategy may not ever be directly suitable for another proposal, awareness of it may trigger another successful strategic idea. Certainly, as in the case of titles and headlines, studying good models helps get the creative juices flowing more freely than a cold start does! And so a file of strategic ideas is also a valuable idea bank.

Indexing strategic ideas is much the same as indexing headlines and captions. Some starter ideas for the fields and possible entries in the fields are offered here. Note that there are possible tie-ins such that some items should appear in more than one retrieval. For example, a method for cutting costs should be considered for both the cost strategy and technical or program design strategy discussions.

Presentation
  Cover
  Color
  Formats
  Exhibits
Competitor
  Exclusivity of ideas
  Proprietary claims
  Special skills/experience/resources
Cost
  True costs
  Low costs
  Total cost of ownership
  Cost options
Technical/program design
  Greater efficiency
  True need or problem
  Innovative approach/ideas
  Conservative/low-risk approach
  Time-saving approach
  Cost-saving approach

Boilerplate, Swipe Files, and the Computer Library

In proposal writing, as in many things, the first one you write is usually the most difficult; it does get at least a little easier as you gather experience in all the skills and problem solving required. However, something more than accumulating experience contributes to reducing the difficulty—and reduces the labor, as well—if you start building that other important resource: materials you can use again and again. Two items, swipe files and boilerplate, are especially important. They are first cousins and important elements of the proposal library. The distinction between *boilerplate* and *swipe files* is relatively fine. The terms are virtually interchangeable, but I find it useful to make this distinction: Boilerplate material may be used over and over without change—charts and descriptions of your organization and its facilities, formal reports, and some other kinds of material. Swipe files are files of material that are easily adaptable to each new application, raw material that can be molded again and again to meet a new need.

Resumes in Swipe Files

Those items many refer to as boilerplate actually include some material that qualifies as swipe files. One item often carried as boilerplate about your own organization, for example, is the file of staff resumes. But resumes do change in more than one respect:

1. As the individual's experience accumulates, his or her resume needs to be updated to reflect added experience and accomplishments.

2. Each project requires staff members with specific qualifications. Most individuals have many kinds of experience and achievements after a few years in the working world. It is difficult—impossible, in most cases—to create a resume for an individual that is optimally well suited to each proposal, so it is necessary to revise one's resume for each new need.

3. Each resume should include the individual's regular position and title in the organization and the position and title he or she will have in the proposed program. The latter position/ title obviously will change with each new project, and the former usually changes from time to time in one's career, even a career spent in a single organization.

The most effective method is to keep a fully detailed resume of each individual in the computer data bank and draw on it to customize a suitable resume for each proposal requirement, adding each new resume to the bank. In that manner, it becomes easier and easier to find the resume model that is most appropriate and, hence, easiest to adapt to the new need.

To further this system, a flexible resume format should be designed. Figure 11–1 suggests a model. The suggested format is highly flexible, allowing you to select and copy or adapt the most appropriate paragraphs or write new ones, as each application requires. And you can, of course, easily change the titles and position descriptions that are part of the head data of the form. (An additional benefit is that this ensures a consistent and uniform resume format.)

Facility and Resources Descriptions

Descriptions of your physical facility and resources do not change often, unless your organization is in a growth mode and adding resources. So this is usually true boilerplate, although you may wish to draw paragraphs and charts selectively from your data banks. This kind of material generally includes both verbal descriptions and line drawings that portray physical layouts.

Current and Past Projects

Most requests for proposals ask for information about relevant other projects your organization is currently performing or has performed in the past. Here, again, such descriptions should be maintained as swipe files rather than as pure boilerplate, preferably as a collection of project descriptions that can be drawn on selectively, as in the case of resume files.

Figure 11–2 offers a suggested format for such descriptions, reflecting the specific kinds of project information often requested by clients. By making each project description a separate paragraph or module, you can easily choose those most appropriate to the current requirement and assemble a table presenting this data. Clients are

Name

Title and Position in the Organization

Title and Position in Proposed Project

Summary paragraph(s) of most relevant experience and other qualifications (relevant to proposed project, that is)

Supporting information (relevant and important, vis-à-vis the proposed project, but secondary)

FIGURE 11–1. Suggested format for resumes

Relevant Projects, Current and Past

Project No. 1:

Name and summary description of project, including client
Dates (start and finish)
Completion within budget?
Completion within schedule?
Contact for verification: Name, title, telephone/FAX

Project No. 2:

FIGURE 11–2. Suggested format for current and past project descriptions

interested in knowing whether you usually finish on schedule and budget or overrun, but if you can claim completion ahead of schedule and significantly under the budget, you certainly should point that out. Finally, clients are usually interested in knowing who they can call to verify your representations.

Differences from the Conventional Library

I have been using that term *library* in a special context. The proposal library is not the classical array of books on shelves. Part of it does exist in the form of bound volumes—books, manuals, reports, and other such items—on shelves. But part of it is in the form of typed or printed documents in metal filing cabinets; and part of it, an increasingly large part, if you are maintaining your library as efficiently as possible, is on computer disks and, perhaps, on tapes also.

The Data Base as a Useful Proposal Asset

As noted, the dbm is a useful writing tool. But it is more than that. Data in machinable media are the most useful form for most of our purposes because the items stored in that form are the easiest to locate, gain direct access to, and use—that is, to copy, modify, adapt, cite, or quote. With the most modern hardware and software available today, searching files, copying from them, and cut-and-paste operations become almost absurdly simple. That is what makes customizing of resumes and other proposal elements so easy.

I use such facilities frequently in writing books and articles, as well as proposals. In my case, because I almost always use the latest version of WordStar (Professional Release 7, at the moment) for my work, I am using a program packaged with it called *ProFinder*. Among other things, it has the capability of searching an entire subdirectory for occurrences of one, two, or three terms in the text or titles of the files. The user decides what those one, two, or three key words (search terms) are to be. And just as they might use an approved key word to search the index of a public data base to which they subscribe, users can invent their own key words to search their own files.

ProFinder and other such programs search an entire text file or the titles of the files in this application. But it is also possible to create an index and have a search program of this type search the index for you, as in the case of using a public data base. Certainly, the computer will search an index for you much more rapidly than you can scan a printed index with your own eyes, and so it is a great time-saver when the bulk and variety of data stored are simply too great to be handled efficiently by simpler means.

Special Programs for the Purpose

There are many data base managers available. In fact, there is a simple program that is known as a file manager, but the dbm program has superior capabilities in general for searching, manipulating, and otherwise managing the data that constitute the data base. Even so, there are numerous differences among the many data base managers available, differences that dictate the size of the various fields and records and even of the total dbm capacity.

The most significant thing about a dbm is that it permits you, the user, to construct files in almost any form you want them. For example, I set up several of my own dbm files, dedicated to use primarily for addressing labels and other chores, as follows:

Name _____

Company _____

Address _____

Address _____

City, St, Zip _____

Tel _____

Notes1 _____

Notes2 _____

Some people would find it useful to break the listing down more, using separate lines for first and last names and for city, state, and zip codes. The advantage of this, for many users, is that the list can then be sorted by last name, city, zip code, or company name. So it is not unusual to set up these files with as many as 15 or 20 different lines (*fields*, in the jargon of dbm, with each collection of fields identified as a *record*).

You can have all the names in a single file, with fields that enable you to sort them in any way you want. I prefer to have a number of lists, each for a different purpose.

You can put the data directly into each record if there is not too much of it for ease of handling. Otherwise, it is probably more efficient and more practical to store and code the data in some set of files and index those files in the dbm. (There is nothing unusual in this. In some manual indexing schemes of years past, the indexes occupied entire volumes, and it was necessary to have a volume that served as a key to the index before one could look anything up with any kind of reasonable efficiency. And so it is here: The complexity of the indexing depends primarily on the size of the data base.)

Suppose, for example, you are a small organization and have all your staff resumes stored away in only five floppy diskettes. You can probably simply store the resumes alphabetically and mark the diskettes accordingly: A–F, G–L, M–Q, R–T, U–Z. But suppose you require 30 or 40 floppy diskettes to hold your entire store of resumes. Searching out any specific one can be a bit of a task; you would probably not know which disk held the resume you wanted. But if you had the disks properly numbered and indexed them in a dbm file, the index would tell you immediately what diskette held the resume. That is, you might set up the dbm file *RESUMES* along the following lines:

Name _____

Diskette no. _____

File name _____

That is a bit too simple; it fails to take advantage of what the dbm can do for you. It fails to serve you in capacities other than retrieval. Before you set out to retrieve a given resume, you need to know what resumes you want to look at. Suppose, for example, you need a half-dozen people to staff a proposal effort, and the boss says, "Who do you want?" That doesn't mean you can have anyone you ask for, of course, but it does mean you need to have an answer ready. If you want six people, you had probably best have at least a dozen resumes you have surveyed and found suitable for your need. That is, you need to be able to use your system for research, as well as for retrieval of data. Suppose, then, you set the file up along these lines:

Name _____

Title _____

Position _____

Education _____

Special skills _____

Experience summary _____

Exp. cont'd _____

Diskette no. _____

File name _____

You can still do everything with this file you could with the original, but you can do a great deal more: You can review these records of resumes, looking for qualifications. That is, you can pull up a list of everyone by education, position, special skills, experience summaries, or any other parameter you wish to and have planned for. You can set up any kind of fields you wish, and you can search the whole file by any field.

That is why it is usually impractical to store or index everything in a given file; each kind of file requires different kinds of fields to serve as key words and help you in your research. Consider some of the kinds of information you might need to support your proposal effort. Consider that you probably have most of what you need in-house—in that great collection of data stored on your shelves, in your filing cabinets, and on those hundreds of disks. (About one-half of my own filing cabinet is given over to the storage of 5.25-inch floppy disks, despite the existence of a hard disk and a 3.5-inch disk drive in my own system, and mine is a one-man office!)

Much of the data you will want each time you are working on a proposal probably exists already in items you need to survey or research (not search for and *retrieve* yet, because you are still trying to find out just what is in your files that you can use). Your files may include any or all of the following kinds of information items, whether in paper or machinable-disk media:

Magazine articles	Project descriptions
Reports	Sales representatives' reports
Manuals	Memoranda
Books	Clip art
Our old proposals	Software manuals
Company literature	Old RFPs and SOWs
Competitors' proposals	Notes of meetings
Competitors' literature	Miscellaneous other literature
Newsletters	Newspaper clippings
Reports from public data bases	Engineering drawings
Annual reports	Laboratory logs
Test results	Commercial catalogs

Other Useful dbm Capabilities

Data base managers have numerous other useful capabilities. One you will use often is the ability to sort the data base in various ways, usually by any of the fields and in at least two orders and several levels. Another, logically linked to this, is the ability to search out redundant items and, if ordered, to discard the additional copies of the item. So new items can be added and integrated into the file indefinitely, obsolete items can be deleted, and with the other capabilities mentioned, maintenance of the file is relatively simple: The computer—the software, that is—does most of the work, on command. Another popular use, especially when the data base is used to manage a mailing list, is the ability to print out labels and reports.

These capabilities include that for designing the labels and reports as you wish, within the parameters of the software design. For example, if I want a list of the editors of periodicals I have listed in a file of periodicals I maintain as one of my own data bases, I might print it out as in Figure 11–3. I can choose the items I want listed and the way I want them listed and organized. I want only a simple listing, in this case.

I did not print this report out directly from the data base program, although I could have easily enough. However, the dbm permits me other options: I can "print" the file out to the screen and read it there, or I can send it to a disk file. I did the latter, opting to import the file to my word processor, where I could incorporate it with the file containing this portion of my manuscript for this book. I was thus afforded a great convenience of having my data base compile this simple table while adding it directly to my manuscript and yet being able to edit it, if necessary. (I did, in fact, make a couple of minor editorial changes to the report.)

This opens up another door for support of your proposal effort: Not only does the dbm serve you as a valuable tool—a key element, in fact—of your proposal library system, establishing and maintaining swipe files and efficient access to them, but it can be used to make other direct contributions to your proposal writing by your taking full advantage of what it can do.

Periodical Editors

Title	Editor
Across the Board	Sarasue French, Asst. Ed.
American Salesman, The	Barbara Boeding, Editor
Barrons	Alan Abelson, Ed.
Better Business	John FR. Robinson, Publ'r.
Business Age Magazine	Claire Bremer, Editor
Business Marketing	Bob Donath, Ed./Assoc. Publ'r.
Business Today	Melody Haakenson, Editor
Business View	Eleanor K. Somer, Publ'r.
Byte Magazine	Frederic Langa, Editor
Common Sense	David Durgin, Editor
Communications Briefings	Frank Grazian, Editor
Compute!	Gregg Keizer, Editor
Computer Product Selling	Karen Paxton, Exec. Ed.
Creating Excellence	David Robinson, Editor
D & B Reports	Patricia W. Hamilton, Ed.
Entrepreneur	Maria Anton, Sr. Editor
Entrepreneur	Rieva Lesonsky, Editor
Globe	Donald McLachlan, Editor
Government Executive	Timothy Clark, Editor
Grit	Naomi L. Woolever, Editor
High-Tech Marketing	Candace Port, Editor
Home Business News	Ed Simpson, Editor
Home Office Computing	Claudia Cohl, Ed.-in-Chief
In Business	Nora Goldstein, Managing Ed.
Inc.	George Gendron, Editor
Income Opportunities	Lance Gould, Asst. Editor
Modern Electronics	Art Salsburg, Ed.-in-Chief
Nation's Business	Managing Editor
National Examiner	Bill Burt, Editor
New Business Opportunities	Rieva Lesonsky, Editor
New Career Ways Newsletter	William J. Bond, Editor
PC Magazine	Lance Elko, Editor
Personal Computing	Fred Abatemarco, Ed.-in-Chief
Personal Publishing	Dan Brogan, Editor
Popular Electronics	Julian S. Martin, Editor
Small Business Opportunities	Susan Rakowski, Editor
Sylvia Porter's Active	Retirement Newsletter
The Star	Leslie Hinton, Editor
The Worksteader News	Lynie Arden
Training Magazine	Jack Gordon, Editor
Venture Magazine	Jeannie Mandelker, Editor
Woman's Enterprise	Caryne Brown, Ed.-in-Chief
Writer's Digest	William Brohaugh

FIGURE 11–3. A dbm report printout

CHAPTER 12

Special Buying

Arrangements

and Opportunities

Everybody keeps his own store.

If You Sell Common Commodities

The Federal Supply Service, one of the major divisions within the General Services Administration (GSA), operates 20 supply depots and 75 stores in the United States. Those establishments store nearly six million separate items, which the Federal Supply Service stocks to supply the rest of the federal establishment. In addition to stocking and distributing these huge numbers of "common-use" items, the Federal Supply Service arranges annual supply contracts for other products it does not carry in stock and for services, spending approximately $3 billion a year for this.

Another major division of the GSA, the Automated Data and Telecommunications Service (ADTS), "manages" the procurement of many other items, principally those required in connection with computers and telecommunications systems.

In addition, the Department of Veterans Affairs also buys centrally for the large number of VA hospitals and is a major government purchaser of food and hospital supplies.

The Department of Defense must supply and support the various forces and their many military bases and is therefore also a major buyer of foods and many other items, both military and nonmilitary in nature. DOD buying is handled through the Defense Logistics Agency (DLA), which operates six Defense Supply Centers in the United States.

There is also the U.S. Postal Service, which buys centrally for the vast chain of post offices and the huge Postal Service motor vehicle fleet of over 100,000 vehicles (second in size only to that of the U.S. Army). The Postal Service main supply depot is at Topeka, Kansas.

To reduce the duplication of purchasing that resulted inevitably from this multiplicity of procurement and supply organizations, a National Supply System has been created, on paper, at least. Gradually, agreements are being worked out among the several procurement organizations to assign responsibility for each class of supplies to one or the other. For example, despite the size of the Postal Service motor vehicle fleet and the estimated $25 million annual purchase of spare parts and maintenance supplies, the Postal Service orders its tires through the GSA. Nonperishable food items are "managed" by the VA and the DLA, the Federal Supply Service having surrendered management of all nonperishable food items to these agencies.

These agencies do not stock all the supplies the U.S. government needs and buys every year, but only common-use items, which are used regularly and predictably and are usually available commercially.

Such items may be bought for stock as the stocks dwindle, by competitive bids, or they may be bought from suppliers with whom contracts for an entire year's supply have been negotiated, usually following normal competitive bids.

But these are not the only buying arrangements. Several other conditions and situations must be accommodated. The various purchasing arrangements are not whimsical or arbitrary, but represent an effort to solve the many different kinds of supply problems encountered by the various government establishments.

There are many items federal agencies are almost sure to buy during the year, yet it is almost impossible to predict which agencies will want them, when, and in what quantities. For example, it's likely that there will be some demand for valves of various kinds, but no one can predict what kind, how many, or where they will be needed. For many of these items, individual orders may be rather small; however, the overall total of such orders will be great enough to make buying at retail or using imprest funds (a form of petty cash fund) prohibitively expensive. In addition, the individual orders are often small enough that competitive bidding is impractical; the need is often for quick delivery, so the time necessary for competitive bidding would be unacceptably long. In some instances, the nature of the procurement is such that it is necessary to buy locally: A military base cannot afford to order milk and eggs from a supplier 2,000 miles away or have laundry and dry cleaning service provided by a distant firm.

These varying needs and conditions can account for the rationale behind the many procurement methods and instruments. They explain, too, why one bid is for a single, one-time order, another is for a year's supply, another is for a multiple of shipments to various points, and so on. And they help explain why a given agency may choose to order something independently, although it could purchase the item through one of the centralized purchasing and supply services.

Figure 12–1 shows several items from a recent issue of the *Commerce Business Daily* that illustrate some of what I've said. Among these notices, which are typical and may be found almost every day in the CBD, are represented the annual supply contract, the multiple-shipment contract, and the single-shipment contract.

Procurements such as these tend to be formally advertised (sealed bids with public openings), but they may also be negotiated contracts, for any of the reasons explained earlier.

The same considerations apply to services, as the notices in Figure 12–2 appear as negotiated procurements. Although many of them are for rather standardized services, many others are for novel

85 Toiletries.

85 - - TOOTHPASTE Definite Quantity—IFB BO/DQ-M-00133, Bid opening: 21 May 79. (107)
GSA, Business Service Center, Rm L-1, J.W. McCormack PO and Courthouse Bldg, Boston MA 02109

99 Miscellaneous.

99 - - ARKANSAS RIVER WATER, 1400 Acre-Feet for FOB delivery to any one of the following 3 Bureau of Reclamation East Slope, Storage Facilities: 1) Twin Lakes Reservoir, 2) Pueblo Dam, 3) Turquoise Reservoir. RFQ 9-01-73-00570 to be issued about 8 May 79.(109)
Department of the Interior, Bureau of Reclamation, LM Region, Building 20, Denver Federal Center, Denver, CO 80225, ATTN: MS. Meyer (303) 234-3135

● 99 - - IDENTIFICATION PLANTES—Fabricated from No. 18 gage aluminum. 1½"x3", letters no less than 3/16" gothic or futura. holes ⅛". IFB DLA002-79-B-0004. Bid opening 18 May 79. See notes 12, 32, 56 and 80. (109)
Defense Industrial Plant Equipement Center, Attn: DIPEC-TC, Memphis, TN 38114

99 - - CONDENSER TUBES AND FERRULES Tubes shall be ¾" O.D. x 13'- 2½" long x #18 B.W.G.—IFB DACW66-?S-B-0044—Bid opening 3 May 79. (107)
Memphis District, Corps of Engineers, Attn: C. P. Williamson, 668 Clifford Davis Federal Bldg, Memphis TN 38103

99 - - ARTS AND CRAFTS MATERIAL, NSC 9999-NONE. IAW description cited in IFB—Quantity and Destns unknown—IFB —Quantity and Destns unknown—IFB DLA400-79-B-2003—Bid opening 18 May 79—For Tech. info. contact Mrs. Sarnecky, 804/275-4473. See notes 72, 73 and 80. (106)
Defense General Supply Center, Richmond, VA 23297, Tel: 804/275-3350

FIGURE 12–1. Notices for goods from *Commerce Business Daily*

---

84 Clothing, Individual Equipment, and Insignia.

---

84 - - COVERALLS with elastic waistband 6.0 oz. polyester long sleeve, navy blue, one piece—RFQ 17-095-79 Bid opening 3:00 PM—26 Apr 79. (088).
>   Procurement Officer, Seventeenth Coast Guard District, PO Box 3-5000, Juneau AK 99802.

---

88 Live Animals.

---

88 - - SWINE, unbred females. Delivered f.o.b. destination within consignee's premises to Beltsville, Maryland, RFQ 11427 due 6 Apr 79. (082)
>   U.S. Dept. of Agriculture, SEA/GSB, Rm 318H, Administration Bldg., Agricultural Research Center-West, Beltsville, MD Attn: Dawn Foster 301/344-3360

● **88 - - HORSES, GELDING**, 15 hand high, 3 to 7 years old, broke for riding and packing, Stehekin District, North Cascades National Park Complex. Verbal quotes approximately 16 Apr 79. (088).
>   National Park Service North Cascades National Park 800 State Street Sedreo Wolley, WA 98284

---

89 Subsistence.

---

89 - - POTATO CHIPS AND CORN CHIPS for Naval Air Station Memphis, Millington, TN—Requirements Type Contract for period 1 Oct 79 through 30 Sep 80—Estimated requirements as specified in IFB N00612-79-B-0119—Deliveries required within 7 days after receipt of order—Opening date o/a 18 Jun 79—Mrs. Mary F. Southard, 803-743-4781—Availability of the solicitation is limited and will be furnished on a first received, first served basis.
89 - - BEVERAGE BASE, FRUIT FLAVOR—Requirements Contract—Estimated annual quantities Fruit Punch, 2000 GL, Grape, 1500 GL, Orange 2000 GL, Black Cherry, 1000 GL—Delivery to NAS Memphis, Millington, TN—IFB N00612-79-B-0121—Opens o/a 12 Jun 79—J.J. Bridges—803-743-6483—Availability of the solicitation is limited and will be furnished on a first received, first served basis.
89 - - BEVERAGE BASE—Cola, Lemon-Lime and Root Beer flavors—Indefinite quantities for period 1 Oct 79 through 30 Sep 80—Estimated annual requirements as specified in IFB N00612-79-B-0120—Deliveries within 72 hours after receipt of order—Opening date o/a 11 Jun 79—J. Bridges, 803/743-6483—Availability of the solicitation is limited and will be furnished on a first received, first served basis. (135)
>   Commanding Officer, Code 200, Naval Supply Center, Charleston, SC 29408

FIGURE 12–1. *(continued)*

---

❶ **Z - - MAINTENANCE PAINTING** Exterior, Bldgs. 102, 103, 409, 416 and 436 at the Air National Guard Base, 8030 Balboa Blvd., Van Nuys CA 91409 (Los Angeles County)—DAHA04-79-B-0031—Bid opens 25 May 79— Magnitude of Proposed construction is between $25,000 and $100,000. (110)

Office of the U.S. Property and Fiscal Officer for California, PO Box G, San Luis Obispo, CA 93406, Attn: Contracting Office, Mrs. Roulis, Tel: 805/544-4900, Ext 214

---

❶ **Z - - REMOVING OLD AND INSTALLING NEW GUTTERS,** various buildings, VAMC Dublin, Georgia. Project 79-105. Bid opening 30 May 79. Bid material available 1 May 79. Estimateds $25,000 - $40,000.

❶ **Z - - REPLACING LOUVER DOORS,** VAMC Dublin, Georgia, Proj. 79-112. Bid opening 30 May 79. Bid Material availalbe 1 May 79. Estimated $12,000 - $18,000. (113)

Veterans Administration Medical Center /134, Dublin, GA 31021

---

❶ **Z - - REPAIR ROOF,** building 94 (R18-78) Naval Air Station, North Island, San Diego, CA. The work includes, but is not limited to, removal of existing gravel surfacing and installation of new roofing and clean gutters and down spouts, complete and ready for use. N62474-78-B-9096—between $100,000 & $500,000—21 May 79. (113)

OICC, Navy Public Works Center, Box 113, Naval Station, San Diego, CA 92136.

---

❶ **S - - CUSTODIAL SERVICE,** VA Drug Dependence, Clinic, Houston, TX — 1 year(s) - IFB GS-07B 20687. Bid Opening 6-7-79 (134)

GSA Business Service Center, 819 Taylor Street, Fort Worth, TX 76102

---

❶ **S - - FIRE PREVENTION AND PROTECTION SERVICES** for Castle Dome Heliport, US Army Yuma Proving Ground, AZ—IFB DAAD01-79-B-0049. Estimated opening date 8 Jun 79—See note 18. (134)

Procurement Directorate, US Army Yuma Proving Ground, AZ 85364.

---

❶ **S - - GARBAGE, TRASH AND REFUSE COLLECTION &DISPOSAL** at Marine Corps Air Station, Laurel Bay, Station Housing and Naval Hospital, Beaufort, S.C. Job IFB 06-79-42442. Bid opening 12 June 79.

Officer in Charge of Construction, MCAS, Beaufort, S.C. P.O. Drawer Y, Burton, SC 29902

FIGURE 12–2.   Notices for services from *Commerce Business Daily*

S Housekeeping Services.

❶ S - - NIGHT DESK CLERK SERVICES—The Contractor will disburse additional linens, receive and issue dormitory keys, control and issue dormitory recreational equipment, assist in the even to fdormitory disturbance, and monitor the National Mine Health and Safety Academy s cardkey control system. Performance shall be during night and weekend periods. IFB S2701005. Estimated bid opening July 6, 1979. See Note 12.

S - - GARBAGE AND TRASH REMOVAL at the National Mine Health and Safety Academy. Beckley, West Virginia. The Contractor will furnish all necessary labor and materials to render complete trash, edible and non-edible garbage removal daily except Sunday. Dumpster type containers are required. Containers shall have a minimum of 16 cubic yards. IFB S2701004. Estimated Bid Opening 2 Jul 79.

S - - LINEN AND LAUNDRY SERVICES at the National Mine Health and Safety Academy. Beckley, West Virginia. Pickup, delivery and professional laundering of aprons, wash cloths, bathtowels, sheets, pillowcases, tablecloths and similar items. IFB S2701002. Estimated bid opening 3 Jul 79. (130)

U.S. Department of Labor, Mine Safety and Health Administration, Branch of Management Operations, PO Box 25367, Denver Federal Center, Denver, CO 80225.

X - - ASA SOFTBALL OFFICIALS for 400 Intramural games and 86 playoff games, 16 May 79 - 11 Aug 79, Fort Richardson, Alaska. RFP DAKF70-79-R-0062. Negotiations will be conducted with Polar Bear Sports Officials Association, Fort Richardson, Alaska. (110)

Department of the Army, Procurement Division, P.O. Box 5-525, Fort Richardson, AK 99505, Attn: Mrs. Lyon 907/863-8283

❶ J - - PREVENTATIVE MAINTENANCE ON ELECTRICAL EQUIPMENT at Federal Center, 74 N. Washington Avenue, Batttle Creek, MI Solicitation No. 5PF7B-79-0041. Offers Due by 21 May 79. Willnot exceed $10,000.00. Contract period 1 Jun 79 through 31 Aug. 79 (113)

General Services Administration, PBS, Federal Center, 74 N. Washington Avenue, Battle Creek, MI 49017

J - - MAINTAIN INTRABASE RADIO SYSTEM at Altus, AFB, Oklahoma—IFB F34612-79-B0016—O/A 26 Jun 79—1 Oct 79 through 30 Sep 80—See Note 56. (131)

Base Contracting Div., Altus Air Force Base, OK 73521 ATTN: Dorotha Lovett 405/481-7321

FIGURE 12–2. (continued)

services. So success in winning government business may, and often does, depend on the bidder's willingness and ability to adapt the services to the needs expressed or to design a set of services to meet the need.

The Federal Supply Schedules

The Federal Supply Service maintains approximately 300 Federal Supply Schedules, plus approximately 200 other similar annual supply agreements. (See Appendix 4 for a list of Federal Supply Schedules.) The general purpose of the schedules is to arrange for the various federal agencies to be able to buy from suppliers in any quantity at wholesale prices and to be able to buy from suppliers who are nearby and/or can fill orders spontaneously and on short notice.

A supply schedule is therefore a basic ordering agreement with each supplier, under which the supplier agrees to fill orders at some stipulated discount from his or her normal list prices for some term, usually one year. The discounts may be on a sliding scale, depending on quantities ordered.

There are three general types of Federal Supply Schedules:

Multiple-award schedules, which cover ordering agreements entered into with a number of contractors for the same types of supplies and/or services

Single-award schedules, which cover ordering agreements entered into with a single supplier for the class of goods or services listed in the schedule

New-item introductory schedules, which enable contractors to introduce new and/or improved items to the supply system

Under these schedules, contractors may enter even unique or proprietary items into the system. For example, many publishers of books, manuals, and newsletters enter their publications in the 76 group of schedules (see Appendix 4, listings 76 I through 76 III B).

Generally speaking, the multiple-award schedules afford the agencies an opportunity to select from among a large number of suppliers so they can take advantage of the largest discounts or the most convenient delivery or otherwise accommodate the service to their needs. Contractors listed in multiple-award schedules are usually required to supply catalog sheets to the agencies describing their listed products and providing ordering information.

In most cases, the single-award schedules are for items covered by federal specifications, although in some cases, the contractors are required to furnish descriptive literature and ordering information to those agencies listed as the relevant "buying activities."

The Federal Supply Service reviews applications for entering items on the new-item introductory schedule and decides whether an item merits inclusion there. Ultimately, if the item generates sufficient demand among the buying activities, it may be transferred to a regular supply schedule, or there may be a new supply schedule established to cover it.

A typical multiple-award schedule is reproduced in Appendix 4. That one is for publications of several kinds, as listed on the cover page. A copy of the schedule is supplied to each of approximately 2,500 federal buying activities that are usual buyers of the products listed, for example, schools, libraries, military installations, laboratories, and so on. The contractor is furnished a list of the buying activities, on labels, and is required to send each a catalog or price list that includes ordering information and discounts and a form listing the contract number and other specifics of the contract terms.

Getting on the Schedule

Getting on the schedule means bidding for and being issued a contract or ordering agreement. No money is committed in this agreement. When a buying activity wishes to order, the buying activity issues a government purchase order, citing the contract as authority.

In the schedule shown in Appendix 4, both publishers and their dealers are listed, but the schedule does not indicate what publications are offered by each or the prices asked. That's why contractors must mail a catalog or price list to the many buying activities. In practice, many of the buying activities, having received their copies of the schedule, will write to each contractor listed and request copies of their catalogs.

Figure 12–3 is an example of the information the contractor must send along with the catalog sheets. The government does not have an official price-list form, but the GSA furnishes a sample for the contractor to follow. Note the sliding discount scale, according to the size of individual orders. Note, too, that the minimum order size is set (contractors may select from a range to stipulate their minimum order) and so is the maximum order size. That points up another feature of the supply schedules: Ordinarily, under the Small Purchases Act, a federal agency is limited to $10,000 maximum per purchase order. However, when an agency issues purchase orders under an existing ordering agreement, the limit is set by the ordering agreement, rather than by statute, and can go quite high; even $50,000 purchase orders are not unusual in these circumstances.

Being listed on a schedule and getting such a contract is actually not at all difficult. In fact, it's virtually routine, as long as all procedures are followed and some discount is offered. However, there are no guarantees that orders will be issued; it's up to the contractor to go out and do some selling, to pursue the business. (For that reason, some contractors call the Federal Supply Schedule a hunting license.) There are no limits placed on the total amount of business you can do under these schedules, and they can be a valuable source of business and an entree to federal procurement offices that might otherwise be all but closed to you.

One difficulty with these schedules is that there is really no central coordination. Different schedules are issued by different GSA regional offices (and there are ten of those) at different times of the year. Moreover, you can apply for some schedules at any time of the year, whereas others are "open" for new contractors only once a year. The Federal Supply Service does not maintain a list of where schedules are issued and when they are open for applications. The list shown in Appendix 4 is handled in Boston, at the Region I GSA

```
                    GENERAL SERVICES ADMINISTRATION
                       FEDERAL SUPPLY SERVICE

AUTHORIZED FEDERAL SUPPLY SCHEDULE CATALOG AND/OR PRICE LIST

SCHEDULE TITLE:  FSC Group 76, Part I, Publications

GSA MAILING CODE:                        CONTRACT NO: GS-01S-06899
CONTRCATOR:  Government Marketing News, Inc.
             P.O.Box 6067                 PERIOD:  February 9, 1979 through
             Wheaton, MD 20906                     January 30, 1980

CONTACT:  Ms. Sherrie Holtz     TELEPHONE:  301-460-1506

MANUFACTURER'S CODE:            BUSINESS SIZE:  Small

AWARDED SPECIAL ITEMS:  426-3, 4


GEOGRAPHIC COVERAGE:  The 50 States, Washington, DC, and Puerto Rico

MINIMUM ORDER:  $10

TIME OF DELIVERY:  45 days

PROMPT PAYMENT TERMS:  1% 10 days, ½% 20 days

PRICES:  Prices as approved on original offer dated 11/10/78 and letter of 12/14/78


FOB POINT:  Destination

QUANTITY DISCOUNTS:  1-50 copies, 10% discount
                     51-99 copies, 20% discount
                     100 or more copies, 30% discount


FOREIGN ITEMS:  None

POINTS OF PRODUCTION:  Washington, DC

ORDERING ADDRESS:  3110 Whispering Pines
                   P.O. Box 6067
                   Wheaton, MD 20906

PAYMENT ADDRESS:  Same as above

WARRANTY PROVISIONS:  Replacement of copies received in damaged condition.
```

FIGURE 12–3. Contractor's price-list form

office, and is for the period February 1 to January 31 of the following year. That means bids are accepted late in the year and must be in the contracting officer's hands well before the end of the calendar year to qualify. Note on that schedule that although the contract is to run—nominally—from February 1, 1979, to January 31, 1980, the schedule was not issued until March 9, and the contract was mailed from the Region I GSA office on February 9, 1979.

To run down a particular schedule, under present conditions, it is necessary to call or write the Federal Supply Service Information Center in Arlington, Virginia. Their mailing address and telephone number are as follows:

General Services Administration
Schedule Information Center (FPS)
Washington, D.C. 20406
(703) 557-8177

In the Information Center in Arlington is a room containing stored copies of every Federal Supply Schedule, and the people who work there can check the cover page of any schedule that interests you and advise you as to which regional office of the GSA handles it and what the issue date is. Other than this, it is a laborious task, involving many letters and/or telephone calls to track down the schedule so that you can determine where to apply for inclusion!

Once you do ascertain that, the matter becomes somewhat simpler. You just write the appropriate GSA contracting officer, request a solicitation package, and submit your bid, as you would any other. If it is a multiple-award schedule, you are likely to receive a telephone call from the contracting officer some weeks later to pursue a telephone negotiation, in which the official strives to get from you the best discounts you are willing to offer. Once that is settled, it is only a matter of time until you receive your contract and are finally listed on the schedule. Ultimately, you will also receive the mailing list, although that will probably come from the Denver GSA office, regardless of where the schedule is managed.

Most schedules are for supplies of various kinds. There are, however, a few for services. One of the more popular of these is

Schedule 733 III, for providing graphic arts services of various kinds. These are necessarily on a local basis because they are for small orders. The Washington area schedule for these services, for example, is issued to contractors who maintain offices within a 50-mile radius of the GSA Region III office, which is in Washington. Other regions operate their own local 733 III Schedules, but all are issued from the Region III GSA office, for some reason. At the same time the Region III GSA office was required to take over all 733 III Schedules, it became available for new contractors only once a year, whereas it was once open the entire year for additional contractors.

The procedure you must follow, then, is to check the listing of Federal Supply Schedules (see Appendix 4 for the current listing), reach the Information Center by letter or telephone, and check (1) whether the schedule is still operative (they do change), (2) which GSA regional office manages it, and (3) what the dates of the term are. Then you apply to the GSA office concerned and get on the bidders list.

The Defense Logistics Agency

The Defense Logistics Agency (DLA), referred to in many older government publications as the Defense Supply Agency (DSA), is the major buyer and supplier of common-use items for the various military arms. The DLA operates six Defense Supply Centers, administers the Federal Supply Catalog, and manages the Defense Contract Administration Service, among other things. In addition to the six Defense Supply Centers, the DLA operates six Defense Service Centers and four Defense Depots.

Like the GSA, the DLA buys both centrally and locally and both by one-time procurements and by annual ordering agreements. However, the DLA does not do all the buying for the military departments, just as the GSA does not do all the buying for the civilian departments. Each department has its own centralized procurement and supply organizations, and each separate establishment does at least some buying of its own. (See Appendix 2 for listings.)

DCAS Small Business Specialists

One of the several functions of the Defense Contract Administration Service (DCAS) is to help small business win a share of government contracts and subcontracts. Each of 21 DCAS offices has at least one small business representative to whom you may apply for counseling and other assistance in pursuing Defense Department business. (See Appendix 2 for listings.)

Doing Business with the Military

Many firms do business entirely with the military agencies. The range of military needs is such that although many of their needs are unique (for supplies and services that only a military organization would have use for), they also buy almost everything else that any other agency might need.

The Department of Defense and the military departments that make it up have always depended on commerce and industry for their supplies and equipment and were, until recently, at least, always the largest market in the government. It is therefore not illogical that the Defense Department and the various military organizations have the most highly organized procurement systems. (Most other federal procurement is patterned after military procurement regulations, forms, and procedures.)

When you request a Form 129 (application for bidders list) from the military, you are usually given, in addition, a form that lists many items of supplies and services, and you are asked to check off those that interest you. This information is then supplied to a computer and stored, so the agency may ask the computer to select a candidate list of potential bidders for any given procurement. (Similar systems are used by NASA and other agencies that do a great deal of procurement and/or buy a variety of goods and services.)

The military agencies also have many more specifications than do most civilian agencies (although some civilian agencies invoke many of the military specifications for their procurements). In most cases, the specifications invoked are available for inspection or may be ordered from the Navy Publications Forms Center, 5801 Tabor Road, Philadelphia, Pennsylvania 19120.

To assist small businesses and implement the socioeconomic requirements of federal procurement generally, DOD places certain requirements on its major prime contractors. For example, any prime contract of $500,000 or more carries with it a requirement that the contractor maintain a Defense Small Business, Minority Business Subcontracting, and Labor Surplus Area Program and designate within the organization a small business–minority business liaison officer to administer (implement) the program. Recent regulations require that bidders for larger contracts actually furnish specific subcontracting plans before awards are made.

There are, however, many opportunities for sales within the military establishments:

- Direct sales, on a local basis, to the military bases
- Both central and local sales to military exchanges
- Central and local sales to military commissaries
- Local sales to military R&D centers

Department of the Army

The major organizations within the army, as far as procurement is concerned, are the following:

- U.S. Army Corps of Engineers
- U.S. Army Medical Department
- U.S. Army Forces Command
- U.S. Army Training and Doctrine Command
- U.S. Army Ballistic Missile Defense Advanced Technology Center
- U.S. Army Communications Command
- U.S. Army Materiel Development and Readiness Command (DARCOM)

Specific installations and procurement offices of the army are listed in Appendix 2.

Department of the Navy

The major portion of procurement in the navy is the responsibility of the chief of naval material, who heads the Naval Material Command. Within that command are five major subdivisions:

- Naval Air Systems Command
- Naval Electronic Systems Command
- Naval Facilities Engineering Command
- Naval Sea Systems Command
- Naval Supply Systems Command

The chief of naval material also is responsible for some of the procurement for the U.S. Marine Corps, which is part of the navy.

A separate navy organization, which does some buying, is the Military Sealift Command. Some buying, especially of R&D services, is also done under the command of the Office of Naval Research.

Buying offices and commands of the navy are listed in Appendix 2.

Department of the Air Force

Major air force organizations that do most of the buying for various air force needs include the following:

- Air Force Logistics Command
- Air Force Systems Command
- Military Airlift Command
- Air Training Command
- Air Force Communications Service
- Aerospace Defense Command

Buying offices and organizations of the air force are listed in Appendix 2.

Research and Development

Research and development (R&D) is carried out by many government agencies, with the bulk of the work done under contract with private industry. The military agencies provide by far the greatest opportunity for such contracts, but other technological agencies also offer some contracting possibilities in R&D. The largest of these are NASA (National Aeronautics and Space Administration) and DOE (Department of Energy). However, some R&D is also carried out by the Department of Transportation, which includes the coast guard and the Federal Aviation Administration among its divisions.

All three military services (army, navy, and air force) maintain a number of R&D facilities that conduct both basic and applied research in many areas, including communication, weapons, medicine, human behavior, electronics, and data processing. Some of the projects are funded by grants, rather than contracts, although grants are almost always awarded to nonprofit organizations, such as universities. (There are occasional exceptions, and grants can go to for-profit organizations.)

Federal R&D facilities are among those listed in Appendix 2.

Unsolicited Proposals

Unsolicited proposals are offered voluntarily by an individual or organization. These are more commonly found in R&D areas than in most others because they are almost inherently offers to do something innovative, based on a proprietary idea, product, or capability. Because they are unsolicited, they have no competition; if the customer likes it, negotiations follow.

There is no prescribed format for an unsolicited proposal, but the Department of Defense suggests submitting two copies. The proposal should contain at least the following information and elements:

1. A cover sheet
2. An abstract
3. A narrative
4. A cost proposal (separate)

It is recommended that the cover sheet include the following information:

1. Name of agency to which offered
2. Name of proposer
3. Address of proposer
4. Title of proposer
5. Proposed project manager or principal investigator, with telephone number
6. Address of project manager, if different from that of proposer
7. Individual to contact for discussion, negotiations, and so on
8. Address of contact
9. Date of submittal

The abstract, which should be part of the "front matter" (that is, appears before the first page of the proposal proper), should state the basic purpose of the proposed effort, give a brief summary of the work to be done, and describe the expected end result and end product of the proposed work. The DOD suggests that the abstract be approximately 200 to 300 words long, but obviously that will vary, depending on the size of the proposal being abstracted.

The narrative should make clear how the proposed work relates to the mission of the agency to which it is submitted, the problems it will solve, and whatever other justification the proposer believes appropriate. The proposer's qualifications should be presented also, of course. The objectives of the proposed contract should be made clear and should be detailed as clearly as possible. The customer is not likely to fund a fishing expedition. It is necessary to present a convincing case for the proposed contract and good evidence that the proposed work will contribute substantially to the agency's mission and have a good prospect for success in achieving the stated objectives. Any preliminary or preparatory work out of which the proposal grew should be mentioned, as it will contribute to the probability that the proposal will be accepted by the customer.

In general, what has been said about competitive proposals applies for the most part to unsolicited proposals as well—perhaps even more so because the customer has not felt the need for such work prior to submittal of the unsolicited proposal and must be convinced that the work and result will be a worthwhile and justified contribution.

In presenting the offeror's qualifications, the suggestions made earlier in connection with proposing competitively should be followed, but the information submitted should also include the following:

(Name of proposer) _____ is a (type of organization) _____ , organized under the laws of the state of _____ , having its principal office and doing business in the city of _____ .

If the firm is incorporated, furnish names of its chief officers; if it's a partnership or sole proprietorship, furnish names of the principals. Indicate the number of employees, state whether yours is a small business, a minority enterprise, or a women-owned business, and whether it is in a labor-surplus area (as defined by the Department of Labor in quarterly designations of labor-surplus areas). State where the proposed work will be performed, whether you are currently doing related work or have done it in the past, and your other general qualifications.

State whether subcontracts are contemplated. If they are, state what will be subcontracted and to whom, if known.

State whether you have or have not retained a company or person to secure the proposed contract, and express willingness to furnish information to the contracting officer regarding this.

State whether working capital is available or, if not, where you intend to turn for working capital.

Describe where the work is to be done, describe the facilities and resources to be used, and mention any other pertinent details.

In practice, it is unwise to offer an unsolicited proposal with no advance discussion because it is most unlikely the customer will buy an unsolicited proposal that comes in cold and completely unexpected. However, many unsolicited proposals are funded every year and are a major source of income to many firms.

One word of caution: Many, if not most, contracting officers are automatically skeptical about proposals purporting to be unsolicited because many government people "arrange" to have favored suppliers submit "unsolicited" proposals that have actually originated in the government executive's mind. It is highly advisable to take all possible steps to document the unsolicited proposal as truly unsolicited.

Military Exchange Services

Military exchanges buy merchandise such as foods and other consumer goods for resale. Officially, army and air force exchanges buy everything offered in the various exchanges through one or more of five regional exchange offices. In practice, some goods may be sold to individual exchanges, particularly if the item is suitable for local sale only. For example, the cost of some local products would be excessively high if they were shipped elsewhere, and custom orders are taken for some items, such as custom-stenciled T-shirts. Most purchases, however, are via regional offices.

For overseas exchanges, all buying is done via the Army and Air Force Exchange Service headquarters in Dallas, Texas 75222. Any information on army and air force exchange procurement may be addressed to the Command and Public Relations Division there. The telephone number is (214) 330-2763.

The navy invites suppliers to sell navy exchanges through the Navy Resale System Office (NRSO) in Brooklyn, New York, or the NRSO Branch Office in Oakland, California, or by sale directly to the individual exchanges.

To sell to marine corps exchanges, contact the Marine Corps Exchange Service.

Specific name and address listings for the various exchange offices are included in Appendix 2.

Military Commissary Stores

Most commissary resale items are purchased by brand-name contracts issued by Headquarters, Defense Personnel Support Center, Defense Supply Agency, 2800 South 20th Street, Philadelphia, Pennsylvania 19101. However, each commissary store may also make direct purchases of resale goods and services, within prescribed dollar limits. Navy commissary stores do most of their purchasing through the Navy Resale System Office, the same organization that buys for navy exchanges.

The U.S. Postal Service

The U.S. Postal Service is a government corporation today, but it is still an official agency within the U.S. government and subject to the same statutory control as other agencies in its purchasing. Its needs are somewhat different from other civilian agencies, and the Postal Service has long had its own centralized purchasing and supply system, with its main warehouses and depot at Topeka, Kansas.

The Postal Service orders some of its supplies from the GSA and the Federal Supply Service. At one time, it used a great deal of military surplus, especially motor vehicles. However, it requires many specialized supplies and types of equipment, such as sorting machines, cancelers, carts, computers, scales, vending equipment, and other devices to support its automation efforts. Much of that equipment is custom designed under contract, some developed at the Postal Service R&D laboratory in Rockville, Maryland. However, aside from extensive purchases of capital equipment, the Postal Service buys a great deal of transportation services to move the mail from city to city and a great deal of service and supplies to maintain its huge fleet of motor vehicles.

Motor vehicle maintenance is carried out by a number of Vehicle Maintenance Facilities (VMFs), which are part of the Postal Service, and many VMFs are supported by "satellite" VMFs. The Baltimore VMF, for example, maintains a satellite VMF in Annapolis to avoid the long tow of a disabled Postal Service vehicle from Annapolis to Baltimore. However, many localities have no VMF within reasonable range, and in such cases, the Postal Service relies on local commercial facilities (service stations and garages) to service its vehicles.

Each VMF has its own parts room and parts clerk and attempts to stock those parts considered necessary to keep vehicles in good operating condition and minimize "down time." However, many occasions inevitably arise when the needed part is not in stock. In such cases, the VMF buys the part locally from nearby dealers. (Because most Postal Service vehicles are standard commercial models, this is entirely feasible.)

One major need of the Postal Service is for construction services. As suburban communities continue to grow, new post offices must be built. Hardly a day passes that the Postal Service cannot offer opportunities to bid for new construction and/or renovation and repairs to existing buildings.

When it was reorganized as a government corporation, the Postal Service employed approximately 670,000 workers, with an annual budget of approximately $10 billion. The budget has grown as a result of both inflation and increased load (about 92 billion pieces of mail per year, currently), although the work force has grown more slowly since the Postal Service invested heavily in automation to become slightly less labor intensive. However, there are some 30,000 post offices, plus a number of other buildings in the Postal Service system, making it a major market for many services and supplies. Buying is done through both the Procurement and Supply Office at Postal Service headquarters in Washington, D.C., and through its many offices. A list of major offices is located in Appendix 2.

The Government Printing Office

The U.S. Government Printing Office (GPO) is one of the old-time agencies of the government, dating back to June 23, 1860. Unlike most of the other agencies, the GPO is not part of the executive branch and therefore does not report to the president, but is part of the legislative branch and reports to Congress, which has a Joint Committee on Printing that acts as the board of directors for the GPO.

Virtually all printing done for the government must be done either through the GPO or by other means authorized by it. Agencies that want to have a private contractor do printing for them must persuade the GPO to authorize it through a waiver. There are, however, a number of agencies operating their own small printing plants, presumably with the GPO's blessing.

The GPO handles hundreds of millions of dollars' worth of printing for the various agencies every year. However, it contracts out about 70 percent of this work to commercial printers through its own headquarters in Washington, D.C., and its 13 Regional Printing Procurement Offices in Atlanta, Boston, Chicago, Columbus, Dallas, Denver, Hampton (Virginia), Los Angeles, New York, Philadelphia, St. Louis, San Francisco, and Seattle. The GPO also buys paper, ink, and other supplies, as well as equipment of various kinds.

In addition to printing, the GPO contracts out typesetting and some special services, such as maintaining subscription lists for periodicals, soliciting subscriptions, and so on.

Many small print shops do GPO work exclusively or as a large portion of their total volume. Satisfactory GPO contractors can expect continuous invitations to bid. To apply for inclusion on the GPO's many bidders lists, first ask for the GPO's standard package of materials, which includes forms on which to list and describe your facility and equipment. This enables the GPO to determine what kinds of jobs you can handle and therefore which bid sets your company should receive. The large number of bids every day would make it too time-consuming and difficult to require sealed bids and to hold public openings, but the bids are normally let on the basis of low bid.

The bidder receives a *detailed* estimating form on which to calculate prices—even to the extreme of pricing the staples used in binding, for example. However, the GPO usually gives a generous amount of time to complete a job.

The GPO has many different types of printing requirements, from newsletters to slick magazines; from simple, side-stitched manuals to casebound books; from letterheads to snap-out forms and other specialties. Many are simple, one-time requirements; others are annual "programs," which furnish continuing work for an entire year, just as many other agencies do.

Locations of key offices of the GPO are listed in Appendix 1.

Opportunities for Individuals

There are many self-employed individuals who find frequent employment on small government jobs, usually arranged by informal purchase order, sometimes by a simple letter contract. Individuals are frequently retained to lecture, write, consult, and handle other small assignments usually performed more efficiently by an individual than by an organization.

In some cases, an individual is retained to do a study or write a book for an agency because he or she is peculiarly qualified, perhaps uniquely so. In others, it is simply because the individual has taken the trouble to track the need down and sell the job. For such small tasks, simply "making the calls" is appropriate and adequate for the need. And the individual can develop a "following" of satisfied customers who will call back again and again. Or such jobs can lead to long-term assignments.

For example, some consultants furnish two or three days a week to an agency for many months, on a semipermanent basis. At OSHA (Occupational Safety and Health Administration, Labor Department), a fairly large staff of "consultants," all contracted for individually, handles the public information, writes press releases, publishes a monthly magazine, and performs a variety of such chores.

Many of those who lecture in government classrooms are outside "consultants," hired because of special competence in some subject and an acceptable "platform" presence.

Only about $10 billion worth of government services are considered to be necessarily done by federal employees because of the nature of the duties. All the rest, probably in excess of $100 billion (no one, in or out of the government, knows exactly how much), is done by outside contractors. Work is done by federal employees in-house only if and when it is deemed to be less costly to do it that way. The federal employee gets 20.4 percent of his or her base salary in retirement benefits, plus up to ten weeks paid time off from work, plus almost guaranteed annual increases and promotions; so it is increasingly difficult for agencies to demonstrate that they can do the job less expensively than an outside contractor. Therefore, the opportunities for government contracts have been growing steadily, rather than declining. Paradoxical as it may seem, presidential moves toward austerity and economy invariably lead to additional contracting opportunities. "Economizing" almost always means reducing the federal payroll—without reducing the work federal agencies are required to do. They must still carry out the same programs. Frequently, the requirement for a consultant is precipitated by and directly due to the fact that the agency has had a freeze put on hiring and therefore uses money available for contracting to get the job done.

APPENDIXES

Agencies and Offices

of Special Interest

to Business People

The United States is divided into ten federal regions, and most government agencies maintain an office in each one. However, several of the agencies are designed to help business in various ways, through their programs, and these usually maintain a large number of district or field offices, in addition to their regional offices, so everyone may have ready access to the services.

Those of special interest to business people seeking information and help in selling to the U.S. government or getting the aid offered in federal programs are listed in this appendix.

The Small Business Administration and the Department of Commerce maintain an unusually large number of field offices because both are concerned almost entirely with supporting American businesses. The General Services Administration and the Government Printing Office, which also maintain many offices for the convenience of the public, are listed here to help readers find those closest to them.

Note that these are offices and agencies offering information and help to those seeking government business. Appendix 2 lists many government procurement offices—which do the actual buying.

Small Business Administration: regional and district offices

Headquarters office: 1441 L St. NW, Washington, DC 20416

Region I

60 Batterymarch, Boston, MA 02110

150 Causeway St., Boston, MA 02203

302 High St., Holyoke, MA 01040

40 Western Ave., Augusta, ME 04430

55 Pleasant St., Concord, NH 03301

1 Financial Plaza, Hartford, CT 06103

87 State St., Montpelier, VT 05602

57 Eddy St., Providence, RI 02903

Region II

26 Federal Plaza, New York, NY 10007*

111 W. Huron St., Buffalo, NY 14202

Carlos Chardon Ave., Hato Rey, PR 00918

970 Broad St., Newark, NJ 07102

100 S. Clinton St., Syracuse, NY 13202

180 State St., Elmira, NY 14904

99 Washington Ave., Albany, NY 12207

100 State St., Rochester, NY 14604

1800 E. Davis St., Camden, NJ 08104

Franklin Bldg., St. Thomas, VI

Region III

1 Bala Cynwyd Plaza, Bala Cynwyd, PA 19004*

Charleston National Plaza, Charleston, WV 25301

109 N. 3rd St., Clarksburg, WV 26301

1500 N. 2nd St., Harrisburg, PA 17108

1000 Liberty Ave., Pittsburgh, PA 15222

400 N. 8th St., Richmond, VA 23240

*Regional and district offices

7800 York Rd., Towson, MD 21204

1030 15th St. NW, Washington, DC 20417

20 N. Pennsylvania Ave., Wilkes-Barre, PA 18701

844 King St., Wilmington, DE 19801

Region IV

1375 Peachtree St. NE, Atlanta, GA 30309

1720 Peachtree Rd. NW, Atlanta, GA 30309

111 Fred Haise Blvd., Biloxi, MS 39530

908 S. 20th St., Birmingham, AL 36205

230 S. Tryon St., Charlotte, NC 28202

1801 Assembly St., Columbia, SC 29201

1802 N. Trask St., Tampa, FL 33607

215 S. Evans St., Greenville, NC 27834

200 E. Pascagoula, Jackson, MS 39205

400 W. Bay St., Jacksonville, FL 32202

502 S. Gay St., Knoxville, TN 37902

600 Federal Pl., Louisville, KY 40202

404 James Robertson Pkwy., Nashville, TN 37219

211 Federal Office Bldg., Memphis, TN 38103

701 Clemantis St. W, Palm Beach, FL 33402

Region V

219 S. Dearborn St., Chicago, IL 60604*

550 Main St., Cincinnati, OH 45202

1240 E. 9th St., Cleveland, OH 44199

34 N. High St., Columbus, OH 43215

477 Michigan Ave., Detroit, MI 48226

575 N. Pennsylvania St., Indianapolis,
IN 46204

122 W. Washington Ave., Madison,
WI 53703

500 S. Barstow St., Eau Claire, WI 54701

540 W. Kaye Ave., Marquette, MI 49855

517 E. Wisconsin Ave., Milwaukee,
WI 53202

12 S. 6th St., Minneapolis, MN 55402

1 N. Old State Capitol Plaza, Springfield,
IL 62701

Region VI

1720 Regal Row, Dallas, TX 75202

5000 Marble Ave. NE, Albuquerque,
NM 87110

4100 Rio Bravo St., El Paso, TX 79901

500 Dallas St., Houston, TX 77002

611 Gaines St., Little Rock, AR 72201

222 E. Van Buren, Lower Rio Grande
Valley, Harlingen, TX 78550

1205 Texas Ave., Lubbock, TX 79408

3105 Leopard St., Corpus Christi,
TX 78408

500 Fannin St., Shreveport, LA 71163

1001 Howard Ave., New Orleans,
LA 70113

50 Penn Place, Oklahoma City, OK 73118

727 E. Durango, San Antonio, TX 78205

Region VII

911 Walnut St., Kansas City, MO 64106

1150 Grand Ave., Kansas City, MO 64106

210 Walnut St., Des Moines, IA 50309

19th & Franam Sts., Omaha, NE 68102

1 Mercantile Tower, St. Louis, MO 63101

110 E. Waterman St., Wichita, KS 67202

Region VIII

1405 Curtis St., Denver, CO 80202

721 19th St., Denver, CO 80202

100 E. B St., Casper, WY 82601

653 2nd Ave. N, Fargo, ND 58102

618 Helena Ave., Helena, MT 59601

125 S. State St., Salt Lake City,
UT 84111

8th & Maine Aves, Sioux Falls,
SD 57102

515 9th St., Rapid City, SD 57701

Region IX

450 Golden Gate Ave., San Francisco,
CA 94102

211 Main St., San Francisco, CA 94105

1130 O St., Fresno, CA 93721

Ada Plaza Center Building, Agana, Guam

1149 Bethel St., Honolulu, HI 96813

301 E. Stewart St., Las Vegas, NV 89101

350 S. Figueroa St., Los Angeles,
CA 90014

112 N. Central Ave., Phoenix, AZ 85004

880 Front St., San Diego, CA 92101

2800 Cottage Way, Sacramento,
CA 95825

300 Booth St., Reno, NV 89509

Region X

710 2nd Ave., Seattle, WA 98104

915 2nd Ave., Seattle, WA 98104

1016 W. 6th Ave., Anchorage, AK 99501

501 1/2 2nd Ave., Fairbanks, AK 99701

216 N. 8th St., Boise, ID 83701

1220 S.W. 3rd Ave., Portland, OR 97204

651 U.S. Courthouse, Spokane,
WA 99210

General Services Administration

Headquarters office:
18th & F Sts. NW, Washington, DC 20405

Headquarters, Federal Supply Service
1941 Jefferson Davis Highway
Arlington, VA 22202
Mailing Address:
Washington, DC 20406

Regional Offices and Business Service Centers

Region I: John W. McCormack Federal
Building, Boston, MA 02109

Region II: 26 Federal Plaza, New York,
NY 10007

Region III: 7th & D Sts. SW, Washington,
DC 20407
600 Arch St., Philadelphia, PA 19106

Region IV: 1776 Peachtree St. NW,
Atlanta, GA 30309

Region V: 230 S. Dearborn St., Chicago,
IL 60604

Region VI: 1500 E. Bannister Rd.,
Kansas City, MO 64131

Region VII: 819 Taylor St. and
24000 Avila Rd., Fort Worth,
TX 76102
515 Rush St., Houston, TX 77002

Region VIII: Denver Federal Center,
Denver, CO 80225

Region IX: 525 Market St.,
San Francisco, CA 94105
300 N. Los Angeles, Los Angeles,
CA 90012

Region X: 915 2nd Ave., Seattle,
WA 98174

Department of Commerce

Headquarters office:
14th & Constitution NW
Washington, DC 20230

Field Offices

505 Marquette Ave. NW, Suite 1015
Albuquerque, NM 87102

412 Hill Bldg.
Anchorage, AK 99501

1365 Peachtree St. NE, Suite 600
Atlanta, GA 30309

415 U.S Customhouse, Gay &
Lombard Sts., Baltimore, MD 21202

908 S. 20th St., Suite 200
Birmingham, AL 35205

441 Stuart St., 10th floor
Boston, MA 02116

1312 Federal Bldg., 111 W. Huron St.
Buffalo, NY 14202

632 6th Ave., 3000 New Federal
Office Bldg., 500 Quamer St.
Charleston, WV 25301

6022 O'Mahoney Federal Center
2120 Capitol Ave., Cheyenne, WY 82001

1406 Mid-Continental Plaza Bldg.
55 E. Monroe St., Chicago, IL 60603

10504 Federal Office Bldg.
Cincinnati, OH 45205

666 Euclid Ave., Room 600
Cleveland, OH 44114

2611 Forest Dr., Forest Center
Columbia, SC 29204

1100 Commerce St., Room 7A5
Dallas, TX 75242

New Customhouse, 19th & Stout Sts.
Room 165, Denver CO 80202

817 Federal Bldg., 210 Walnut St.
Des Moines, IA 50309

445 Federal Bldg., 231 W. Lafayette
Detroit, MI 48226

203 Federal Bldg., W. Market St.
P.O. Box 1950, Greensboro, NC 27402

Federal Office Bldg., 450 Main St.
Room 610-B, Hartford, CT 06103

4106 Federal Office Bldg.
300 Ala Moana Blvd.
Honolulu, HI 96850

2625 Federal Bldg., Courthouse
515 Rusk St., Houston, TX 77002

357 U.S. Courthouse and
Federal Office Bldg., 46 E. Ohio St.
Indianapolis, IN 46204

11777 San Vincente Blvd.
Los Angeles, CA 90049

147 Jefferson Ave., Room 710
Memphis, TN 38103

City National Bank Bldg.
25 W. Flagler St., Room 821
Miami, FL 33130

Federal Bldg., U.S. Courthouse
517 E. Wisconsin Ave.
Minneapolis, MN 55401

Gateway Bldg., 4th Floor
Market St. & Penn Plaza
Newark, NJ 07102

432 International Trade Mart
2 Canal St., New Orleans, LA 70130

Federal Office Bldg.
26 Federal Plaza, Foley Square
New York, NY 10007

Capitol Plaza, 1815 Capitol St.
Suite 703A, Omaha, NE 68102

9448 Federal Bldg., 600 Arch St.
Philadelphia, PA 19106

Valley Bank Center
201 N. Central Ave., Suite 2950
Phoenix, AZ 85037

2002 Federal Bldg., 1000 Liberty Ave.
Pittsburgh, PA 15222

1220 S.W. 3rd Ave., Room 618
Portland, OR 97204

2028 Federal Bldg., 300 Booth St.
P.O. Box 50026, Reno, NV 89509

8010 Federal Bldg., 400 N. 8th St.
Richmond, VA 23240

120 S. Central Ave.
St. Louis, MO 63105

1203 Federal Bldg., 125 S. State St.
Salt Lake City, UT 84138

Federal Bldg., Box 36013
450 Golden Gate Ave.
San Francisco, CA 94102

Federal Bldg., Room 659
San Juan, PR (Hato Rey) 00918

222 U.S. Courthouse, P.O. Box 9746
125–29 Bull St., Savannah, GA 31402

Lake Union Bldg.
1700 Westlake Ave. N, Room 706
Seattle, WA 98109

Government Printing Office: bookstores and procurement centers

Main office:
North Capitol and H Sts. NW
Washington, DC 20402

Federal Bldg., 275 Peachtree St. NE
Atlanta, GA 30303*

9220 Parkway East-B
Roebuck Shopping City
Birmingham, AL 35206

John F. Kennedy Federal Bldg.
Sudbury St., Boston, MA 02203*

Everett McKinley Dirksen Bldg.
219 S. Dearborn St., Chicago, IL 60604*

Federal Office Bldg., 1240 E. 9th St.
Cleveland, OH 44114

Federal Bldg., 200 N. High St.
Columbus, OH 43215*

Federal Bldg., 1100 Commerce St.
Dallas, TX 75242*

Federal Bldg., 1961 Stout St.
Denver, CO 80202*

Patrick V. McNamara Federal Bldg.
477 Michigan Ave., Detroit, MI 48226

45 College Center, 9319 Gulf Freeway
Houston, TX 77017

Federal Bldg., 400 West Bay St.
Box 35089, Jacksonville, FL 32202

Federal Office Bldg., 601 E. 12th St.
Kansas City, MO 64106

Federal Office Bldg.
300 N. Los Angeles St.
Los Angeles, CA 90012*

Federal Bldg., 519 E. Wisconsin Ave.
Milwaukee, WI 53202

26 Federal Plaza
New York, NY 10007*

Federal Office Bldg., 600 Arch St.
Philadelphia, PA 19106*

Majestic Bldg., 720 N. Main St.
Pueblo, CO 81003

Federal Office Bldg.
450 Golden Gate Ave.
San Francisco, CA 94102*

Federal Office Bldg., 915 Second Ave.
Seattle, WA 98104*

Government Printing Office
710 N. Capitol St. NW
Washington, DC 20402*

Dept. of Commerce, 14th & E Sts. NW
Washington, DC 20230

Dept. of State, Rm. 2817, North Lobby
21st & C Sts. NW
Washington, DC 20520

Pentagon, Main Concourse, South End
Washington, DC 20310

USIA, 1776 Pennsylvania Ave.
Washington, DC 20547

HHS, Room 1528
330 Independence Ave. SW
Washington, DC 20201

---

*Procurement center

Directory of

Key Government

Installations

and Offices

Approximately 130,000 government employees are kept busy in about 15,000 "buying activities," handling purchasing for the U.S. government. No one has ever compiled a complete directory of these, although there are a number of brief listings. In fact, each regional GSA office can furnish a partial list of buying activities in its own region, but this list is far from complete.

The offices listed in Appendix 1 can steer you to most of the routine buying of the government. Much of the remaining buying includes some $18 billion of "R&D" at current levels, which is distributed among many agencies, and much of that is readily available to small firms.

All federal agencies are required to have a small business representative or advisor and a minority business representative. In large agencies, there are often individuals assigned full time to these functions, and there are often several individuals in the agency. In other cases, someone in the agency, often the contracting officer, wears several hats and handles these functions. In any case, in making initial contacts, it is wise to seek out the individual(s) who handle(s) these functions and ask for assistance.

In the following listings, many of the programs are identified specifically. But there are other cases in which the agency has advised us to have those seeking business communicate with the appropriate representative. In many cases, the agency can and will supply a brochure or manual free of charge to familiarize applicants with the agency's programs and contract or grant opportunities.

The information presented here is reasonably accurate at the time of this writing. However, things do change, even in the government. And because personnel inevitably change, the names of individuals are not supplied. Relatively few would be useful, in any case. It is necessary to know only that there is a small business representative or advisor available to help and that additional, detailed information is available for the asking.

Department of Agriculture

Federal Research, Science and Education
   Administration
Cooperative Research, Science and
   Education Administration
Both above:
U.S. Department of Agriculture
Washington, DC 20250

Competitive Grants Office, Science and
   Education Administration
U.S. Department of Agriculture
1300 Wilson Blvd.
Arlington, VA 22209

Department of Commerce

Experimental Technology Incentives
   Program
National Bureau of Standards
Administration Bldg., Room A-739
Washington, DC 20234

Maritime Administration
Department Commerce Room 4884
Programs & Technology Dept. Office
National Oceanic and Atmospheric
RD1, Rockville, MD 20852

Department of Defense

Director, Defense Civil Preparedness
   Agency
Department of Defense, The Pentagon
Washington, DC 20301

Director, Defense Communications
   Engineering Center
Derey Engineering Bldg.
1860 Wiehle Ave.
Reston, VA 22090

Director, Command and Control
   Technical Center
Defensive Communications Agency
Washington, DC 20301

Director, Defense Communications
   Agency
ATTN: MILSATCOM Systems Office
Code 800
Washington, DC 20305

WWMCCS System Engineer
WWMCCS System Engineering
   Organization
Washington, DC 20305

Defense Nuclear Agency
Washington, DC 20305

Armed Forces Radiobiology Research
Institute
Defense Nuclear Agency
Bethesda, MD 20014

Field Command, DNA
Kirtland AFB, NM 87115

Department of the Air Force

Space and Missile Systems
Organization (BC)
Los Angeles Air Force Station
Box 92960, Worldway Postal Center
Los Angeles, CA 90009

Aerospace Medical Division
Directorate of R&D Procurement (BC)
Aeronautical Systems Div.
Wright-Patterson AFB, OH 45433

Air Force Electronic Systems Div. (BC)
Hanscom AFB
Bedford, MA 01731

Space and Missile Test Center
Vandenberg AFB
Lompoc, CA 93437

Air Force Aeronautical Systems Div.
Wright-Patterson AFB, OH 45433

Air Force Flight Test Center (BC)
Edwards AFB, CA 93523

Kirtland Procurement Center (BC-39)
Air Force Contract Management Div.
Kirtland AFB, NM 87115

Air Force Eastern Test Range (BC)
Patrick AFB, FL 32925

Rome Air Development Center
Griffis AFB, NY 13441

Armament Test and Development
Ctr. (BC)
Eglin AFB, FL 32542

Arnold Air Force Station, TN 37389

Air Force Office of Scientific Research
Bolling AFB, Washington, DC 20332

Department of the Army

BMD Systems Command
Box 1500
Huntsville, AL 35807

HQ DARCOM
5001 Eisenhower Ave.
Alexandria, VA 22333

Human Engineering Laboratories (HEL)
Aberdeen Proving Ground, MD 21005

Army Material Systems Analysis
Agency (AMSAA)
Aberdeen Proving Ground, MD 21005

Harry Diamond Laboratories
2800 Powder Mill Rd.
Adelphi, MD 20788

Army Materials and Mechanics Research
Center
Watertown, MA 02172

Army Natick R&D Center
Natick, MA 01760

Army Mobility Equipment R&D
Command
Fort Belvoir, VA 22060

ARRADCOM, ATTN: DRDAR-SB
Dover, NJ 07801

Chemical Systems Laboratory
ATTN: DRDAR-SB
Aberdeen Proving Ground, MD 21010

Benet Weapons Laboratory
ATTN: DRDAR-LCB
Watervliet, NY 12189

Ballistic Research Laboratories (BRL)
ATTN: DRDAR-BL
Aberdeen Proving Ground, MD 21010

Army Aviation R&D Command
St. Louis, MO 63166

Army Electronics R&D Command
2800 Powder Mill Rd.
Adelphi, MD 20788

Army Communications R&D Command
Fort Monmouth, NJ 07703

Army Missile R&D Command
Redstone Arsenal
Huntsville, AL 35809

U.S. Tank-Automotive R&D Command
Warren, MI 48090

Army Yuma Proving Ground
Yuma Proving Ground, AZ 85364

Office of the Chief of Engineers
Washington, DC 22314

Army Eng. Waterways Experiment Station
Box 631, Vicksburg, MS 39180

Army Cold Regions Research and
Engineering Laboratory
Box 282
Hanover, NH 03755

Army Construction Engineering
Research Laboratory
Box 4005
Champaign, IL 61820

Army Engineer Topographic Laboratories
Fort Belvoir, VA 22060

Army Coastal Engineering Research
Center
Kingman Bldg.
Fort Belvoir, VA 22060

Army Medical R&D Command
ATTN: SGRD-RP
Forrestal Bldg.
Washington, DC 20314

Walter Reed Army Institute of Research
Washington, DC 20012

Department of the Navy

Office of Naval Research
Room 718
800 N. Quincy St.
Arlington, VA 22217

Chief of Naval Personnel
Department of the Navy
Washington, DC 20370

Naval Medical R&D Command
National Naval Medical Center
Bethesda, MD 20814

Naval Air Systems Command
Washington, DC 20361

Naval Electronics System Command
Washington, DC 20360

Naval Facilities Engineering Command
200 Stovall St.
Alexandria, VA 22322

Naval Sea Systems Command
Washington, DC 20362

Naval Supply Systems Command
Washington, DC 20376

Naval Research Laboratory
4555 Overlook Ave. SW
Washington, DC 20375

Naval Civil Engineering Laboratory
Naval Construction Battalion Center
Port Hueneme, CA 93043

Naval Underwater Systems Center
New London Laboratory
New London, CT 06320

Naval Coastal Systems Laboratory
Panama City, FL 32401

Naval Surface Weapons Laboratory
White Oak Laboratory
Silver Spring, MD 20910

Naval Underwater Systems Center
Newport Laboratory
Newport, RI 02840

Naval Ship Engineering Center
Washington, DC 20362

Naval Air Test Center
Patuxent River, MD 20670

Naval Air Propulsion Test Center
Trenton, NJ 08628

Naval Air Development Center
Warminster, PA 18974

Naval Air Engineering Center
Lakehurst, NJ 08735

Naval Surface Weapons Center
Dahlgren Laboratory
Dahlgren, VA 22448

Naval Weapons Center
China Lake, CA 93555

Naval Missile Center
Point Mugu, CA 93042

Naval Ocean Systems Center
San Diego, CA 92152

Naval Training Equipment Center
Orlando, FL 32813

Naval Ship R&D Center
Bethesda, MD 20084

Naval Weapons Support Center (Code 50)
Crane, IN 47522

Naval Avionics Facility
6000 East 21st St.
Indianapolis, IN 46218

Naval Explosive Ordnance Disposal
Facility
Indian Head, MD 20640

Naval Ordnance Missile Test Facility
White Sands Missile Range, NM 88002

Naval Ship Missile Systems Eng. Station
Port Hueneme, CA 93043

Naval Ordnance Station
Indian Head, MD 20640

Naval Weapons Station
Yorktown, VA 23691

Naval Oceanographic Office
NSTL Branch (Code 4130)
Bay St. Louis, MS 39522

Department of Energy

DOE Div. of Procurement
Railway Labor Bldg., Rm. 308
401 First St. NW
Washington, DC 20545

National Institutes of Health

National Institute of Allergy and
  Infectious Diseases
Westwood Bldg., Rm. 707
5333 Westbard Ave.
Bethesda, MD 20016

National Institute of Arthritis,
  Metabolism, and Digestive Diseases
Bldg. 31, Rm. 2B19
9000 Rockville Pike
Bethesda, MD 20014

National Cancer Institute
Research Contracts Branch
Bldg. 31, Rm. 10A20
9000 Rockville Pike
Bethesda, MD 20014

National Institute of Child Health and
  Human Development
Contracts Management Section
Landow Bldg., Rm. C619
Bethesda, MD 20014

National Institute of Dental Research
Contracts Management Section
Westwood Bldg., Rm. 539
5333 Westbard Ave.
Bethesda, MD 20016

National Institutes of Health
Research Contracts Branch
Bldg. 31, Rm. 1B32
9000 Rockville Pike
Bethesda, MD 20014

National Heart, Lung, and Blood Institute
Westwood Bldg., Rm. 650
5333 Westbard Ave.
Bethesda, MD 20016

National Institute of Neurological
  Diseases and Stroke
Federal Bldg., Rm. 1012
7550 Wisconsin Ave.
Bethesda, MD 20014

National Library of Medicine
Bldg. 38, Rm. C1
Rockville Pike
Bethesda, MD 20014

Department of Housing and Urban Development

Principal small business opportunities in HUD are in the Office of Development and Research, in connection with the following programs:

Housing Assistance Research
Safety and Standards Research
Housing Economic Data and Analysis
Consumer and Equal Opportunity Research
Community Conservation Research
Community Development Research
Energy Conservation and Standards Research
Data Collection and Analysis
HUD Program Evaluation, Dissemination and Research Support
Office of Procurement and Contracts
Department of Housing and Urban Development
451 7th St. SW
Room B-133 (711 Bldg.)
Washington, DC 20410

Department of the Interior

Office of Mineral Information
Bureau of Mines, Dept. of the Interior
2401 E St. NW
Washington, DC 20241

Geological Survey
Department of the Interior
12201 Sunrise Valley Dr.
Reston, VA 22092

Department of Justice

Grants and Contracts Management Div.
Office of the Comptroller
633 Indiana Ave. NW
Washington, DC 20531

Department of Transportation

The DOT conducts many studies and researches connected with transportation and its problems. For contracts emanating from the Office of the Secretary, contact the following:

Procurement Operations Division
Department of Transportation
Office of the Secretary of Transportation
Washington, DC 20590

Federal Aviation Administration ALG-380
800 Independence Ave. SW
Washington, DC 20590

National Aviation Facilities Experimental Center, ANA-51
Atlantic City, NJ 08405

Federal Highway Administration
400 7th St. SW
Washington, DC 20590

Federal Railroad Administration
National Highway Traffic Safety Admin.
400 7th St. SW
Washington, DC 20590

Urban Mass Transportation Administration
400 7th St. SW
Washington, DC 20590

U.S. Coast Guard Academy
New London, CT 06320

U.S. Coast Guard
Headquarters (G-FCP)
400 7th St. SW
Washington, DC 20590

Environmental Protection Agency

Contracts Management Division, EPA
Research Triangle Park, NC 27711

Contracts Management Division, EPA
Cincinnati, OH 45268

Headquarters Contract Operations
(PM-214), EPA
Washington, DC 20460

National Aeronautics and Space Administration

NASA Headquarters Contracts Division
Washington, DC 29546

NASA/Ames Research Center
Moffett Field, CA 94035

NASA/Dryden Flight Research Center
Box 273
Edwards, CA 93523

NASA/Goddard Space Flight Center
Greenbelt, MD 20771

Jet Propulsion Laboratory
4800 Oak Grove Dr.
Pasadena, CA 91103

NASA/Johnson Space Center
Houston, TX 77058

NASA/Kennedy Space Center, FL 32899

NASA/Langley Research Center
Langley Station
Hampton, VA 23365

NASA/Lewis Research Center
2100 Brookpark Rd.
Cleveland, OH 44135

NASA/Marshall Space Flight Center
Huntsville, AL 35812

NASA/National Space Technology Labs
Bay St. Louis, MS 39520

NASA/Wallops Flight Center
Wallops Island, VA 23337

National Science Foundation

Applied Science and Research
Applications Directorate
National Science Foundation
1800 G St. NW
Washington, DC 20550

U.S. Postal Service

R&D Program Dept.
Advanced Mail Systems Development
    Office
Postal Technology Research Office
Letter Mail Systems Development Office
General Systems Development Office
Support Services Division
All are at:
11711 Parklawn Dr.
Rockville, MD 20852

APPENDIX 3

Federal Information
Centers

Most of us know the U.S. government operates many programs and offers information and other services to the public. But most of us have no idea how to track down the desired information or service. (In fact, a Washington, D.C., firm, Washington Researchers, makes a business of helping firms locate information and even teaches others how to find it in Washington, D.C.!)

The government has made an effort to help the poor, bewildered citizen by establishing Federal Information Centers as a function and responsibility of the General Services Administration. The service is designed to aid the public, which can visit or call any of the offices listed here with whatever questions they have to ask. The service is meant to provide answers and guidance. When it can't do so immediately, the service will track down the information on behalf of the requestor. In many cases, a toll-free tie line is provided.

Location	Tel. No.	Address	Toll-Free Tie Line to
Alabama			
Birmingham	(205) 322-8591		Atlanta, GA
Mobile	(205) 438-1421		New Orleans, LA
Arizona			
Tucson	(602) 622-1511		Phoenix, AZ
Phoenix	(602) 261-3313	230 N. 1st Ave. 85025	
Arkansas			
Little Rock	(501) 378-6177		Memphis, TN

Location	Tel. No.	Address	Toll-Free Tie Line to
California			
Los Angeles	(213) 688-3800	300 N. Los Angeles St. 90012	
Sacramento	(916) 440-3344	650 Capitol Mall 95814	
San Diego	(714) 293-6030	880 Front St. 92188	
San Francisco	(415) 556-6600	450 Golden Gate Ave. 94102	
San Jose	(408) 275-7422		San Francisco, CA
Santa Ana	(714) 836-2386		Los Angeles, CA
Colorado			
Colorado Springs	(303) 471-9491		Denver, CO
Denver	(303) 837-3602	1961 Stout St. 80294	
Pueblo	(303) 544-9523		Denver, CO
Connecticut			
Hartford	(203) 527-2617		New York, NY
New Haven	(203) 624-4720		New York, NY
District of Columbia			
Washington	(202) 755-8660	7th & D Sts. SW 20407	
Florida			
Fort Lauderdale	(305) 522-8531		Miami, FL
Miami	(305) 350-4155	51 S.W. 1st Ave. 33130	
Jacksonville	(904) 354-4756		St. Petersburg, FL
St. Petersburg	(813) 893-3495	144 1st Ave. S 33701	
Tampa	(813) 229-7911		St. Petersburg, FL
West Palm Beach	(305) 833-7566		Miami, FL
Georgia			
Atlanta	(404) 526-6891	275 Peachtree St. NE 30303	
Hawaii			
Honolulu	(808) 546-8620	300 Ala Moana Blvd. 96850	
Illinois			
Chicago	(312) 353-4242	219 S. Dearborn St. 60604	
Indiana			
Gary	(219) 883-4110		Indianapolis, IN
Indianapolis	(317) 269-7373	575 N. Pennsylvania St. 46204	
Iowa			
Des Moines	(515) 284-4448		Omaha, NE

Location	Tel. No.	Address	Toll-Free Tie Line to
Kansas			
Topeka	(913) 297-2866		Kansas City, MO
Wichita	(316) 263-6931		Kansas City, MO
Kentucky			
Louisville	(502) 582-6261	600 Federal Place 40202	
Louisiana			
New Orleans	(504) 589-6696	701 Loyola Ave. 70113	
Maryland			
Baltimore	(301) 962-4980	31 Hopkins Plaza 21201	
Massachusetts			
Boston	(617) 223-7121	John F. Kennedy Federal Bldg. 02203	
Michigan			
Detroit	(313) 226-7016	447 Michigan Ave. 48226	
Grand Rapids	(616) 451-2628		Detroit, MI
Minnesota			
Minneapolis	(612) 725-2073	110 S. 4th St. 55401	
Missouri			
Kansas City	(816) 374-2466	601 E. 12th St. 64106	
St. Joseph	(816) 233-8206		Kansas City, MO
St. Louis	(314) 425-4106	1520 Market St. 63103	
Nebraska			
Omaha	(402) 221-3353	215 N. 17th St. 68102	
New Jersey			
Newark	(201) 645-3600	970 Broad St. 07102	
Paterson/			
Passaic	(201) 523-0717		Newark, NJ
Trenton	(609) 396-4400		Newark, NJ
New Mexico			
Albuquerque	(505) 766-3091	500 Gold Ave. SW 87101	
Santa Fe	(505) 983-7743		Albuquerque, NM
New York			
Albany	(518) 463-4421		New York, NY
Buffalo	(716) 846-4010	111 W. Huron St. 14202	
New York	(212) 264-4464	26 Federal Plaza 10007	
Rochester	(716) 546-5075		Buffalo, NY
Syracuse	(315) 476-8545		Buffalo, NY
North Carolina			
Charlotte	(704) 376-3600		Atlanta, GA
Ohio			
Akron	(216) 375-5638		Cleveland, OH

Location	Tel. No.	Address	Toll-Free Tie Line to
Cincinnati	(513) 684-2801	550 Main St. 45202	
Cleveland	(216) 522-4040	1240 E. 9th St. 44199	
Columbus	(614) 221-1014		Cincinnati, OH
Dayton	(513) 223-7377		Cincinnati, OH
Toledo	(419) 241-3223		Cleveland, OH
Oklahoma			
Oklahoma City	(405) 231-4368	201 N.W. 3rd St. 73102	
Tulsa	(918) 584-4193		Oklahoma City, OK
Oregon			
Portland	(503) 221-2222	1220 S.W. 3rd Ave. 97204	
Pennsylvania			
Philadelphia	(215) 597-7042	600 Arch St. 19106	
Allentown/			
Bethlehem	(215) 821-7785		Philadelphia, PA
Pittsburgh	(412) 644-3456	1000 Liberty Ave. 15222	
Scranton	(717) 346-7081		Philadelphia, PA
Rhode Island			
Providence	(401) 331-5565		Boston, MA
Tennessee			
Chattanooga	(615) 265-8231		
Memphis	(901) 521-3285	167 N. Main St. 38103	
Nashville	(615) 242-6167		Memphis, TN
Texas			
Austin	(512) 472-5494		Houston, TX
Dallas	(214) 749-2131		Fort Worth, TX
Fort Worth	(817) 334-3624	819 Taylor St. 76102	
Houston	(713) 226-5711	515 Rusk Ave. 77002	
San Antonio	(512) 222-4544		Houston, TX
Utah			
Ogden	(801) 399-1347		Salt Lake City, UT
Salt Lake City	(801) 524-5353	125 S. State St. 84138	
Virginia			
Newport News	(804) 244-0480		Norfolk, VA
Norfolk	(804) 441-6723	Stanwick Bldg., E. Virginia Beach Blvd. 23502	
Richmond	(804) 643-4928		Norfolk, VA
Roanoke	(703) 982-8591		Norfolk, VA
Washington			
Seattle	(206) 442-0570	915 2nd Ave. 98174	
Tacoma	(206) 383-5230		Seattle, WA
Wisconsin			
Milwaukee	(414) 271-2273		Chicago, IL

APPENDIX 4

Federal Supply

Schedules

Explanation

The Federal Supply Service (FSS), General Services Administration, has three basic buying programs.

The *Federal Supply Schedule Program* is a system of approximately 300 Federal Supply Schedules, which are, in effect, annual supply agreements with a number of suppliers of both goods and services. Some schedules are national agreements with single suppliers; others are multiple-award schedules, entered into with many competitive suppliers. Being on a schedule may therefore qualify you to supply your services or goods on a purely local basis, within the geographical limits set by the schedule (but it is possible to get on schedules for more than one area, in these cases), to be a supplier on a national basis, and even to be virtually the sole supplier of some class of goods or services. These schedules account for about $2 billion annually, at current procurement levels.

In the *Stock Program*, the FSS buys goods for warehousing and distributing from 20 supply depots and 75 GSA self-service stores.

Through the *Special Buying Program*, the FSS provides a service to the other federal agencies to help them buy items not listed regularly in the schedules or stocked in the stock program.

The Federal Supply Service buys about $3 billion worth of goods and services every year, accounting for three-fifths of the GSA procurement.

This appendix contains a generalized listing of Federal Supply Schedules in force at the time of this writing (schedules do change, however, and it is necessary to verify the appropriateness of a schedule at the time you wish to apply for inclusion) and a reproduction of a typical multiple-award schedule.

List of Schedules

Schedule Number	Name	Description or Typical Items
NIIS	New Item Introductory Schedule	All types items and services
19	Small Craft and Marine Equipment	Boats, motors, accessories
23	Wheel and Track Vehicles	Snowmobiles, autos, trailers, carts
25 I	Vehicular Equipment Components	Tire chains and clutch facings
25, 28, 29, 38, 39	Parts and Accessories	Automotive, construction, excavating, mining, materials handling, highway maintenance
26 II	Pneumatic Tires and Inner Tubes	Highway, off-highway, industrial
26 IV A	Tires	Industrial, solid and cushion
29 IA	Engine Accessories	Spark plugs, oil filters, and elements
30	Power Transmission Equipment	V-belts
32, 34	Woodworking and Metalworking	Spare parts and accessories
35 II	Machinery and Equipment Electrical Trash Compactors and Balers	Industrial, institutional, and mobile
35 IV A	Appliances	Household and commercial washers, dryers
36 II A,B	Special Industrial Machinery	Lithographic printing plates and solutions; printing, duplicating, binding equipment
36 II C	Special Industry Machinery	Security shredding machines
36 IV	Special Industry Machinery	Copying equipment, supplies, services
37 I A	Special Industry Machinery	Chain saws

Schedule Number	Name	Description or Typical Items
37 I A	Agricultural Equipment	Cattleguards
37 II A	Lawn and Garden Equipment	Lawn mowers, edgers, shredders, and so on
38 I A	Cleaning and Equipment	Rider- or walker-operated, self-propelled
39 II A	Materials Handling Equipment	Conveyors, hand trucks, towveyer trucks
41 I A	Air Conditioning Equipment	Domestic and window units
41 I B	Air Conditioning Equipment	Central air and export-use window units
41 III A	Appliances	Household refrigerators
41 III B	Refrigeration Equipment	Drinking water dispensers
42 I	Firefighting Equipment and Supplies	Fire extinguishers, accessories
42 II	Safety and Rescue Equipment	Breathing apparatus, safety climbing equipment, welders' protective equipment
42 III	Safety Equipment	Shoe decontamination unit
42 IV A	Safety Equipment	Nonprescription safety glasses
44 I A	Air Treatment and Conditioning Equipment	Air cleaners, portable humidifiers, dehumidifiers, heat pumps
45 IV A	Sanitation Equipment	Industrial incinerators
45 VII A	Plumbing and Heating Equipment	Domestic water heaters, gas and electric
45 VIII A	Plumbing and Sanitation Equipment	Household garbage disposers
46 I A	Water Purification Equipment	Water stills, storage tanks, purity conductivity meters, and reverse osmosis systems
47	Pipe	Culvert, steel and aluminum
47 II A	Pipe	Plastic
49 I A	Maintenance and Repair Shop Equipment	Hydraulic jacks, heat guns, and auger machines
49 I B	Maintenance and Repair Shop Equipment	Motor vehicle and miscellaneous maintenance and repair shop equipment

Schedule Number	Name	Description or Typical Items
49 II	Maintenance and Repair Shop Equipment	Ultrasonic cleaning systems and accessories
51 I A	Hand and Power Tools	Pneumatic, hydraulic, powder-actuated, gasoline engine, and special-purpose drill bits
51 II A	Hand and Power Tools	Electric
52	Measuring Tools	Measuring tapes
54 I A	Prefabricated Structures	Buildings, enclosures, and sound controlled rooms
54 II A	Scaffolding, Shoring, Work and Service Platforms, Steps	Portable
56 III A	Construction and Building Materials	Solar control film and screens
58 II	Communication Equipment	Message- and data-transmitting equipment and background music systems
58 III B	Communication Equipment	Professional audio and video recording equipment
58 V A	Communication Supplies	Audio magnetic tape, reels, and cartridges; video magnetic tape, cassettes, and so on
58 V C	Communication Supplies	Instrumentation recording tape, reels
58 V D	Communication Supplies	Recording tapes, audio cassettes, reels
58 VI	Communication Equipment	Telephone, intercom PA systems
58 VII	Communication Equipment	Radio transmitting-receiving equipment
58 IX	Communication Equipment	Telemetry, laser, radionavigation, radar, underwater sound, signal data
59 III	Electronic Components	Microelectronic circuit devices
61 I	Batteries	6- and 12-volt lead acid, automotive
61 II	Batteries	Heavy duty, storage
61 III	Batteries	Dry cell
61 IV A	Batteries	Automotive, storage, wet-charged

Schedule Number	Name	Description or Typical Items
61 V A	Power and Distribution Equipment	Portable generators
61 V B	Power and Distribution Equipment	Nonrotating battery chargers
61 VII A	Transformers	For refrigerators
62 I	Lighting Fixtures and Lamps	Household
62 II	Lighting Fixtures and Lamps	Light sets, emergency and auxiliary
62 III	Lighting Fixtures and Lamps	Fluorescent and incandescent
62, 67	Lamps	Electrical and photographic
63	Alarm and Signal Systems	Transit and traffic signals, miscellaneous alarms and signals
65 I A	Drugs and Pharmaceuticals	Drugs and pharmaceutical products
65 I B	Drugs and Pharmaceuticals	Drugs and pharmaceutical products
65 II B	Medical and Veterinary Equipment	Surgical instruments and supplies
65 II C	Dental Equipment and Supplies	Operatory and laboratory
65 II D	Medical and Dental Equipment	Monitoring, electronic, patient aids, tables, physiotherapy equipment
65 III A	Medical and Dental Supplies	Gloves, medical and surgical
65 IV	Medical and Dental Supplies	Prescription ophthalmic lenses, glasses
65 V A	Medical and Dental Supplies	Film, X-ray 90-second processing
65 V B,C	Medical and Dental Supplies	X-ray film, medical and dental
65 VI	Medical and Dental Supplies	Antibacterial deodorant soap
66 I A	Instruments and Laboratory Equipment	Measuring and drafting instruments
66 I B	Instruments and Laboratory Equipment	Magnifiers and reducing glasses, lettering sets, electronic distance-measuring equipment
66 II B	Instruments and Laboratory Supplies	Glass, plastic, metal lab ware; lab distillation and demineralizing systems

Schedule Number	Name	Description or Typical Items
66 II C	Instruments and Laboratory Equipment	Microscopes, centrifuges, pH meters
66 II D	Instruments and Laboratory Supplies	Industrial radiographic X-ray film
66 II E	Instruments and Laboratory Equipment	Analytical balances and scales
66 II F	Instruments and Laboratory Equipment	Amplifiers: low frequency, power, pulse
66 II G	Instruments and Laboratory Equipment	Graphic recording instruments
66 II H	Instruments and Laboratory Equipment	Measuring and test instruments
66 II I,J	Instruments and Laboratory Equipment	Microwave and low-frequency instruments
66 II L	Instruments and Laboratory Equipment	Power supplies, transducers, servos
66 II M	Instruments and Laboratory Equipment	Spectrophotometers, densitometers, and so on
66 II N	Instruments and Laboratory Equipment	Analyzers, chromatographs, colony counters, dilutors, pipetters
66 II O	Instruments and Laboratory Equipment	Laboratory apparatus, furniture, refrigerators, freezers
66 II Q	Instruments and Laboratory Equipment	Oceanographic, environmental, weather
66 III	Instruments and Laboratory Equipment	Time recorders, date and time stamps
66 V A	Instruments and Laboratory Equipment	Solar and wind energy systems and components
66 VI A	Laboratory Equipment	Glassware and supplies
67 II B	Photographic Supplies	Film, chemicals, paper
67 III B	Photo Equipment	Cameras, projectors, developing equipment
67 IV A	Microphoto Supplies and Mobile Projection Stands	Mobile direct-positive and thermal developing, duplicating film, mobile projection stands
68 I A	Chemicals and Chemical Products	Bulk sodium chloride

Schedule Number	Name	Description or Typical Items
68 I B	Chemicals, Chemical Products	Calcium chloride
68 I C	Chemicals, Chemical Products	Bleach, laundry and household
68 II A	Chemicals, Chemical Products	Herbicides
68 III A	Chemicals, Chemical Products	Medical gases
68 III C	Chemicals, Chemical Products	Dry ice
68 III D	Chemicals, Chemical Products	Liquefied petroleum gases
68 III E,F	Chemicals, Chemical Products	Refrigerant fluorocarbons and sulfur hex
68 III G	Chemicals, Chemical Products	Helium
68 III H	Chemicals, Chemical Products	Fire-extinguishing fluorocarbons
68 III K	Chemicals, Chemical Products	Oxygen, aviator's breathing
68 III L	Chemicals, Chemical Products	Industrial gases in cylinders
68 III M	Chemicals, Chemical Products	Industrial gases, liquid, bulk, cylinders
68 V	Chemicals, Chemical Products	Boiler feedwater and a-c compounds
68 VI	Chemicals, Chemical Products	Sanitizers, deodorants, disinfectant cleaners
69	Training Courses, Aids, Devices	Teaching, reading test-scoring machines
70 X	Data Processing Storage and Related Equipment	Storage, handling transport equipment for data processing supplies
70 XI	Data Processing Supplies	Edp 1/2" tape, 1600 and 6250 bpi
71 I A	Household Furniture	Ranch style
71 I B	Household Furniture	Early American and 18th-century English
71 II A	Household Furniture	Upholstered living room
71 II B	Household Furniture	Modular multiple and individual seating
71 III	Household Furniture	Danish, traditional, and modern
71 V A	Office Furniture	Tables, folding legs; folding chairs, wood and metal
71 V B	Office Furniture	Bulletin boards and key cabinets
71 V C	Office Furniture	Steel vertical blueprint filing cabinets, roll drawing files

Schedule Number	Name	Description or Typical Items
71 V D	Office and Field Furniture	Map and plan filing cabinets, modular steel, folding end table
71 V E	Office Furniture	Contemporary steel filing cabinets, shelf files, card files
71 V F	Office Furniture	Freestanding partitions
71 VI A	Office Furniture	Executive traditional wood
71 VII A	Household Furniture	Metal indoor-outdoor, rec room, lobby
71 VII B	Household Furniture	Metal frame dormitory
71 VIII A	Office Furniture	Executive unitized wood
71 X A,B	Furniture	Special purpose, classroom, auditorium
71 XI A,B	Office Furniture	Security filing cabinets, safes, vaults
71 XII A	Office Furniture	Executive, modern, wood and metal
71 XIII A,B	Library Furniture	Wood and metal
71 XIV A	Shop Furniture	Desks, benches, tables
71 XV	Household Furniture	Traditional wood, dinette tables and chairs
71 XVI B	Household Furniture	Motel-type and sofa beds
71 XVII	Hospital Furniture	Patient's room
71 XIX	Furniture	Contemporary wall units, office use
71 XX	Household Furniture	Contemporary oak
71 XXI	Office Furniture	Acoustical partitions
71 XXII	Furniture	Lounge and reception room, recliners
71 XXIII	Household and Office Accessories	Artificial plants, planters, urns, art
71 XXV	Furniture	Storage cabinets
71 XXVI A	Casual Style and Household Furniture	Rattan, plastic, outdoor metal casual
71 XXVII A	Furniture	Office and household, centurion by Federal Prison Industries*

Schedule Number	Name	Description or Typical Items
71 XXVII B	Office Furniture	Contemporary centurion by Federal Prison Industries*
71 XXVIII A	Office Furniture	Lateral files, special sizes and uses
71 XXIX A	Office Furniture	Storage and sorting cabinets, bins
71 XXX A	Office Furniture	Cabinets and desks, card punch and programmer
71 XXXI A	Furniture	Directory boards
72 I A	Household and Commercial Furnishings	Carpets, rugs, carpet tiles, cushions
72 I B	Household and Commercial Furnishings	Floor coverings: tile, linoleum, vinyl
72 I C	Household and Commercial Furnishings	Entranceway carpet mats, mattings
72 I D	Household and Commercial Furnishings	Special-purpose carpet
72 II	Household and Commercial Furnishings	Window shades: cloth, vinyl, fiberglass
72 III A	Commercial Furnishings	Shopping handcarts, nesting
72 V	Household and Commercial Furnishings	Draperies, bedspreads, drapery hardware, cubicle curtains, shower curtains
72 VI A	Household and Commercial Furnishings	Venetian blinds
72 VII A	Household and Commercial Furnishings	Plastic trash receptacles
73 III	Food Service, Handling, Refrigeration, Storage, and Cleaning Equipment	Cabinet/shower (nonrefrigerating, nonheating), cooking equipment, dishwashing equipment, food preparation equipment
73 IV A	Appliances	Household gas ranges
73 IV B	Appliances	Commercial and household electric ranges
73 V A	Appliances	Household dishwashers
74 I	Office Machines	Electric typewriters, composing, photocomposing, and word-processing machines

Schedule Number	Name	Description or Typical Items
74 II,III	Office Machines	Adding, calculating, dictating, miscellaneous
74 IV	Visible Record Equipment	Book, cabinet, individual style frames, posting and ledger trays, tub files, and so on
74 V	Office Machines	Manual typewriters, portable and nonportable
74 VIII	Office Machines	Electric erasers, embossing, and stencil cutting machines
74 XIII A	Word-Processing Supplies	Magnetic data recording cards
75 I C	Office Supplies	Special-use papers, overlay sheets, and so on
75 I D	Office Supplies	Plotting paper and supplies
75 II A	Office Supplies	Pencils, marking tapes, chart supplies, and so on
75 II B	Office Supplies	Looseleaf binders, label tapes, staplers, map tacks, and so on
75 IV A,B	Office Supplies	Rubber stamps
75 IV C	Office Supplies	Pre-inked rubber stamps
75 V	Office Supplies	Envelopes, mailing
75 VII	Office Supplies	U.S. government national credit cards
75 VIII A	Office Supplies	Tab cards, aperture cards, copy cards
75 IX	Office Devices	Contemporary desk accessories
76 I	Publications	Dictionaries, encyclopedias, maps, and so on
76 II	Publications	Law, tax, reporting periodicals
76 III A	Publications	Medical, trade, text, technical
76 III B	Publications	Medical, trade, text, technical
77 I	Home Entertainment Equipment	Phono records, cassettes
77 II	Musical Instruments	Instruments, amplifiers, accessories
77 III	Home Entertainment Equipment	TV, radio, phonographs, recorders
78 I A	Recreational, Athletic Equipment	Athletic and sporting goods
78 I B	Athletic, Recreational Equipment	Indoor recreational, gym equipment

Schedule Number	Name	Description or Typical Items
78 I C	Athletic, Recreational Equipment	Outdoor
79 I A	Cleaning Equipment, Supplies	Vacuum cleaners, shampooers, polishers
79 I B	Cleaning Equipment, Supplies	Vacuum cleaners, shampooers, polishers
79 II A	Cleaning Equipment, Supplies	Detergents
80 I A	Paint	Tree-marking paint
80 II A	Paint	Gloss and semi-gloss latex
81 I A	Packaging, Packing Supplies	Cushioning materials
81 II A	Packaging, Packing Supplies	Steel and nonmetallic strapping
84 II A	Clothing and Furnishings	Special-purpose clothing
84 II B	Clothing and Furnishings	Footwear and special-purpose clothing
84 III A	Clothing and Furnishings	Men's and young men's
84 III B,C	Clothing and Furnishings	Misses', women's, boys', girls', infants'
84 IV	Jewelry	Civilian career service emblems, plaques
84 V A	Clothing and Footwear	Athletic and recreational
87 IV	Agricultural Supplies	Seeds
87 V	Agricultural Supplies	Fertilizers and hydrated lime
89 I	Subsistence	Nonperishable
89 IV A	Subsistence	Freeze-dried foods
91 II	Miscellaneous Supplies	Cutout letters, numbers, striping tape
93 II	Nonmetallic Fabricated Materials	Reflectorized fabric, sheeting, tape
99 IV A	Signs	Signs and components, mounting fixtures
99 VI A	Trophies and Awards	Trophies, awards, plaques, pins, cups
733	Transcripts	Stenographic reporting services
733 III	Services	Visual arts, graphics
739 I A	Services	Rental and servicing of portable toilets
739 VI B	Services	Rental of measuring and test instruments

Schedule Number	Name	Description or Typical Items
739 VII A	Services	Microfilming, surveys, filming, film processing, aperture card mounting, roll to roll
751	Motor Vehicle Rental/Travelers Pocket Guide	Without driver
781 I,II	Professional Film Processing and Videotape Processing	Motion picture, filmstrip and slide, videotape duplication
782	Distribution of Audiovisual Materials (Free Loan)	Motion picture films, videotapes, cassettes, filmstrips, slides, audiotapes
807 I A	Services	Clinical laboratory tests (human or animal), electrocardiogram analysis, tissue microslide preparation, rental and servicing of specialized medical equipment
823	Services	Lending library

---

*Supplied exclusively by Federal Prison Industries, part of the Bureau of Prisons, Department of Justice

FEDERAL SUPPLY SCHEDULE
Multiple Award

FSC 76   PART I
CLASSES 7610 & 7640
PUBLICATIONS
DICTIONARIES, ENCYCLOPEDIAS, OTHER REFERENCE
BOOKS AND PAMPHLETS, MAPS, ATLASES, CHARTS,
AND GLOBES

GENERAL SERVICES ADMINISTRATION

FEDERAL SUPPLY SERVICE   O1SC 7601

GSA DC-01902753

CONTENTS	ORDERING INSTRUCTIONS

GENERAL INSTRUCTIONS

1. **INFORMATION CONTAINED IN THIS SCHEDULE.** This Schedule lists contractors to whom awards have been made. Contractors who were listed in the previous Schedule but have not been awarded contracts are not listed herein and, if awarded contracts, will be published in cumulative editions to this Schedule. New information will be identified by a vertical line in the right hand margin. Ordering offices should review this Schedule to determine: special item numbers; item name and description; contractor's address, telephone number, and contract number; effective date of award; and ordering instructions.

2. **INFORMATION CONTAINED IN THE CONTRACTOR'S PRICELIST/ CATALOG.** Ordering offices should review the pricelist to determine: ordering address; payment address; delivery point; delivery time; discounts; prices; business size; foreign items; maximum order limitations; models offered; and, if applicable, warranties, terms and conditions of rental, maintenance, and/or repair; export packing and point of production.

3. **GEOGRAPHIC COVERAGE.** The 50 States, Washington, DC, and Puerto Rico.

4. **MANDATORY USERS.** All departments and independent establishments, including wholly-owned Government corporations, in the executive branch of the Federal Government (except the U.S. Postal Service) and the DC Government.

5. **NONMANDATORY USERS.** The following activities are authorized to use this Schedule on a nonmandatory basis: (i) Federal agencies other than those covered by the mandatory use provision and nonappropriated fund activities as prescribed in FPMR 101-26.000, (ii) Government contractors authorized in writing by a Federal agency pursuant to 41 CFR 1-5.9, and (iii) mixed ownership Government corporations (as defined in the Government Corporation Control Act). Contractors are encouraged to honor orders from these activities. In the event the contractor is unwilling to accept such an order, the contractor will return it by mailing or delivering it to the ordering office within seven working days after receipt. Failure to return an order will constitute acceptance whereupon all provisions of the contract shall apply with respect to such order.

   NOTE: Questions regarding agencies/activities authorized to use this Schedule should be directed to the Schedules Information Center. (See Paragraph 1a, ORDERING INSTRUCTIONS)

6. **MULTIPLE AWARDS.** Multiple award Federal Supply Schedules cover contracts made with more than one supplier for comparable items at either the same or different prices for delivery to the same geographic area.

7. **CATALOGS AND PRICELISTS.** If catalogs and/or pricelists have not been received and are required or if additional copies are required, ordering offices should communicate directly with the contractor for copies of such material. See LIST OF CONTRACTORS for telephone numbers.

8. **INCORPORATION OF FORMS.** The following forms apply to this Schedule:

   a. Standard Form 32, General Provisions (Supply Contract), April 1975 edition, with the following modification: Article 15 is amended by deleting the words "at hard labor".

   b. GSA Form 1424, GSA Supplemental Provisions, June 1977 edition, except Clause 4, Variation in Quantity, is deleted and no variation in quantity is permitted in deliveries.

   c. GSA Form 2891, Instructions to Users of Federal Supply Schedule, May 1977 edition; except paragraph 9, PAYMENTS is deleted and paragraph 20 of the ORDERING INSTRUCTIONS is substituted.

1. **GSA ASSISTANCE.**

   a. For information of a general nature write or call:

   > GENERAL SERVICES ADMINISTRATION (FPS)
   > SCHEDULES INFORMATION CENTER
   > WASHINGTON, DC 20406
   >   Telephone: (703) 557-8177
   >   AUTOVON: 225-9684

   b. For additional copies of Schedules or for copies of the Federal Supply Schedule Program Guide, write or call:

   > GENERAL SERVICES ADMINISTRATION (8BRC)
   > PUBLICATIONS DISTRIBUTION CENTER
   > DENVER, CO 80225
   >   Telephone: (303) 234-4195

   c. Contracting Officer mailing address:

   > GENERAL SERVICES ADMINISTRATION (1FPQ)
   > CONTRACTING OFFICER (FSC 76 PART I)
   > J W McCORMACK P O & CTHSE BLDG
   > BOSTON, MA 02109

2. **PROMPT PAYMENT DISCOUNTS.** Discount terms should be shown on all ordering documents.

3. **POINT OF DELIVERY.** At destination within the area defined in GENERAL INSTRUCTIONS, Paragraph 3, Geographic Coverage.

4. **TIME OF DELIVERY.** See contractor's catalog/pricelist.

5. **IMPREST FUNDS (PETTY CASH).** The contractor agrees to accept cash payment for purchases made under the terms of the contract in conformance with FPR 1-3.604.

6. **SMALL REQUIREMENTS.** No ordering activity is obligated to place orders amounting to $50 or less.

7. **MINIMUM ORDER.** See contractor's catalog/pricelist under "Small Requirements" for lowest value order which will be accepted.

8. **MAXIMUM ORDER LIMITATIONS.** Purchase orders cannot exceed the amount(s) shown in the contractor's pricelist/ catalog.

9. **INSPECTION.** This Schedule provides for inspection at destination.

10. **PACKAGING AND PACKING.** Standard commercial practice (Level C of Federal Standard 102).

    If special or unusual packing is required, such packing requirements should be arranged with the contractor by the ordering activity.

11. **BUY AMERICAN DIFFERENTIALS.** Buy American differentials must be applied by the ordering activity before placing an order if foreign and domestic products are listed under the same special item number and both products will satisfy the requirement.

12. **RECEIVING DOCK HOURS.** State on the purchase order the time (local daylight or standard) that material can be received at destination.

13. **RECEIVING DOCK LIMITATIONS.** If there are limitations on size (height, width, or length) or weight of vehicle that can be accommodated at delivery point, state them on the purchase order.

14. **DELIVERY ADDRESS.** If delivery address is vague, include instructions on the purchase order that will assist the carrier in reaching the delivery point.

15. **JUSTIFICATION.** When orders are placed at other than the lowest price available under a special item number and (1) the cost is more than $500 per line item, ordering activities must justify the purchase of the higher priced item; (2) the cost is $500 or less per line item, ordering activities should refer to their agency procurement regulations to determine if justification is required.

16. COPIES OF INVOICES. If more than one copy of the invoice is required, state clearly on purchase orders the number of invoices needed.

17. AGENCIES SUBMITTING REQUISITIONS TO GSA FOR PURCHASE. For items contained in this Schedule, the requisition, if citing National Stock Numbers, must also contain Special Item Number, as shown in the Schedule, manufacturer's name or manufacturer's code, brand name, model, and/or part number.

18. LATEST EDITIONS REQUIRED. All books shall be the latest edition and shall be identified. In the event a revised or new edition is published during the contract period, the following provisions shall apply:

    (a) CONTRACTOR will notify the contracting officer of the change 60 days prior to the publication date or as soon as information is available.

    (b) If the list price of the new edition remains the same as the one contracted for, there shall be no change other than to note that the new edition is available. If there is a list price change, the Government will compute the discount reflected from the list price and apply the same percentage discount indicated in the contractor's pricelist/catalog to the new list price, to reach the new contract price. No revision or amendment to the contract will be issued and the contractor is obligated to perform on a continuing basis.

    (c) Upon publication of a new or revised edition, the earlier edition will no longer be on contract and contractor is expressly prohibited from shipping same. If orders are received showing the old edition and/or price and the computed price of the new edition is not more than 25% higher than the previous edition, the contractor is authorized to ship without prior approval of the ordering office. No amendment to the purchase order is required and payment will be made on properly computed invoice in accordance with sub-paragraph (b) above. If increase in price is more than 25%, contractor is to promptly notify ordering office of the availability of the new edition and price, and upon approval shall ship new edition. Amendment to the purchase order is required and payment will be made accordingly.

19. OUT-OF-STOCK. Contractors will be obligated to notify ordering offices, within delivery time specified in contract, of books which are out-of-stock at publisher's warehouse, advising approximate availability date. Ordering offices shall instruct contractors within 20 days after date of notification to "Back Order" or "Cancel". However, contractor shall not be requested to "Back-Order" unless books are expected within 60 days after date of notice. If instructions are not received by contractor within the time specified, item shall be automatically canceled from order.

20. PAYMENT. Advance payment for periodicals and subscription items is authorized by the Act of June 12, 1930, 46 Statute, 580, as amended by Public Law 87-91 (31 USCA 530) enacted July 20, 1961. Therefore, contractors shall be paid for such items by ordering offices, upon submission of properly certified invoices or vouchers, at prices stipulated in contractor's pricelist/catalog, less deductions, if any, as provided. "Subscription" items include any publication that covers a series printed on a periodic basis or any series of a predetermined number of issues the price of which is set in advance:

    (a) Partial Payment. Partial payment of invoices WILL BE MADE without undue delay provided the items have been received. It is not necessary for complete delivery to be made before partial payment is due. Payment of invoices will not be withheld because of failure of the contractor to supply books which are out-of-print, out-of-stock, to be published at a later date, or in case of shortages, i.e., discrepancies between invoices and receiving documents. In such cases, items in question will be deleted on the voucher by indicating the item number and reason for deduction. Contractor will be advised of such deduction. This information will be placed on the face of the voucher at the time the voucher is prepared for payment. INVOICES WILL NOT be returned to the contractor for correction due to any of the above mentioned conditions. Payment for items received subsequent to administrative deductions taken on partial payment of invoices may be effected by cross-referencing the voucher on which the administrative deduction was taken when effecting prior payments, after receipt of invoice from supplier.

    (b) Time Discount. In the event it is necessary to return invoices to the contractor for correction, such invoices must be returned by the fiscal officer within the time discount period specified. The discount will be computed from date of delivery or from date a correct invoice is received in the office specified by the Government, whichever is later.

    (c) Shortages or Damage in Transit. Contractor shall be notified within 15 days of shortage or damage in shipment. Prompt notification is necessary so that carrier's records may still be available.

21. BLANKET PURCHASE ARRANGEMENTS. Blanket Purchase Arrangements are authorized under this Schedule. The overall dollar value of a Blanket Purchase Arrangement may exceed the contract maximum order limitation; however, no single order or series of orders placed within a short period of time under the Blanket Purchase Arrangement may exceed the contract Maximum Order Limitation.

LIST OF CONTRACTORS

CONTRACTS AWARDED AS A RESULT OF NEGOTIATION PURSUANT TO SECTION 302 (C)(10) OF THE FEDERAL PROPERTY AND ADMINISTRATIVE SERVICES
ACT OF 1949, 63 STAT. 393, AS AMENDED (41 U.S.C. 252 (C)(10))

Listed in the Contract Number column is the business size indicator "s" for small business and "o" for other than small business,
"a" for minority business enterprises, and "b" for other than minority enterprises

CONTRACT GS-01S-	CONTRACTOR, ADDRESS & TELEPHONE	CONTRACT EFFECTIVE	CONTRACT GS-01S-	CONTRACTOR, ADDRESS & TELEPHONE	CONTRACT EFFECTIVE
s/b 06901	S W BOND BOX 253 MINOT, ND 58701 (701) 839-5513	13 FEB 79	s/b 06897	L G HARKINS & CO INC 239 FOURTH AVE PITTSBURGH, PA 15222 (412) 281-3229	8 FEB 79
s/b 06898	CARROLL PUBLISHING CO 1058 THOMAS JEFFERSON ST NW WASHINGTON, DC 20007 (202) 333-8620	8 FEB 79	o/b 06852	HOUGHTON MIFFLIN CO DICTIONARY DIV 2 PARK ST BOSTON, MA 02107 (617) 725-5172	13 FEB 79
s/b 06889	MARSHALL CAVENDISH CORP 147 W MERRICK RD FREEPORT, NY 11520 (516) 546-4200	8 FEB 79	s/b 06855	INSTRUCTIONAL RESOURCES CORP 251 E 50TH ST NEW YORK, NY 10022 (212) 688-4646	8 FEB 79
s/b 06900	COPLEY & ASSOC SA 2030 M ST NW - SUITE 602 WASHINGTON, DC 20036 (202) 223-4934	9 FEB 79	s/b 06858	JOYNER & ASSOC INC 11250 ROGER BACON DR RESTON, VA 22090 (703) 437-5060	15 FEB 79
s/b 06859	GEO F CRAM CO INC 301 S LA SALLE ST INDIANAPOLIS, IN 46206 (317) 635-5564	13 FEB 79	o/b 06851	MacMILLAN PROFESSIONAL & LIBRARY SERVICES DIV OF MacMILLAN PUBLISHING CO INC 866 THIRD AVE NEW YORK, NY 10022 (212) 935-5620	13 FEB 79
s/b 06854	DRAY PUBLICATIONS INC ROUTE 5 DEERFIELD, MA 01342 (413) 773-5491	8 FEB 79	s/b 06838	MacRAE'S BLUE BOOK CO 100 SHORE DR HINSDALE, IL 60521 (312) 325-7880	13 FEB 79
o/b 06834	EASTMAN KODAK CO 343 STATE ST ROCHESTER, NY 14650 (716) 724-4423	9 FEB 79	o/b 06842	G & C MERRIAM CO 47 FEDERAL ST SPRINGFIELD, MA 01101 (413) 734-3134	8 FEB 79
s/b 06895	EMERSON BOOKS INC REYNOLDS LANE BUCHANAN, NY 10511 (914) 739-3506	9 FEB 79	s/b 06893	MICRO FORM REVIEW INC 520 RIVERSIDE AVE WESTPORT, CT 06880 (203) 266-6967	13 FEB 79
s/b 06831	FEDERAL EMPLOYEES NEWS DIGEST INC BOX 457 MERRIFIELD, VA 22116 (703) 533-3031	7 FEB 79	s/b 06843	NATIONAL LEARNING CORP 212 MICHAEL DR SYOSSET, NY 11791 (516) 921-8888	13 FEB 79
s/b 06832	THE FEMINIST COMMITTEE 3921 LAND O'LAKES DR NE ATLANTA, GA 30342 (404) 231-0988	8 FEB 79	s/b 06856	NATIONAL STANDARDS ASSOC 4827 RUGBY AVE WASHINGTON, DC 20014 (301) 951-0333	13 FEB 79
s/b 06844	FOLLETT PUBLISHING CO 1010 W WASHINGTON BLVD CHICAGO, IL 60607 (312) 666-5858	8 FEB 79	o/b 06835	NYSTROM DIV OF CARNATION 3333 ELSTON AVE CHICAGO, IL 60618 (312) 463-1144	13 FEB 79
o/b 06840	REGINALD BISHOP FORSTER & ASSOC INC 121 W FRANKLIN MINNEAPOLIS, MN 55404 (612) 871-1395	13 FEB 79	s/b 06896	OXBRIDGE COMMUNICATIONS 183 MADISON AVE NEW YORK, NY 10016 (212) 689-8524	9 FEB 79
o/b 06903	H M GOUSHA CO BOX 6227 SAN JOSE, CA 95150 (408) 296-1060	13 FEB 79	s/b 06857	PALMER/PAULSON ASSOC 7400 WAUKEGAN RD NILES, IL 60648 (312) 647-7466	13 FEB 79
s/b 06899	GOVERNMENT MARKETING NEWS INC 1001 CONNECTICUT AVE - SUITE 1019 WASHINGTON, DC 20036 (202) 293-6225	9 FEB 79	o/b 06833	POLITICAL RESEARCH INC TEGOLANO AT BENT TREE 16850 DALLAS PARKWAY DALLAS, TX 75248 (214) 386-5827	8 FEB 79
o/b 06841	GROLIER EDUCATIONAL CORP SHERMAN TURNPIKE DANBURY, CT 06816 (203) 792-1200	9 FEB 79			

LIST OF CONTRACTORS - Continued

CONTRACT GS-01S-	CONTRACTOR, ADDRESS & TELEPHONE	CONTRACT EFFECTIVE	CONTRACT GS-01S-	CONTRACTOR, ADDRESS & TELEPHONE	CONTRACT EFFECTIVE
s/b 06893	PROCUREMENT ASSOC INC 733 N DODSWORTH AVE COVINA, CA 91724 (213) 966-4576	13 FEB 79	s/b 06873	UNIFORMED SERVICES ALMANAC INC BOX 76 WASHINGTON, DC 20044 (703) 532-1631	13 FEB 79
s/b 06860	UNDINE CORP 221 E 78TH ST NEW YORK, NY 10021 (212) 355-2689	13 FEB 79	s/b 06894	GEO WATSON & CO 913 RIDGE RD GREENBELT, MD 20770 (301) 345-8891	8 FEB 79
s/b 06839	UNIFORMED SERVICES ALMANAC INC BOX 76 WASHINGTON, DC 20044 (703) 532-1631	13 FEB 79			

CROSS-REFERENCE TO RELATED SCHEDULES

FSC	PART	SECTION	RELATED ITEMS
			PUBLICATIONS:
76	II	-	law, tax, and reporting periodicals
76	III	A	medical, trade, text, and technical books; and pamphlets
76	III	B	medical, trade, text, and technical books; and pamphlets

-o-

Your Marketing

Library

There are a few publications you can get without charge from government agencies, even in these straitened times when our government has by necessity become far less generous in its handouts to the general public. The Government Printing Office now charges for virtually everything it prints, but the agencies for which it prints often will supply you the books free of charge. Here are a few of the books and other documents that should be a permanent part of your marketing library, especially if you write proposals:

- *United States Government Manual* (current year), GPO bookstore
- GPO *Style Manual*, GPO bookstore
- Any good dictionary
- The free marketing guides from as many government agencies as possible
- The *Commerce Business Daily* (Department of Commerce or GPO), subscription to paper or electronic (on-line) edition
- Directory of minority businesses, your area (SBA)
- *Proposal Preparation Manual*, DOT Report No. DOT-RSPA-DPB-50-7816 (National Technical Information Service, Springfield, VA 22161). (Many agencies have free proposal guides of equal merit.)

- *Small Business Guide to Federal R&D* (National Science Foundation, Office of Small Business R&D, 1800 G Street NW, Washington, D.C. 20550)
- *Program Guide,* Federal Supply Schedule, Stock No. 02200500120 (GPO bookstore)

If you write proposals, keep the following information on file. These items should be readily available so you do not need to begin a search for them in the frantic last hours of proposal writing.

- Up-to-date resumes of incumbent, permanent staff
- Roster and resumes of available special consultants
- Copies of all your own past proposals, particularly the successful ones
- Copies of all competitor proposals you can acquire
- Information on all competitors, such as annual reports, brochures, capability statements, and so on
- Standard capability statements for your own organization

How to Get on

Mailing Lists for

Surplus Bids

The government sells surplus property, sometimes by holding public auctions, more frequently by soliciting sealed bids. The property is enormously variable, reflecting the variety of government purchasing, and includes all kinds of equipment, raw materials, land, timber, buildings, furniture, and other goods. Some of it is in excellent condition, and in some cases may even be new and unused. Some is in such poor condition that its chief value lies in what may be salvaged.

Sales of surplus are listed in the *Commerce Business Daily* almost every day of the year. However, you can have your name placed on mailing lists so you will automatically receive solicitations to bid for those items or classes of items you indicate some interest in.

The two federal agencies that handle most of the surplus sold are the General Services Administration and the Department of Defense. Each GSA regional office (see listing in Appendix 1) conducts surplus sales in its own region, and you must address a request to the

GSA office in each region of interest. To get on the list for GSA surplus sales, address your letter(s) to:

General Services Administration
Federal Supply Service
Personal Property Division
(Use address(es) from Appendix 1 list)

To apply for DOD surplus sales, request an application form from:

DOD Surplus Sales
P.O. Box 1370
Battle Creek, MI 49016

Organization

Charts of Major

Agencies

The following are the official charts of the major federal agencies, as published by the U.S. government. No presentation of an agency is quite so enlightening as its organization chart. From these charts, you can tell rapidly what the reporting order is, how high in the agency hierarchy any given office or officer is, and how much importance the agency attaches to its various functions and missions. Whether you are already doing business with one of the agencies, preparing to make preliminary marketing contacts, or writing a proposal to the agency and seeking intelligence to aid in that effort, studying the agency's organization chart is always a helpful first step.

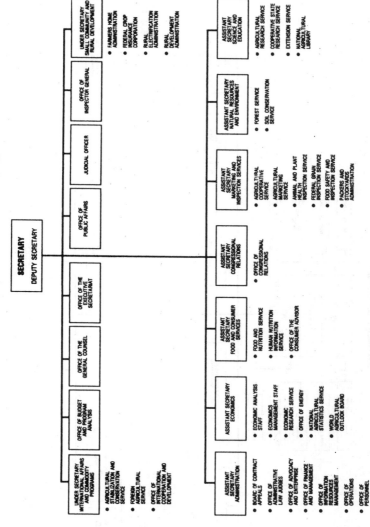

DEPARTMENT OF AGRICULTURE

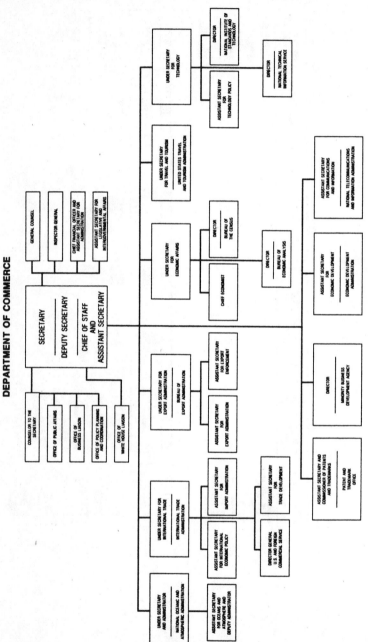

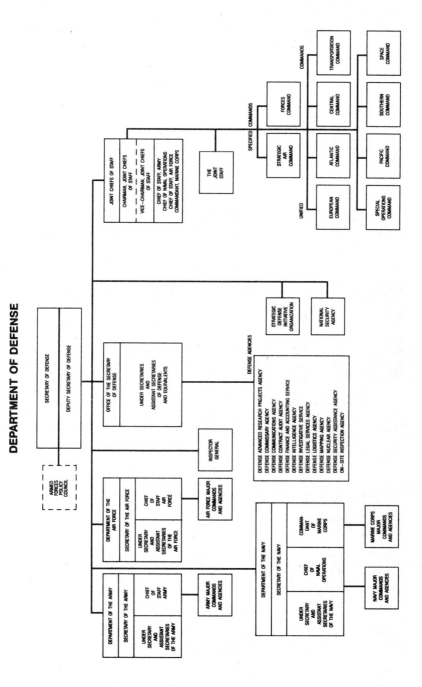

DEPARTMENT OF DEFENSE

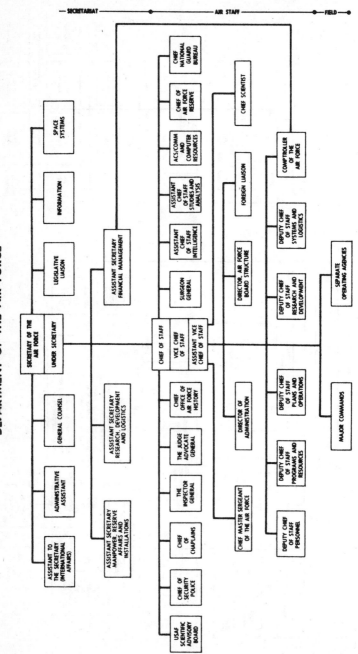

DEPARTMENT OF THE AIR FORCE

DEPARTMENT OF THE ARMY

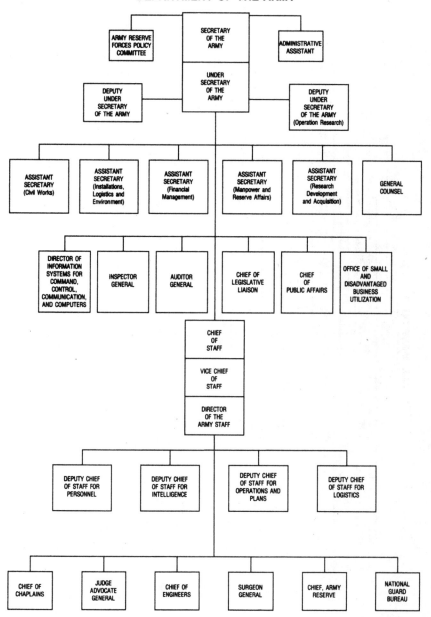

DEPARTMENT OF THE NAVY

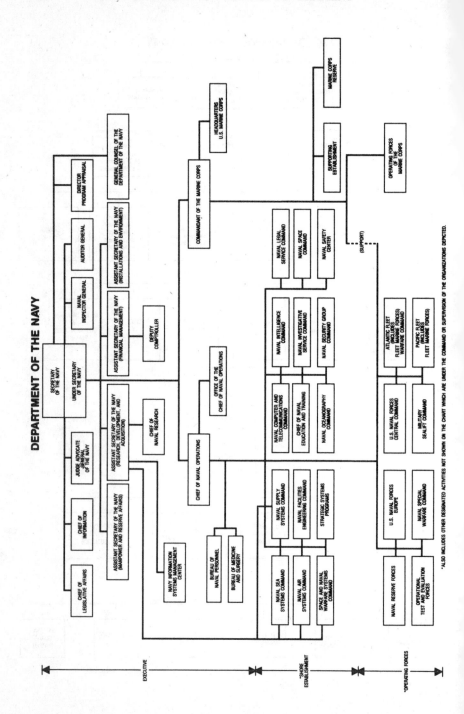

*ALSO INCLUDES OTHER DESIGNATED ACTIVITIES NOT SHOWN ON THE CHART WHICH ARE UNDER THE COMMAND OR SUPERVISION OF THE ORGANIZATIONS DEPICTED.

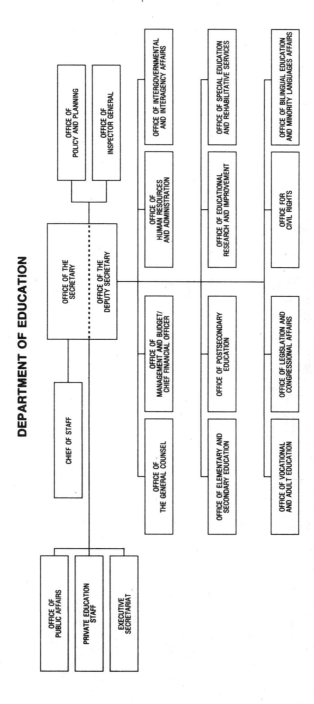

DEPARTMENT OF EDUCATION

OFFICE OF THE SECRETARY

OFFICE OF THE DEPUTY SECRETARY

CHIEF OF STAFF

OFFICE OF PUBLIC AFFAIRS

PRIVATE EDUCATION STAFF

EXECUTIVE SECRETARIAT

OFFICE OF POLICY AND PLANNING

OFFICE OF INSPECTOR GENERAL

OFFICE OF INTERGOVERNMENTAL AND INTERAGENCY AFFAIRS

OFFICE OF SPECIAL EDUCATION AND REHABILITATIVE SERVICES

OFFICE OF BILINGUAL EDUCATION AND MINORITY LANGUAGES AFFAIRS

OFFICE OF HUMAN RESOURCES AND ADMINISTRATION

OFFICE OF EDUCATIONAL RESEARCH AND IMPROVEMENT

OFFICE FOR CIVIL RIGHTS

OFFICE OF MANAGEMENT AND BUDGET/ CHIEF FINANCIAL OFFICER

OFFICE OF POSTSECONDARY EDUCATION

OFFICE OF LEGISLATION AND CONGRESSIONAL AFFAIRS

OFFICE OF THE GENERAL COUNSEL

OFFICE OF ELEMENTARY AND SECONDARY EDUCATION

OFFICE OF VOCATIONAL AND ADULT EDUCATION

DEPARTMENT OF ENERGY

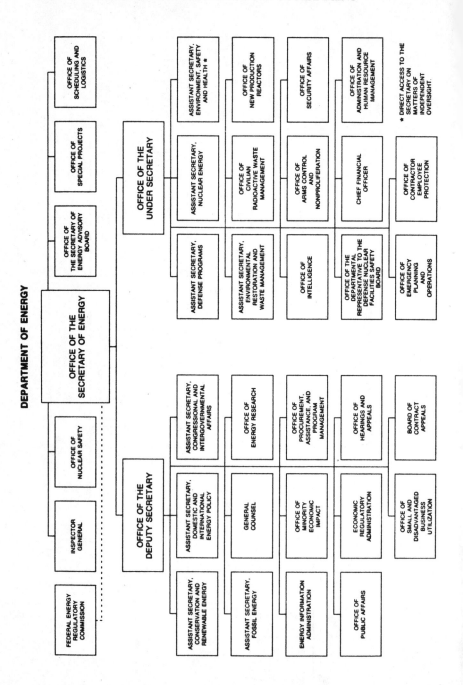

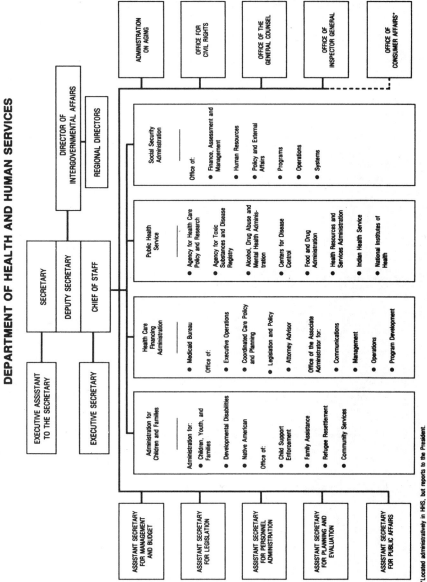

DEPARTMENT OF HEALTH AND HUMAN SERVICES

*Located administratively in HHS, but reports to the President.

DEPARTMENT OF HOUSING AND URBAN DEVELOPMENT

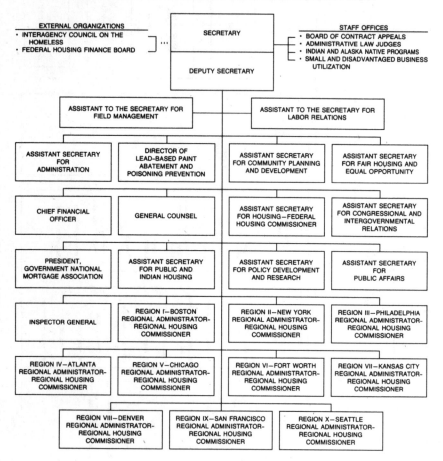

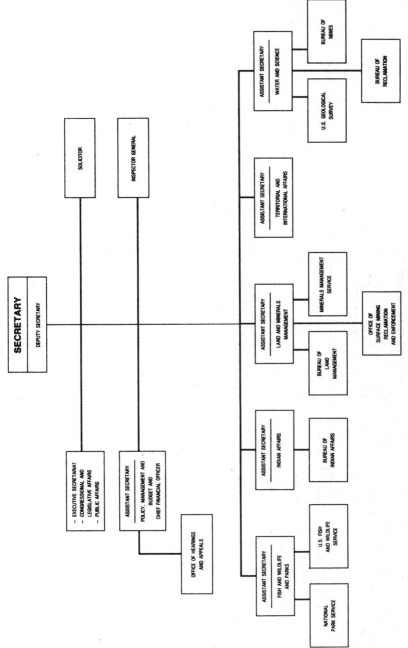

DEPARTMENT OF THE INTERIOR

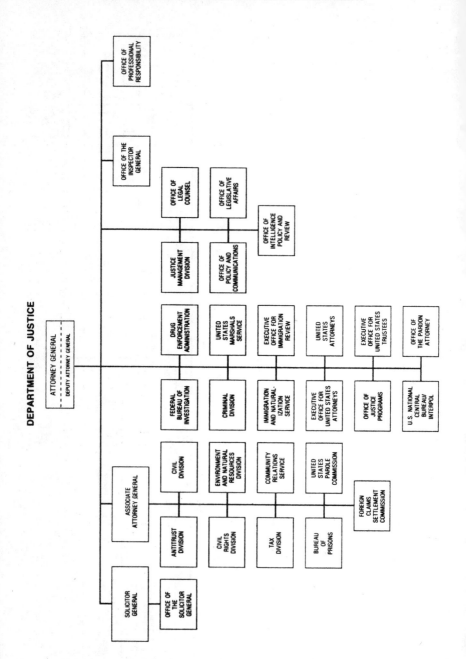

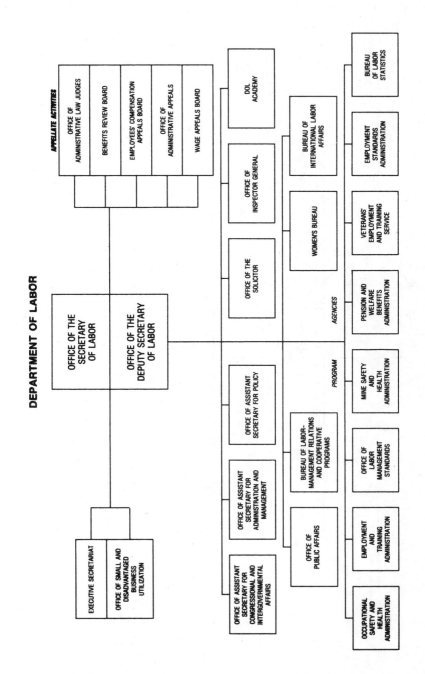

DEPARTMENT OF LABOR

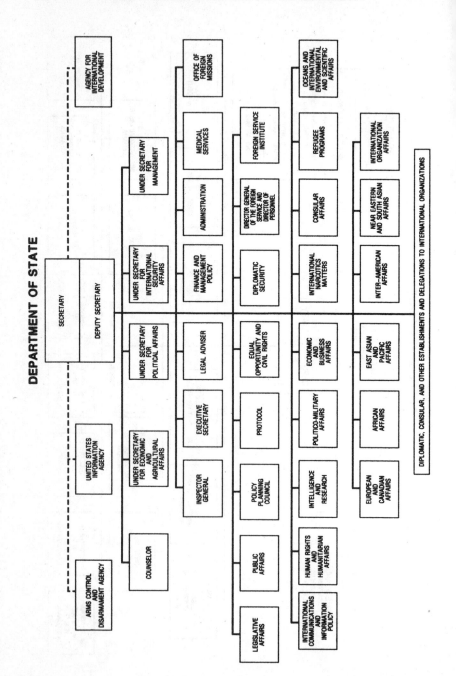

DEPARTMENT OF STATE

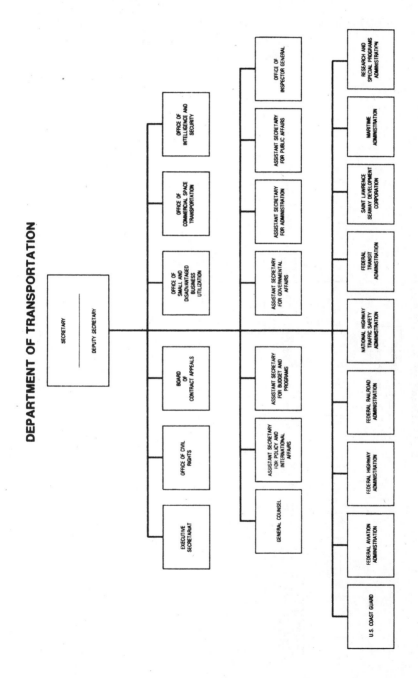

DEPARTMENT OF TRANSPORTATION

DEPARTMENT OF THE TREASURY

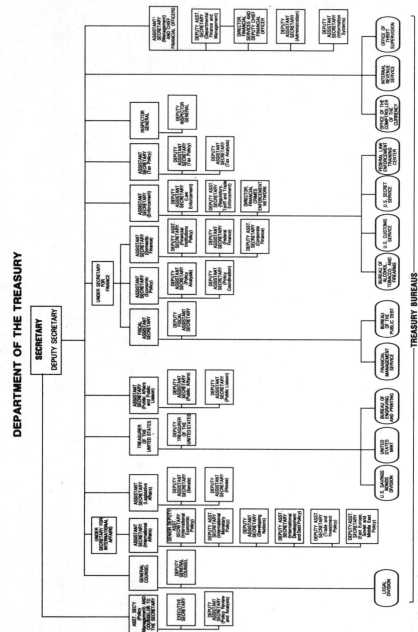

[1] Assistant Secretary (Management) is the Chief Financial Officer (CFO).

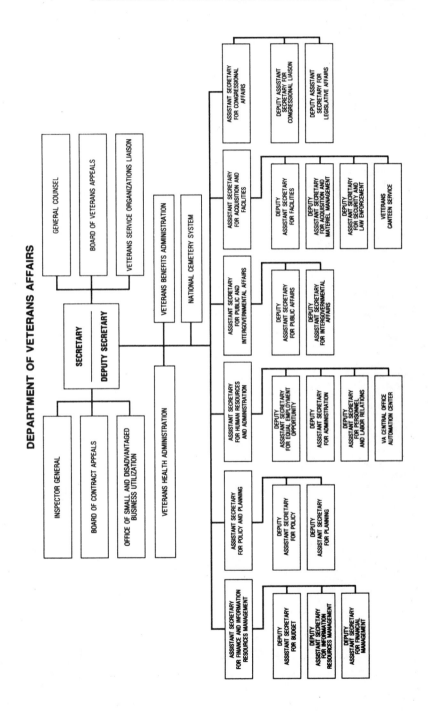

DEPARTMENT OF VETERANS AFFAIRS

ENVIRONMENTAL PROTECTION AGENCY

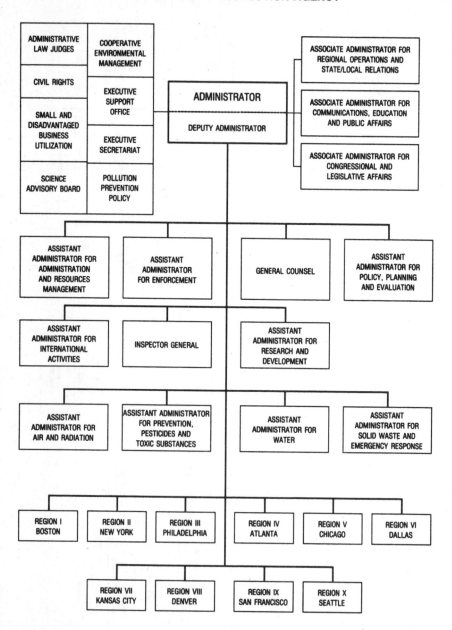

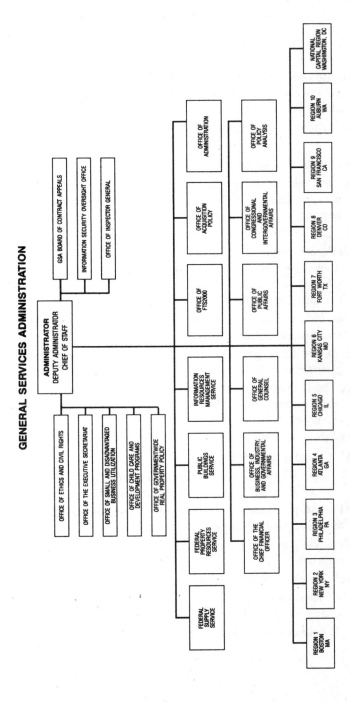

GENERAL SERVICES ADMINISTRATION

GLOSSARY

advertised bid/procurement (also formally advertised) sealed bid with public opening, using IFB (information for bid) form; bids must be read aloud; award to low bidder

AEC Atomic Energy Commission

AMC Army Materiel Command

below the line cost items on which no profit is taken

best and final offer invitation to cut price offered in proposal, often with presentation and/or discussions, sometimes considered final negotiation

BIA Bureau of Indian Affairs (part of DOI)

bidder's conference preproposal conference held to answer questions from prospective bidders; usually used for very large procurements where there are many questions or where the customer finds it difficult to explain all in RFP

bid set, bid package solicitation, including IFB or RFP, work statement, specifications, other information required for bid

B/L bill of lading, government bill of lading; when contract so stipulates, government will pay freight costs by providing shipping documents

BOA basic ordering agreement; term contract, with unit prices, under which customer may order goods or services on demand, as stipulated and priced

CBD *Commerce Business Daily*

CIA Central Intelligence Agency

COB close of business (specific time varies among agencies); often given, with a date, as the deadline for submittal of bids or proposals

CPAF cost-plus-award-fee contract; type of contract with incentive fees to reward good performance and cost reductions

CPFF cost-plus-fixed-fee contract, well known as "cost-plus" type of contract

CPSC Consumer Product Safety Commission

DACA days after contract award; often used in scheduling to stipulate milestones or due dates for project products or functions

DC District of Columbia

340

DCAA Defense Contract Audit Agency; auditing agency of Defense Department, often utilized by other agencies to audit contractors' accounts or verify overhead rates

DOC Department of Commerce

DOD Department of Defense

DOE Department of Energy

DOI Department of the Interior

DOJ Department of Justice

DOL Department of Labor

DOT Department of Transportation

EEOC Equal Employment Opportunity Commission

EPA Environmental Protection Agency

FAA Federal Aviation Commission (part of DOT)

FCC Federal Communications Commission

FDA Food and Drug Administration

FOB Free on board; stipulation in solicitation requiring contractor to pay freight (include in cost estimates) to destinations given

FOI Freedom of Information (Act)

FRA Federal Railroad Administration (part of DOT)

FSC Federal Stock Code; government identifying number for standard commodity

FSS Federal Supply Service (part of GSA)

FTC Federal Trade Commission

GAO General Accounting Office; arm of Congress, conducts investigations, studies, prepares reports for congressional members; headed by Comptroller General of the United States

GPO Government Printing Office

GSA General Services Administration; main supply arm of government (nonmilitary)

HHS Department of Health and Human Services

HUD Department of Housing and Urban Development

ICC Interstate Commerce Commission

IFB information for bid; form used for formally advertised procurement

IG industrial group; used to classify supplies by major groups; also Inspector General, an office in most major agencies

indef qty   indefinite quantity; usually used for BOAs and other term contracts where unit prices are established for ordering supplies

labor hour contract   similar to BOA, but contract rates established for labor classes

LEAA   Law Enforcement Assistance Administration (division of DOJ)

NASA   National Aeronautics and Space Administration

NBS   National Bureau of Standards (part of DOC)

NHTSA   National Highway Traffic Safety Administration (part of DOT)

NIDA   National Institute of Drug Abuse (part of HHS)

NIH   National Institutes of Health (part of HHS)

NIMH   National Institutes of Mental Health (part of HHS)

NIOSH   National Institute of Occupational Safety and Health (part of HHS)

NLM   National Library of Medicine (part of HHS)

NOL   Naval Ordnance Laboratory

NRL   Naval Research Laboratory

NSA   National Security Administration

NSF   National Science Foundation

NSN   National Stock Number; number assigned to standard commodities; often used as specification in procurement

OFPP   Office of Federal Procurement Policy (part of OMB)

OMB   Office of Management and Budget

OPM   Office of Personnel Management; replaces former Civil Service Commission

OSHA   Occupational Safety and Health Administration (part of DOL)

PBS   Public Buildings Service (part of GSA)

PHS   Public Health Service (part of HHS)

RFP   request for proposal

RFQ   request for quotation

SBA   Small Business Administration

T&M   time and material (contract); similar to BOA and labor hour contracts

USA   U.S. Army

USAF   U.S. Air Force

USCG U.S. Coast Guard
USDA U.S. Department of Agriculture
USMC U.S. Marine Corps
USN U.S. Navy
USPS U.S. Postal Service

INDEX

More Business Books
from Prima Publishing

The Complete Franchise Book, updated and revised 2nd edition
by Dennis L. Foster $19.95

Now you can benefit from the pithy advice and guidance of one of
America's foremost franchise consultants. Each step, from answering
a newspaper ad and choosing the right company to negotiating a fair
contract and opening your doors, is covered in detail.

How to Become a Successful Consultant in Your Own Field
by Hubert Bermont (hardcover) $21.95

Here is the help you need to make the transition from employee to
consultant. Topics covered include: what it takes to be a consultant,
how to get hired, how to determine what to charge, how to operate a
consulting business, and how to avoid pitfalls and mistakes.

The Complete Work-at-Home Companion, 2nd edition
by Herman Holtz (available Sept. 1993) $21.50

Your guide to successfully making it in your own home-based
business. Holtz offers clear advice on setting up the ideal office as
well as getting maximum mileage from computer hardware and software. Learn how to overcome distractions; price your products;
handle taxes and insurance; choose incorporation, partnership, or sole
proprietorship; and more!

Mail-Order Success Secrets
by Tyler G. Hicks $14.95

Is owning your own business your goal? Then mail order is the low-
cost, high-profit way to go. Among the areas covered are: how to start
your own business, where to find your product, how to get low-cost
publicity, the overseas mail-order market, tapping into the 800-
number boom, and more. Includes real-life examples as well as Ty
Hicks' insights after nearly 25 successful years in the mail-order business.

FILL IN AND MAIL . . . TODAY

PRIMA PUBLISHING
P.O. BOX 1260BK
ROCKLIN, CA 95677

USE YOUR VISA/MC AND ORDER BY PHONE:
(916) 786-0426 (Mon–Fri 9–4 PST)

Please send me the following titles:

Quantity	**Title**	**Amount**
_____	_____	_____
_____	_____	_____
_____	_____	_____
_____	_____	_____

	Subtotal	$_____
	Postage & Handling	$ 3.95
	7.25% Sales Tax (California only)	$_____
	TOTAL (U.S. funds only)	$_____

Check enclosed for $_____ (payable to Prima Publishing)

Charge my ❑ MasterCard ❑ Visa

Account No. _____ Exp. Date _____

Signature _____

Your Printed Name _____

Address _____

City/State/Zip _____

Daytime Telephone ( )_____

Satisfaction is guaranteed—or your money back!
Please allow three to four weeks for delivery.

❖ THANK YOU FOR YOUR ORDER ❖